Mutual Recognition as a New Mode of Governance

Mutual recognition is generally forgotten in debates about new modes of governance, even though it is a particular powerful example. Its invention was crucial for the completion of the European Union's single market, and in the late 1990s it was transferred to the field of Justice and Home Affairs.

Outside of the EU, mutual recognition is also gaining in importance. This book discusses mutual recognition in the context of the debate on new modes of governance and analyzes its potential to solve governance problems, focusing on the preconditions it needs for its functioning (e.g. trust of the Member states), the positive implications of achieving coordination through it, as well as its negative side effects (e.g. the danger of a regulatory race to the bottom). Particular focus is on the contentious services directive as a prominent example of using mutual recognition. In addition, contributions look at the application of mutual recognition in the market for goods, in the area of Justice and Home Affairs, in tax policy, and in the World Trade Organization, so that the book achieves a comprehensive assessment of mutual recognition as a new mode of governance.

This book was previously published as special issue of the *Journal of European Public Policy*.

Susanne K. Schmidt has worked widely on European integration and its impact on the Member states. Her articles have appeared in the *Journal of European Public Policy (JEPP)*, the *Journal of Public Policy, Politische Vierteljahresschrift (PVS)* and the *Zeitschrift für Internationale Beziehungen*. She is member of the editorial board of the *Journal of European Public Policy*.

T0316059

Journal of European Public Policy Series

Series Editor: Jeremy Richardson is a Professor at Nuffield College, Oxford University

This series seeks to bring together some of the finest edited works on European Public Policy. Reprinting from Special Issues of the 'Journal of European Public Policy,' the focus is on using a wide range of social sciences approaches, both qualitative and quantitative, to gain a comprehensive and definitive understanding of Public Policy in Europe.

Mutual Recognition as a New Mode of Governance

Edited by
Susanne K. Schmidt

Routledge
Taylor & Francis Group

LONDON AND NEW YORK

First published 2008 by Routledge

2 Park Square, Milton Park, Abingdon, Oxon OX14 4RN
711 Third Avenue, New York, NY 10017, USA

Routledge is an imprint of the Taylor & Francis Group, an informa business

First issued in paperback 2016

Typeset in Agaramond and Franklin Gothic by Techset Composition, Salisbury, UK

British Library Cataloguing in Publication Data
A catalogue record for this book is available from the British Library

ISBN 13: 978-0-415-41853-9 (hbk)
ISBN 13: 978-1-138-97665-8 (pbk)

Contents

Mutual recognition as a new mode of governance

Susanne K. Schmidt

INTRODUCTION

Mutual recognition is generally not mentioned in debates about new modes of governance (Eberlein and Kerwer 2004; Héritier 2003; Scott and Trubek 2002). Yet, mutual recognition is the principle on which the single market is built. Stemming from an innovative interpretation of the freedom to trade goods in the *Cassis* judgment, it allowed the Community in the late 1980s to push the realization of the single market despite its incapability of agreeing on the harmonization of rules. Due to its novelty – the idea being that goods being marketed according to the regulations of any member state could be marketed in principle in all other member states – the principle of mutual recognition roused significant interest. Analyses were related particularly to the danger of a 'race to the bottom' of regulatory standards (regulatory competition), which could occur if products marketed according to lower standards could be sold just as easily as more expensive, higher-standard ones (e.g. Gatsios and Seabright 1989). But as European integration progressed with monetary union, the addition of the second and third pillars, and three enlargement rounds, attention to these issues and the concomitant Treaty negotiations soon diverted interest from mutual recognition and the single market. Therefore, when the debate on the new modes of governance came up in the mid- to late 1990s – particularly in relation to the need for economic policy co-ordination in view of monetary integration – mutual recognition was no longer at the centre of attention. 'The most important of Europe's institutional innovations is hardly mentioned any longer in the debates on the so-called "new modes of governance"' (Joerges and Godt 2005: 95).

Why reconsider the principle of mutual recognition? Here it is useful to start by returning to the underlying distinction between government and governance. While the former implicates the potential for hierarchical steering, the discussion about the latter gained ground with the realization of how little gains from co-ordination and co-operation can be assured on an exclusive hierarchical basis. Domestically, states rely on the co-operation of various associations and other non-state actors (policy networks). Internationally, 'governance without government' (Rosenau and Czempiel 1992) exposes the need for non-hierarchical solutions to co-ordination and co-operation needs. Mayntz points to three distinct uses of the term. Originally, governance was equated with governing. Then the term was 'used to indicate a new mode of governing that is distinct from the hierarchical control model, a more cooperative mode where state and non-state actors participate in mixed public–private networks' (Mayntz 1998: 8). Governance now refers to different forms of social co-ordination, going back to Williamson's analysis of markets and hierarchies, and the extension of his typology to include other forms of co-ordination (Williamson 1985).

As with the definition of governance, there is little agreement as to what 'new' modes of governance (NMG) are. New modes of governance, to start, are those that allow for the provision of governance functions in an innovative, but not yet established, way. Authors who attempt to positively characterize NMG generally emphasize that these new modes achieve governance functions in a less binding way (voluntariness), drawing in a wide range of relevant actors (inclusion). Thus, the legitimacy and effectiveness of political decisions is thought to be enhanced (Héritier 2003: 106). Topics much studied in the context of the debate on NMG are the open method of co-ordination (OMC), comitology, and independent regulatory authorities. Apparently, there is difficulty in distinguishing new modes of governance from governance. Moreover, while OMC has been new for the European Union (EU) and has proliferated into several policy fields, the way member states co-ordinate their policies via OMC is most similar to the non-binding co-ordination achieved in other international regimes such as the Organization for Economic Co-operation and Development (OECD) or the International Monetary Fund (IMF) (Schäfer 2006). Similarly, independent regulatory authorities have been new in the context of the EU but are established in the US.

'New' seems to relate as much to the context of where a particular mode of governance is brought to bear as to the mode itself and its true novelty.[1] Rather than attempting a positive definition of NMG which aims at delineating its features, several authors therefore prefer a negative definition, defining NMG in the EU as deviating from the classic Community method (i.e. the adoption of directives and regulations by the Council and the Parliament based on proposals from the Commission) (Eberlein and Kerwer 2004: 122; Scott and Trubek 2002: 1, 5). This definition makes it possible to take into account all 'new' forms, without limiting the analysis because of previous alternative definitions (e.g. no legal measure or the inclusion of private actors as a precondition) (Eberlein and Kerwer 2004: 136).

We do not need to decide whether it is sensible to speak of new modes of governance or simply of governance modes. Mutual recognition, it is apparent, could be seen to be just as new as other examples studied, such as the OMC, comitology, and independent regulatory authorities. While the principle of mutual recognition originally surfaced in the early 1980s with moves to complete the single market, in the late 1990s it was also transferred to the field of justice and home affairs. Outside of the EU, mutual recognition has gained in importance, especially within the World Trade Organization (WTO) but also in other trading blocks. Considering the other characteristics of NMG, how does mutual recognition relate to them?

If we look at the inclusion of a *broad range of actors*, mutual recognition typically works when actors (such as companies and professionals) offer their goods and services abroad. They need to actively take up their rights under mutual recognition, and act under the assumption that the regulations they abide by are deemed to be equivalent. Thus, as far as mutual recognition provides governance functions, it is due to the extent to which multiple actors act according to the principle. If mutual recognition is not used, it cannot function. Moreover, private actors also seem to play a role in the control of the equivalence of regulations. Established companies in a market have an interest in monitoring the entrance of differently regulated competitors well, and are willing to claim non-equivalence if reasonable.[2]

If we turn to *voluntariness*, the case law of the European Court of Justice (ECJ) requires member states to accept equivalent products of other member states. However, the extent to which equivalence exists is not clearly defined or easily established. In their assessment of equivalence, actors have much leeway, with the ECJ being the final arbiter. For the member states, it is not acceptable to simply let any goods or services which are marketed anywhere into their markets. In his article in this volume, Trachtman (2007: 785) calls this 'rootless recognition'. There is a restriction on equivalent products. Member states retain the right to restrict free trade. The need for exceptions quickly becomes clear when we think of products that, when traded, have particular political implications. Thus, without exemption, the Netherlands could export their liberal drug policy, as it would be possible to sell everything sold on Dutch markets in the Community. Of course, this is an extreme example. As member states remain politically responsible for the products traded in their territory, there are many other instances where clarity is lacking, regarding whether or not products meet the equivalence condition with possible consequences for health, the environment or other important societal goals. In his contribution to this issue, Pelkmans (2007) elucidates how difficult it is to bring mutual recognition to work.

Because of the inherently uncertain nature of where equivalence starts and where it stops, Weiler, for instance, deems mutual recognition inappropriate for building the single market (Weiler 1999: 367f.). Although there is an apparent need for exceptions, in fact, it is also clear that there is a fine line between legitimate exceptions and protectionism. Despite the obligation for mutual recognition stemming from the interpretation of the basic freedoms by the ECJ, mutual recognition therefore has more voluntary aspects than other forms of hard law.

Mutual recognition also embodies many of the claimed benefits of NMG compared to 'old' modes of governance, such as the Community method. Mutual recognition allows for more flexibility, for decentralization, and increased public–private co-operation, all of which are features claimed for NMG thought to improve policy output and compliance, in addition to increasing legitimacy (cf. Kohler-Koch 2005: 14). Thus, mutual recognition may be said 'to realize common concerns while accommodating diversity and respecting the institutional integrity and political autonomy of its Member States in all matters where uniformity and centralization are not necessary or not possible' (Scharpf 2001: 13), which are aspects Scharpf relates to NMG.

There is yet another reason to link mutual recognition to the debate about NMG, irrespective of how convincing its voluntariness and broad inclusion of actors is. If we think of governance as responding to the limits of hierarchical government, mutual recognition is an important alternative. Instead of agreeing on a common regulatory solution, governments agree on a patchwork of equivalent national rules. It is only by focusing on this alternative to hierarchy that the growing transnational activities of national administrations become a focus of analysis. Their relevance is increasingly being analysed on an international level (Raustiala 2002; Slaughter 2004). Within the more deeply institutionalized multi-level system of the EU, these horizontal forms of governance play an even larger role.

If this special issue is about mutual recognition as a new mode of governance, then the idea is not to prove how far mutual recognition meets the criteria of inclusion and voluntariness, or whether efficiency and legitimacy are really enhanced by it, as is claimed for other NMG. As mentioned, 'newness' is a tricky attribute of NMG. Rather, the idea is to take a broader approach to NMG as innovative means of providing governance functions. Instead of trying to establish criteria for categorizing NMG, mutual recognition is taken as a – comparatively new – mode of governance, and the goal is to analyse its potential to solve governance problems. The questions asked aim at an assessment of the way mutual recognition may provide governance functions, including the preconditions it needs for its functioning (e.g. trust of the member states, (Majone 1994: 75, 83)), the positive implications of achieving co-ordination through it, as well as its negative side effects (e.g. the danger of a regulatory race to the bottom). In order to provide for such an assessment, the articles in this volume look at the application of mutual recognition in different areas: in the market for goods (Pelkmans 2007) and services (Nicolaïdis and Schmidt 2007; Kostoris Padoa Schioppa 2007), in the area of justice and home affairs (Lavenex 2007), in tax policy (Genschel 2007), and in the WTO (Trachtman 2007) as well as linking the concept to other forms of recognition in international relations, political philosophy, and international political economy (Nicolaïdis 2007). Before introducing the different contributions, I turn to the concept of mutual recognition in greater detail, in order to provide for an initial understanding of its features.

GOVERNANCE THROUGH MUTUAL RECOGNITION

Mutual recognition allows for the integration of previously distinct markets. This is how the principle is used in the context of the single market (or in other trading blocks). Markets, which are constituted by specific regulations for goods, services or professions, and thereby held distinct, can be integrated through mutual recognition. Mutual recognition thus can act as an alternative to harmonization, which depends on the classic Community method and had been the way to integrate the common market before the turn to mutual recognition. But not only markets can be integrated in this way. The decision to implement mutual recognition in JHA, for instance with the European arrest warrant, is an attempt to integrate potentially all areas marked by different regulations, including core areas of statehood. To approach the issue of how mutual recognition works, and in which policy fields it is an option, it seems best to compare it to the existing alternatives for treating diversity. These alternatives consist of, on the one hand, harmonization, where diversity is overcome by finding a common denominator. On the other hand, diversity can be dealt with by agreeing on the use of the rules of the country where the activity takes place – that is, national treatment or host-country control, compared to home-country control under mutual recognition.

Dealing with diversity: national treatment, harmonization, and mutual recognition

The simplest approach to market integration is *national treatment* (non-discrimination) (cf. Nicolaïdis and Shaffer 2005: 7–15; Maduro 1998: 101–49; Armstrong 2002: 229). Member states open their borders to goods and services of foreign origin, if the providers of these comply with the rules of the host country. The only obligation, then, is not to discriminate against foreign products. This approach leaves the sovereignty of the host country intact. It is responsible for market regulation. Companies, however, are burdened with significant costs of adaptation, with the need to comply with different national rules wherever they are selling their products. This approach establishes the primate of political control. Possible trade benefits are forgone by burdening costs on business, but member states keep their regulatory control over markets.

Under national treatment markets remain separated by different regulations. However, it should be noted that this is the approach largely followed in the United States (Maduro 1998: 143). With *harmonization*, diversity can be overcome. Regulatory obligations are harmonized ex ante. This, however, imposes significant negotiation costs on governments. A vertical transfer of sovereignty results at the supranational level. Once regulations of a sector have been harmonized, member states are no longer free to alter them unilaterally. They can only enact new regulatory goals by starting supranational negotiations again. This is another cost of integrating markets to such an extent. As a result, companies do not face additional adaptation costs when targeting the markets of other member states. Ideally, co-operation in harmonization allows for the balancing of the possible benefits of trade with the political interest in regulation. Trade is no longer hindered by the need of companies to fulfil different regulatory obligations, which may just as well be alternative solutions to the same regulatory problem.

Finally, markets can be integrated via *mutual recognition*. At the lowest level is the assumption that member states' regulations do present alternative solutions to the same underlying problem. By being lawfully marketed in one member state, products may also enter the markets of other member states. Thus, member states do not need to face the bargaining costs of ex-ante harmonization, nor do companies need to face the adaptation costs of having to comply with different national standards. Regulation falls exclusively under the responsibility of the home state. Home-state control, however, implies a *horizontal transfer of sovereignty* (Nicolaïdis 1993: 490–93). Member states can no longer guarantee a certain level of regulation of products marketed to their nationals as these regulations are being determined by other countries. The previous unity of territory, legitimation and the setting of rules is broken up. Governments have to trust other member states to regulate and control their companies sufficiently. Subsequently, we can see that mutual recognition is quite a demanding principle of market integration. While it promises to realize the gains of trade without levying particular ex-ante costs on governments (such as for harmonization) or companies (such as when adopting host-country regulations), consumers may face significant information costs next to profiting from increased variety. Moreover, significant costs may arise ex post. Governments may be held politically accountable for products marketed in their country if these imply risks, even though these governments were never in a position to regulate these companies. As the costs of insufficient regulation are partly being exported, while low regulatory standards give advantages to companies, member states may face incentives to engage in regulatory competition – under the assumption that companies are cost-sensitive to the regulations at issue (Holzinger and Knill 2004: 26). Mutual recognition is therefore often regarded as the market solution to regulatory diversity where competitive pressures lead to an efficient outcome. However, the prisoner's dilemma teaches us that a 'race to the bottom' may result, and member states may end up with a suboptimal level of regulation (Majone 1992; Gatsios and Seabright 1989).[3]

In the Community different legal positions match the different principles of integration. Under the *Cassis de Dijon* case law, the ECJ gives a broad meaning to the market freedoms (for goods, services, persons, and capital). As long as goods or services are legally marketed in a member state, in other words, if they conform to the regulations of their home state, they can also be marketed in all other member states. This is the obligation to *mutually recognize* goods and services from the other member states. There is, however, a caveat. The Treaty of Rome gives member states the right to hinder trade and to regulate their markets, if they can claim overriding concerns. While Article 28 assures the freedom of goods, Article 30 mentions different exceptions. The other freedoms face similar restrictions. Additionally, by broadening the reach of the market freedoms under the *Cassis de Dijon* case law, the ECJ simultaneously enhanced the possibilities of member states to regulate their domestic markets, by invoking mandatory requirements to which goods would have to adhere ('rule of reason'). Despite the need to mutually recognize the regulations of others, member states can individually determine the re-regulations of sensitive areas (Hatzopoulos and Do 2006: 965f.).

With these exceptions, member states maintain areas of regulation they can individually determine; it is here that host-country control applies. As this right of *national treatment* hampers the single market, minimum harmonization is foreseen in these areas under the single market programme. By extending the reach of mutual recognition to all fundamental freedoms (goods, services, persons, and capital), while targeting minimum harmonization at those areas where member states have a legitimate claim to exemptions, the Commission's new approach to the single market was one with no need for national treatment. Consequently, national treatment is rarely mentioned in political science analyses of the single market. However, minimum harmonization faces high agreement costs. Rules under national treatment are common whenever member states cannot be obliged to accept mutual recognition and the Council does not agree on joint rules.

While it is uncommon to associate the principle of national treatment with the Community, it plays a large role in the General Agreement on Tariffs and Trade (GATT). This raises an important question: is it fair to say that national treatment is a way to allow for trade that does not have an impact on the sovereignty of the member state, given that we know market pressures on domestic regulations also result from the GATT? To explain this puzzle, it is necessary to refer to the well-known distinction between product and process standards (Scharpf 1999: 91–101). While the GATT may allow its members to define the product standards for goods according to national treatment, nothing is necessarily said about the process standards being used. While goods travel independent of their production processes, the latter in fact often have to be mutually recognized, even in the GATT. A case in point are the famous tuna/dolphin cases; the US wanted to ban all tuna from its market, in the production of which dolphins were being killed. However, it was not allowed to do so – exemplifying the mutual recognition of production processes in the GATT (Scott 2000: 143).[4] It is this 'implicit' mutual recognition that emanates from market pressures on national regulations, not the national treatment of product standards. See Table 1.

Different from the GATT, the single market officially gets by without national treatment. This is because, in the EU, institutionalized, binding means of co-operation exist, allowing for the definition and implementation of common regulations. These regulations are meant to fill in those areas where member states would otherwise take exception to the market freedoms. However, these institutions are only a necessary condition to arrive at co-operation; actors also have to agree on a common solution. Where actors fail to do so due to heterogeneous preferences and/or technical problems of devising solutions adequate for all member states, member states will sometimes 'agree not to agree', and subsequently pass off this right as one of national treatment (Schmidt 2004: 58).

Table 1 Characteristics of principles of market integration

	National treatment (non-discrimination)	Harmonization	Mutual recognition
Authority of regulation	Host-country control	Unified supranational regulation	Home-country control
Costs	Adaptation costs of companies	Negotiation costs of states	Costs of control of hosts; information costs for consumers
Political consequences	No transfer of sovereignty	Vertical transfer of sovereignty	Horizontal transfer of sovereignty, regulatory competition
Focus	Primate of politics	Possible balance of trade and politics	Primate of trade
Legal basis	Exception from the market freedoms	Secondary law	Market freedoms

Source: Adapted from Schmidt (2004: 75).

The potential of governance through mutual recognition

The discussion of mutual recognition has been notably absent in the context of the debate on NMG, but there has been much controversy on both its benefits and pitfalls in the framework of the single market. As mutual recognition does not unify regulations, it is often perceived as a market approach to regulation, where states compete with their regulatory solutions against each other. This market analogy has much influenced the debate on mutual recognition. Often, depending on the degree to which authors believe markets to be perfect or imperfect, they regard market pressures on regulation through mutual recognition as a blessing or a curse. Thus mutual recognition is intimately linked to an ideological debate about regulatory markets. This is hardly satisfactory.

If this volume is about understanding the potential of mutual recognition as a form of governance with regard to its preconditions and positive and negative implications as mentioned above, a differentiated outlook seems necessary. Thus, (1) mutual recognition is bound to work differently in different policy fields – making it more acceptable in one compared to the other; (2) mutual recognition will have different implications for different people and different geographical areas; (3) mutual recognition is generally applied in a restricted way, mediating its consequences; and (4) for an assessment of mutual recognition a dynamic perspective is needed, taking into account its longer term effects, while being aware of both the advantages and disadvantages of its alternatives.

(1) Having been originally introduced for goods, the implications of home-country control in other areas like the freedom of services and persons do not seem settled. Whether goods comply with the relevant regulations under home-country control can be checked by the home country, which is also responsible for the setting of these rules. This is different with services, which generally cannot be traded independently of their provider. Being provided in a different country under home-country rules, it is much more difficult for home-country control to take place. Moreover, in JHA, police in one state are asked to enact the laws of another state. If there were mutual recognition in taxes, member states would have to collect each others' money. With the number of member states increasing, and therefore the number of regulatory regimes increasing, this divided authority over the setting and control of rules raises particular difficulties for the application of mutual recognition beyond the trade of goods. If mutual recognition relies on trust, this reliance is much enhanced when member states need to trust each other not only in the setting and enforcement of rules on their respective territory (the home country) but also on their own territory (the host country).

The fact that mutual recognition gives rise to complicated control issues in some policy fields is only one relevant matter. Moreover, the kind of rules which are being mutually recognized is important. Depending on the issue area, the democratic legitimation of rules differs starkly. For goods, the definition of technical regulations is often delegated to standards bodies; rules in JHA or for taxes, however, concern individual freedoms or redistributive issues. These are in need of a higher input legitimacy (Scharpf 2003), and are normally subject to parliamentary rule. If these rules require the legitimacy of parliament, it must be more difficult to delegate the responsibility over their setting and control to another member state than it is with rules, for the setting and control of which delegation to standardization or certification bodies is normally used.

(2) Whether mutual recognition leads to positive outcomes like diversity and decentralization or to negative outcomes like social dumping depends much on which perspective is taken. For example, consider the possible application of mutual recognition to social security systems (cf. Kostoris Padoa Schioppa 2005). For highly qualified professionals, for instance university professors, their treatment under home-country rules would most likely increase mobility and personal well-being, as scientists could easily move across borders without the hassle of determining how their healthcare and pensions would be affected if they spent some years abroad. However, for relatively low-qualified builders, mutual recognition of their social security would, on the one hand, help to abolish labour-market rigidities; but, on the other hand, there would be a risk of exploitation of wage differentials to an extent that wages and pension contributions paid in high-wage countries to workers from low-wage countries would not permit them to live in the country where the work is being done (cf. Streeck 2000).

(3) Mutual recognition is never absolute. Kalypso Nicolaïdis (1993) pointed out very early on that mutual recognition is 'managed', meaning that it is applied in a context that buffers competitive pressures. Alternatively, we can think about mutual recognition being combined with other integration principles (Schmidt 2004). This is most obvious when mutual recognition is linked to European minimum harmonization/standardization, creating a common baseline. Thus, for the single market we actually have to differentiate between mutual recognition when it only applies to the testing of the compliance of products with harmonized rules (avoiding the duplication of certification) and mutual recognition of product regulations (Nicolaïdis and Shaffer 2005: 17).

However, mutual recognition can also be combined with national treatment. For instance, in the provision of insurance services, insurance companies act under home-country control, but they also have to comply with different national insurance contract laws because otherwise consumers would not know what their insurance protection is (Schmidt 2004: 122). In combination with other market principles, the impact of mutual recognition is modified. This implies that we need to take into account that actors may – wrongly – perceive competitive pressures and act upon them, although they do not take off.

(4) With regard to the fear of a race to the bottom, the long-term effects of mutual recognition could be said to have dominated the perception of the concept. At the same time, few examples of downward spirals have actually become known, probably because mutual recognition is normally 'managed', mediating competitive pressures. But if instances of a race to the bottom are rare, this does not mean that mutual recognition does not have dynamic implications. Thus, the awareness that mutual recognition operates may make it difficult to adapt existing regulations, due to the potential impact on trade. But if mutual recognition hampers national reforms, these barriers must be seen in the context of existing alternatives. While national treatment leaves national politicians totally free to act, the constraints on domestic reform under mutual recognition may be still less severe than under harmonization. Here a qualified majority of member states – next to the European Parliament – have to agree to any future modification, giving a minority a veto position on all future reforms.

In view of these qualifications, it is doubtful how far the market analogy is appropriate. The amount of trust and mutual reliance needed for mutual recognition to function means that there are no anonymous market participants but well-acquainted co-operators who put mutual recognition to work. It might therefore be likened to a cartel rather than a market. Initiating competition and the search for competitive advantages may well risk destroying co-operative benefits. Member states are likely to perceive competition as a misuse of trust which has been given to a joint approach to co-operation problems rather than as a legitimate attempt of some to acquire competitive advantages over others.

CONCLUDING REMARKS

The following contributions enhance our understanding of the complex characteristics of mutual recognition. Beginning the process, Kalypso Nicolaïdis (2007) embeds mutual recognition in the wider context of the conditions for recognition discussed in political philosophy, international relations, and international political economy. She draws connections between economic mutual recognition and the recognition of states, and then moves on to discuss the conditions of 'integration across Europe' (Nicolaïdis 2007: 694), building on managed mutual recognition. As this implies an internalization of 'the interests and beliefs of others' (p. 695), she makes clear that managed mutual recognition reaches as far as possibly questioning the freedom of speech: 'should limits to free speech be legal or moral questions, should bans be considered in case of disrespect or only incitement to violence' (p. 695). Against these broader, theoretical reflections, Jacques Pelkmans (2007) turns towards the actual working of mutual recognition in goods markets. Interestingly, he provides empirical evidence on the problems that different actors face with mutual recognition. Moreover, he discusses the standstill procedure that member states are obliged to respect when enacting new regulations, in order to provide other member states and the Commission with an opportunity to object and to consider whether European rules are needed. This procedure, Pelkmans convincingly argues, serves as an important institutional backing for mutual recognition. Nicolaïdis and Schmidt (2007) analyse the recently agreed services directive. The contention surrounding this proposal showed how mutual recognition becomes unacceptable if differences among member states are perceived as being large and with them the competitive opportunities relating to mutual recognition. Analysing the problems of mutual recognition in the field of services, the article argues that the original proposal went much beyond the practice of 'managed' mutual recognition while the version which was adopted recovers that spirit. In her comment on the services directive, Fiorella Kostoris Padoa Schioppa (2007) emphasizes the benefits of mutual recognition in fostering competition, and is more pessimistic about the achieved compromise.

Philipp Genschel (2007) analyses why mutual recognition has been adopted in goods markets but not in value added tax (VAT). In an interesting historical analysis he shows that mutual recognition was actually originally considered for VAT and declined for goods regulation. With this comparison, he sheds light on the opportunities and limits of governance through mutual recognition, emphasizing the latter. He closes with praise for national treatment (which contrasts nicely with the argument of Nicolaïdis (2007)), stressing the value of diversity as it allows continuing national policy autonomy. Sandra Lavenex (2007) analyses the problems of applying mutual recognition to JHA. Like Genschel, she delves into the market analogy and questions the transferability of the concept into this core area of statehood. While markets are liberalized through mutual recognition, in JHA it serves as a tool of governmentalization. Joel Trachtman (2007) moves beyond the EU with his contribution and discusses the possibilities of embedding mutual recognition in the WTO. He stresses the need to provide for equivalence as a basis for mutual recognition to be acceptable and draws attention to the lack of harmonization at the international level as a precondition of achieving equivalence. Moreover, he emphasizes the risk of excluding developing countries. As he shows, the principle of most-favoured nations established at the WTO can come into conflict with closed mutual recognition arrangements, as the one established in the EU.

Adrienne Héritier (2007) draws together several contributions of the volume. Her comparison of mutual recognition across different policy areas employs a rational-choice institutionalist framework. She argues that the adoption of mutual recognition depends on an activist court and on well-developed implementation rules. Thus, for mutual recognition as a new mode of governance to function, a support structure easing the requested equivalence is the key. In the final contribution to this volume, Maduro (2007) takes up the theme from Héritier on the role of the judiciary in a more normative analysis. He discusses three paradoxes that mutual recognition entails, which relate to the question of governance, to its impact on sovereignty, and to its dependence on identity. He emphasizes how mutual recognition in different policy areas raises different issues of participation and representation, which have implications for its legitimacy as the balance of power within the states is affected. Given that mutual recognition is frequently contested, the final responsibility over where it should apply is often delegated to the Court. For the Court, to assume this responsibility he concludes, it needs to be accorded sufficient legitimacy. This implies 'that the political process can always regain control over the policy issues that it, frequently and implicitly, delegates to courts' (Maduro 2007: 824).

In conclusion, the different contributions to this volume shed new light on the strengths and weaknesses of mutual recognition, a principle that is fundamental to the European integration process but nevertheless often overlooked.

Biograpichal note: Susanne K. Schmidt is Professor of Political Science at the University of Bremen, Germany.

ACKNOWLEDGEMENTS

The Thyssen Foundation kindly funded a workshop at the University of Bielefeld which allowed discussion of most of the papers which comprise this volume. I would like to thank all participants for their helpful comments, in particular Philipp Genschel, Sandra Lavenex and Kalypso Nicolaïdis. Much of the research for this article was done at the Max Planck Institute for the Study of Societies; I would like to thank Fritz Scharpf in particular. I am also grateful for support under the 6th framework programme of the European Union (Contract No. CIT1-CT-2004-506-392). I would also like to thank Claudia Haase for language corrections in several contributions, and Julia Spreen for her editorial assistance, as well as Tanja Börzel and Jette Knudsen for comments. Last but not least, I am very grateful to Jeremy Richardson for the opportunity to edit this special issue and his support throughout.

NOTES

1 Considering this, it might be better to omit the adjective in order to prevent NMG from being believed to be inherently new, which might stand in the way of useful comparisons between different contexts where a certain mode of governance is being deployed – however long it has been used.
2 I thank Wendy van den Nouland for this information.
3 Under certain conditions also a 'race to the top' can result. I will come back to this point.
4 In an interesting article Howse and Regan argue that the GATT could also be interpreted as allowing the imposition of process standards on imported products (Howse and Regan 2000).

REFERENCES

Armstrong, K. (2002) 'Mutual recognition', in C. Barnard and J. Scott (eds), *The Law of the Single European Market. Unpacking the Premises*, Oxford: Hart, pp. 225–67.

Eberlein, B. and Kerwer, D. (2004) 'New governance in the European Union', *Journal of Common Market Studies* 42(1): 121–42.

Gatsios, K. and Seabright, P. (1989) 'Regulation in the European Community', *Oxford Review of Economic Policy* 5: 37–60.

Genschel, P. (2007) 'Why no mutual recognition of VAT? Regulation, taxation and the integration of the EU's internal market for goods', *Journal of European Public Policy* 14(5): 743–61.

Hatzopoulos, V. and Do, T.U. (2006) 'The case law of the ECJ concerning the free provision of services', *Common Market Law Review* 43(4): 923–91.

Héritier, A. (2003) 'New modes of governance in Europe: increasing political capacity and policy effectiveness?', in T. Börzel and R. Cichowski (eds), *The State of the European Union*. Oxford: Oxford University Press, pp. 105–26.

Héritier, A. (2007) 'Mutual recognition: comparing policy areas', *Journal of European Public Policy* 14(5): 800–13.

Holzinger, K. and Knill, C. (2004) 'Competition and cooperation in environmental policy: individual and interaction effects', *Journal of Public Policy* 24(1): 25–47.

Howse, R. and Regan, D. (2000) 'The product/process distinction – an illusory basis for disciplining "unilateralism" in trade policy', *European Journal of International Law* 11(2): 249–89.

Joerges, C. and Godt, C. (2005) 'Free trade: the erosion of national, and the birth of transnational governance', *European Review* 13(1): 93–117.

Kohler-Koch, B. (2005) 'European governance and system integration', *European Governance Papers* No. C-05-01, New Modes of Governance/Connex.

Kostoris Padoa Schioppa, F. (2005) 'Mutual recognition, unemployment and the welfare state', in F. Kostoris Padoa Schioppa (ed.), *The Principle of Mutual Recognition in the European Integration Process*, Basingstoke: Palgrave Macmillan, pp. 190–223.

Kostoris Padoa Schioppa, F. (2007) 'Dominant losers: a comment on the services directive from an economic perspective', *Journal of European Public Policy* 14(5): 735–42.

Lavenex, S. (2007) 'Mutual recognition and the monopoly of force: limits of the single market analogy', *Journal of European Public Policy* 14(5): 762–79.

Maduro, M.P. (1998) *We the Court. The European Court of Justice and the European Economic Constitution. A Critical Reading of Article 30 of the EU Treaty*, Oxford: Hart.

Maduro, M.P. (2007) 'So close and yet so far: the paradoxes of mutual recognition', *Journal of European Public Policy* 14(5): 814–25.

Majone, G. (1992) 'Market integration and regulation: Europe after 1992', *Metroeconomica* 43: 131–56.

Majone, G. (1994) 'Mutual recognition in federal type systems', in A. Mullins and C. Saunders (eds), *Economic Union in Federal Systems*, Sydney: The Federation Press, pp. 69–84.

Mayntz, R. (1998) *New Challenges to Governance Theory*, Florence: European University Institute.

Nicolaïdis, K. (1993) 'Mutual recognition among nations: the European Community and trade in services', Ph.D. dissertation, Harvard, Cambridge, MA.

Nicolaïdis, K. (2007) 'Trusting the Poles? Constructing Europe through mutual recognition', *Journal of European Public Policy* 14(5): 682–98.

Nicolaïdis, K. and Schmidt, S.K. (2007) 'Mutual recognition "on trial": the long road to services liberalization', *Journal of European Public Policy* 14(5): 717–34.

Nicolaïdis, K. and Shaffer, G. (2005) 'Managed mutual recognition regimes: governance without global government', *Legal Studies Research Paper Series*, Paper No. 1007, University of Wisconsin Law School, <http://ssrn.com/abstract=728383>.

Pelkmans, J. (2007) 'Mutual recognition in goods. On promises and disillusions', *Journal of European Public Policy* 14(5): 699–716.

Raustiala, K. (2002) 'The architecture of international cooperation: transgovernmental networks and the future of international law', *Virginia Journal of International Law* 43(1): 1–92.

Rosenau, J. and Czempiel, E. (1992) *Governance without Government: Order and Change in World Politics,* Cambridge: Cambridge University Press.

Schäfer, A. (2006) 'A new form of governance? Comparing the open method of co-ordination to multilateral surveillance by the IMF and the OECD', *Journal of European Public Policy* 13(1): 70–88.

Scharpf, F.W. (1999) *Governing in Europe: Effective and Democratic?,* Oxford: Oxford University Press.

Scharpf, F.W. (2001) 'European governance: common concerns vs. the challenge of diversity', *MPIfG Working Paper 01/6,* Cologne: Max Planck Institute for the Study of Societies.

Scharpf, F.W. (2003) 'Problem-solving effectiveness and democratic accountability in the EU', *MPIfG Working Paper 03/1,* Cologne: Max Planck Institute for the Study of Societies.

Schmidt, S.K. (2004) *Rechtsunsicherheit statt Regulierungswettbewerb: Die nationalen Folgen des europäischen Binnenmarkts für Dienstleistungen,* Habilitationsschrift, Hagen: FernUniversität Hagen.

Scott, J. (2000) 'On kith and kine (and crustaceans): trade and environment in the EU and WTO', in J. Weiler (ed.), *The EU, the WTO and the NAFTA. Towards a Common Law of International Trade,* Oxford: Oxford University Press, pp. 125–67.

Scott, J. and Trubek, D. (2002) 'Mind the gap: law and new approaches to governance in the European Union', *European Law Journal* 8(1): 1–18.

Slaughter, A.-M. (2004) *A New World Order,* Princeton, NJ: Princeton University Press.

Streeck, W. (2000) 'Vorwort: Europäische? Sozialpolitik?', in W. Eichhorst (ed.), *Europäische Sozialpolitik zwischen nationaler Autonomie und Marktfreiheit. Die Entsendung von Arbeitnehmern in der EU,* Frankfurt/Main: Campus Verlag.

Trachtman, J.P. (2007) 'Embedding mutual recognition at the WTO', *Journal of European Public Policy* 14(5): 780–99.

Weiler, J. (1999) 'The constitution of the common market place: text and context in the evolution of the free movement of goods', in P. Craig and G. de Burca (eds), *The Evolution of EU Law,* Oxford and New York: Oxford University Press, pp. 349–76.

Williamson, O.E. (1985) *The Economic Institutions of Capitalism,* New York: The Free Press.

Trusting the Poles? Constructing Europe through mutual recognition

Kalypso Nicolaïdis

INTRODUCTION

This story could well start with the Dutch embassy in Berlin. From without, it advances like the bows of a ship between monuments symbolizing Germany's multifaceted history. As you wander inside, every space offers at least one vista from which to gaze at an adjacent space and from which one can be gazed at. There is no common grand entrance to awe the visitor with a sense of overarching commonality. Nevertheless, she who journeys through this maze of mutually open spaces cannot help but wonder whether the inspiration behind Kolhaus's design wasn't Europe itself. That is, the Union as it is becoming or as some of us wish it to become. A mosaic of intertwined mental and physical landscapes open to each other's soft influences and hard laws, and bound together not by some overarching sense of common identity or people-hood but by the daily practice of mutual recognition of identities, histories and social contracts – what I have called elsewhere our European 'demoi-cracy' (Nicolaïdis 2004).

Such an idea of Europe is, of course, an idealization. Unlike Kolhaus's embassy, the European Union (EU) is built on the quicksands of archetypes, the construct of lawyers and political scientists fighting the twin perils of a post-modern Napoleonic vision of a harmonized continent and a Westphalian nostalgia for absolute sovereign autonomy. Nevertheless, like the embassy, it rests on solid foundations – in the law and politics of integration. And like the embassy, it is predicated on some prevailing common notion of *appropriately intrusive trust*, the double movement of creating a claim on someone else and accepting the limits of such a claim (I assume your space will be compatible with, since visible from, mine; but in return, you trust that my gaze will not be overly intrusive and insistent, in the manner of Calvino's Palomar routine around the naked bosom on the beach (Calvino 1983)). It is this kind of trust, I believe, that is owed to all new members of the Union, including the Poles.

Perhaps to generalize, 'given the opaqueness of the other's intentions and calculations', trust needs to be predicated on identifying and strengthening the *ties that bind* in order to be sustainable (Seligman 1997: 43; Hoffman 2002). The fabric of human intercourse is less often made of *blind trust* and more often the product of *binding trust* between individuals, groups, organizations or indeed countries. Trust of the first kind may only superficially be seen as deeper in that it is most often predicated on separateness at best, mutual ignorance at worst. But if trusting the other is to seek to bind her to one's expectations, such trust requires prior and continued knowledge about such other. International regimes and institutions can be seen as elaborate mechanisms for mutual monitoring, a consensual form of reciprocal spying predicated on residual amounts of trust, trust that we will each refrain from cheating in the blind spots of our commonly agreed standards. International regimes must strike a balance between acceptable *intervention* in each other's affairs and *deference* to each other's systems. With time, the systems might come to be predicated on increasingly *blind* trust, where it is the mutual spying which becomes residual, only the amount necessary to reassure each other that continued trust is warranted. At some point, changes in the scale and purpose of the interaction and in background conditions – be they political, ideological, social, economic or technological – may call into question the whole design on which such a combination of binding and blind trust rests, requiring new additional amounts of binding trust. A new cycle then begins.

This article is a preliminary exploration of the sources and implications of the subtle balance between autonomy and connection, deference and intervention, *blind* and *binding* trust which underlies political and societal bargains around mutual recognition in the EU. In order to do this, I start with the story of the Polish plumber explored in much greater detail in this volume (Nicolaïdis and Schmidt 2007). I suggest a two-step approach to defining 'managed mutual recognition' which highlights the *preconditions* and the *limits* attached to it. I then seek to generalize this approach and explore the conflicts that lay behind the construction of Europe in other realms (justice and home affairs (JHA), diplomacy and freedom of expression) through the lenses of such managed mutual recognition as applied in the single market.

While the first twofold comparison (with JHA) is undertaken elsewhere in this volume (Lavenex 2007), the other two (recognition of state sovereignty and recognition of identities) can be considered as the two ends of the spectrum – from the broad macro to the micro level – and in this way emblematic of the function of recognition in international relations. Clearly, as the object of recognition changes – other countries' laws, other countries themselves, other 'others' – so do its preconditions, including the type of trust required. But I argue that the main patterns stay the same. Indeed, these areas illustrate the connection between recognition as a technical, legal or regulative norm to a more general form of transnational governance to a philosophical principle (Nicolaïdis 1993, 1997, 2004; Kostoris Padoa Schioppa 2005).

To be sure, recognition has become an increasingly fashionable concept in ethics and political theory as 'liberation movements' around the world have learned to see themselves as objects of dis-recognition and subjects struggling for recognition (Taylor 1994; Fraser 1995). In all social conflicts, in other words, resistance to an established social order is always driven by the moral experience of in some respect not receiving what is taken to be justified recognition (Honneth 1996). On such grounds, the recognition conception of justice, translated in various kinds of non-discrimination laws and multicultural practices, has given rise to considerable debate, including on the virtues of restorative justice.

While this enquiry assumes that developments and ideas related to the economic, political and societal realms cannot but inform one another, I will not revisit these philosophical debates here, but instead focus on the actual and potential meaning of *mutual* recognition in the EU itself. In the EU context, it took a long time for observers and politicians alike to see that, in whatever guise, what I call 'pure mutual recognition' is far from a panacea. It necessarily constitutes a surrender of sovereignty, control, dominance, monopoly. In implementing it, states must constantly fine-tune the balance between the liberal imperative of recognition, on the one hand, and the republican constraints that need to be attached to it, on the other. This article suggests that as we explore different realms, we identify three variants of 'managed recognition' and the binding trust that ought to come along with it: recognition as embedded, constitutive and, indeed, mutual.

1. TRUSTING THE POLES? THE CONTESTED NATURE OF MUTUAL RECOGNITION

I have argued elsewhere that we may think of the current times as a Tocquevillean moment for the EU, an EU poised between its aristocratic past and an uncertain but irrevocable future where citizens enjoy the power of their collective vetoes

(Nicolaïdis 2005b). If so, we need to better understand the tensions that arise in the attempt to adapt the existing ethos of the EU to these changing circumstances. The story of the Polish plumber illustrates the great difficulty which comes with such an adaptation.

It is striking that the 'no' to the draft Constitution started its inexorable rise in the French polls at the same time as discussions on the so-called 'Bolkestein directive' reached a crisis. Ironically, the opponents of the directive claimed with great vehemence that it was not the liberalization of services in itself which they were targeting but only the principle of home-country rule, which they claimed was a new principle for the EU, surreptitiously introduced by a neo-liberal Commission. In their view, this principle represented the soullessness of the market logic at its most extreme. It was symbolized by the infamous-to-be Polish plumber who, by gaining unfair competitive advantage through the application of his home-country rule, threatens the integrity of the host-state social contract (Nicolaïdis and Schmidt 2007). The conflictual nature of mutual recognition should come as no surprise (Nicolaïdis 1993, 1997; Nicolaïdis and Shaffer 2005). This is a Janus-faced norm, usually branded as the 'easy option' and yet the hardest of all. As a horizontal transfer of sovereignty, it is both about respecting sovereignty and radically reconfiguring it – by delinking the exercise of sovereign power from its territorial anchor through a reciprocal allocation of jurisdictional authority to prescribe and enforce laws.

The real puzzle then is why the public trial of recognition in the EU and its unprecedented political visibility came so late. In fact, it has everything to do with our Tocquevillean moment for two reasons. First, because in such a transitional moment, market regulation norms acquire a political resonance which they lacked until then, while the political class is unable to construct a public discourse that would prevent such migration to the public sphere from being captured by populists and demagogues. Second, this tension is made worse as the Union enlarges to encompass a degree of diversity of socio-historical systems now in competition beyond the 'mental absorption' capacity of its citizens. In short, at a turning point in our history, the issue of mutual recognition highlighted the instability of European bargains between both ideological families and between member states, especially old and new ones, shifting from the former to the latter over time.

Introducing managed mutual recognition

In this context, alternative regulative principles for the single market definitely bear different connotations with regard to diversity. The classic construct in the EU narrative on the single market is to contrast recognition with, on the one hand, national treatment (which if narrowly interpreted as a ban on discrimination does not solve the problem of regulatory fragmentation) and, on the others, harmonization (which is both impossible to attain and sustain and irrelevant to problems of jurisdiction of control *per se*) (Nicolaïdis 1989, 1993, 1997; Schmidt 2007). When we wish to generalize, the archetypical contrast, of which this threefold distinction is a category, is that between mutual recognition, that is, the engagement with differences, and, on the one hand, isolation, ghetto-ization or ignorance of these differences; and, on the other hand, assimilation or negation of these differences. In both cases, the other side must become like me, either upon entering my territory or through a process of harmonization. The move to mutual recognition comes with the acknowledgement that such sameness is usually neither feasible nor desirable. The denial of recognition comes in the form of the standard reply: your rules, or those governing the production of your products, the supervision of your firms or the training of your workers and professionals do not have to be the *same as mine* but they need to be *compatible with mine*.

My first conceptual move in the international political economy (IPE) field has been to establish that in fact the deeper and more relevant contrast is one step removed from this one. It is between pure and managed mutual recognition, blind trust and binding trust, or between recognition as an alternative to versus an overarching concept encompassing elements of national treatment and harmonization. To a great extent, the distinction is parallel to that discussed by Joseph Weiler and others between the *Dassonville* jurisprudence – at least on one reading of its implications – of generalizing an *obstacles-based approach* to national regulation (all national rules are potentially subject to an assessment of illegality, and therefore to pure mutual recognition/home-country rule by judicial fiat), and the more circumscribed *Cassis* doctrine of *functional equivalence*, especially as further constrained in *Keck*, which involves precisely the identification of the conditions and limits of recognition (Weiler 2005). It must be noted here that only by migrating from the judicial to the legislative arena is it possible to spell out the full panoply of instruments for the management of recognition, which I have described elsewhere as the attributes of recognition (Nicolaïdis 1993, 1997, 2005a).[1] Therefore, while it is important to analyse the role of the rulings of the European Court of Justice (ECJ) in the European story of mutual recognition, it is also true that all the Court could do when it came to designing this more sophisticated understanding of the principle was to provide a road map for politicians and technical experts later drafting the laws (Nicolaïdis 1993; Nicolaïdis and Egan 2001).

Thus my second conceptual move is to ask what makes for sustainable recognition; in other words, how can institutions contribute in the entrenchment of *binding trust?* Binding trust is not only performative, based on what you do, but also *constitutive*, based on who you are – or who you should be – and involves therefore both an act of delineation of that other with whom I accept to interact and a peek inside her boundaries. Managed mutual recognition encapsulates the various ways in which this subtle balance can be struck through political bargains and the move from ex-ante to ex-post conditions (e.g. with less initial convergence we have to accept more extensive mutual monitoring down the road) as well as between such conditions in general and the limits – in scope and effectiveness – that can be put around recognition. The key to these trade-offs consists in resolving conflicts that unfold over acceptable differences and acceptable deference.

The services directive in perspective

The idea that the working out of legitimate differences constitutes the most progressive challenge for Europe today remains relatively far from the left's ideological repertoire, especially parts of the French left, which shares with its Gaullist counterpart a lingering attachment to Europe as *Grande France* (Nicolaïdis 2005b). Whatever the actual flaws of the Bolkestein directive, and there were many, to reject it wholesale, and to vilify the home-country principle in doing so, is to fail to see the EU for what it has become, a 'mutual recognition space'. In fact, the rules adopted by the EU to 'complete' the single market in the last decade have created many kinds of firewalls against all-out competition *à l'americaine* through the kind of managed recognition discussed above.

This has long been the ambition of the European legislator, following on the ECJ's jurisprudence: to create a wide net for legislation on the single market and from this baseline only harmonize or retain host-country control when differences are illegitimate. When should differences be considered so is the object of a vast literature – any pronouncement here is bound to be contested. Suffice to say that to the extent that recognition ought to be conditional on some sort of convergence, we must first decide if it is for the sake of the Polish plumber himself, in order to avoid *his* (unfair) exploitation, or for the sake of the French plumber, in order to avoid *her* (unfair) displacement. One way to reconcile both concerns is to ask whether a service provider on the move can live on his or her wages in the host country. And there is surely a link between legal transnational recognition and domestic social recognition, as workers struggling for wage increases tend to see the injustice of their situation in terms of misrecognition on the part of their own society too.

Indeed, the fate of the Polish plumber had been sealed a decade earlier by the so-called posted workers directive which, in the wake of the *Rush Portuguesa* judgment, reinterpreted the 1980 Rome convention which had instituted mutual recognition in the first place, precisely in order to avoid what can be called 'face-to-face social dumping' (Nicolaïdis and Schmidt 2007). But national negotiators had fiercely disagreed on the scope of host/home-country jurisdiction, agreeing, for instance, to include only 'universally applicable' collective agreements in the list of standards that host countries were allowed to impose on foreign posted workers.

It may be argued that the Bolkestein directive suffered from the ambiguities arising from this prior settlement, which it sought only to clarify (with a liberal bent) while removing remaining administrative obstacles to the operations of the employing firms themselves. Nevertheless, the draft directive may have floundered precisely because it failed to 'manage' mutual recognition enough: its brand of recognition was too deferential to home state systems. Almost in mirror image, many of the opponents of the directive failed to understand that mutual recognition could be more or less managed with pure home-country control at one end of the spectrum. Interestingly, as the debate reached an ideological stalemate, those seeking a compromise in the European Parliament (EP) and elsewhere tried to convey this idea by seizing on an exaggerated distinction between the (bad) country of origin principle and (good) mutual recognition.[2] There were certainly semantic reasons for this shift (mutual recognition 'sounds' progressive and desirable) but I would argue that the real distinction they were after was between the two forms of mutual recognition contrasted in this article, namely 'pure' and 'managed'.

As the debate on services illustrates, a philosophy of recognition is based not only on reciprocal trust but also on the consensual delineation of the limits of such a trust. Can the Polish authorities be trusted to act in the interests of Polish workers? Can trade unions in the West be trusted to act in solidarity *with*, not in protection *against*, Polish plumbers? And what kind of externalities at the local level are created by such patterns of trust? Any interaction or interdependence and thus any formal integration process are conditioned by the collective determination of where tolerable differences start and end between groups or nations. Obviously, the assumption that differences are legitimate until proved not so is conditioned by some kind of will to live together, some basic sense of commonality. It may well be the case that EU enlargement to east and central Europe has widened the perception of differences to such an extent, and thus so weakened the shared sense of belonging, that this underlying philosophy of 'legitimate differences' as the default option must be reinvented anew.

But enlargement was not the only culprit. Opposition to the directive was based on two changing ideological frames: from the old vision of Europeanization as (good) 'non-discrimination' to Europeanization as (bad) globalization; and from associating the EU single market with *liberismo* to *liberalismo*, from free trade to economic liberalism. Under the first vision, the single market itself is an instrument against nationalism and a conveyor of solidarity; under the second, this solidarity function can only be fulfilled through convergence of rules. Under a progressive understanding of recognition, it is possible as a cosmopolitan and solidarist to defend liberty as free movement, or *liberismo*, without necessarily defending economic liberalism, or *liberalismo*, as an anti-state deregulatory ideology. Decisions by the ECJ may constrain the capacity of host states to police their territory but they do so by upholding *liberismo* not by promoting *liberalismo*. Ultimately, recognition, even in the judicialized EU, has been a political decision. Indeed, as I will stress in the next sections, we are speaking here of recognition *of* acts of states *by* states and therefore a mechanism that highlights rather than denies state power.

2. FROM PLUMBERS TO REFUGEES: RECOGNITION AS EMBEDDED

It is worth noting that the 'no' campaigners in France – often lumping together 'no' to Bolkestein and to Giscard – hardly noticed a critical move contained in the draft Constitution, namely the systematic extension of the principle of mutual recognition to the realm of JHA; in other words the acceptance by judges and police forces throughout Europe of each other's judgments and procedures. While the move had been anticipated in practice, it testifies to the increased prevalence of the recognition paradigm beyond the strict realm of the single market (Lavenex 2007). Most spectacularly, September 11 accelerated the adoption of mutual recognition in the EU in the case of arrest warrants; that is, final judicial decisions: 'wanted in one EU country, wanted everywhere in the EU.' In fact, recognition had been adopted as the goal of the system of state responsibility for the examination of asylum claims since the 1990 Dublin Convention in order to ensure that applications would be constrained by a one-stop entry system: rejected in one country, rejected everywhere. No doubt such recognition was driven by division of labour considerations rather than a sudden conversion to the business of trust. And therefore it is no surprise that the system has not been extended to this day to 'positive recognition' – for refugees, that is, accepted once/accepted everywhere.

What can we learn from contrasting the fate of plumbers and refugees seeking to move *in* or *within* Europe? Lavenex (2007) argues that what serves as an instrument of liberalization in one sector, by expanding the societal *vis-à-vis* the governmental sphere, may work in the opposite direction in another. In JHA, '[t]hose benefiting from mutual recognition are hence not societal actors but state representatives.' In short, the field of JHA does not support the liberal credentials which characterize mutual recognition in the single market realm – neither *liberalismo* nor *liberismo*.

To be sure, there is a difference between recognizing who gets to be a criminal *across borders* and what gets to be a certified aircraft or for that matter who gets to be a certified lawyer – *across borders*, although both of the latter can kill too! Crucially, states have learned to delegate authority vertically to non-state bodies in areas pertaining to markets while parliaments are still in control in areas pertaining to justice; in that sense, recognition affects democratic accountability to different degrees in these different areas (Nicolaïdis and Schaffer 2005; Schmidt 2007).

Yet, Lavenex overstates the difference between the two realms for two reasons. First, we cannot say that recognition allows the free movement of products on the one side and the free movement of (state) judgments on the other. In fact, recognition – at least as it relates to international relations (IR) – is always about granting extra-territorial jurisdiction to the acts of states (or bodies with delegated public authority), be they policies, regulations or laws and the ways in which states may help each other in enforcing these acts. The object of recognition is always embedded in a system of state practices (Nicolaïdis 1997; Nicolaïdis and Egan 2001).

Second, the insight that recognition is not *in and of itself* a liberal principle is fundamental but in fact not specific to JHA. When it comes to the movement of professionals, if a doctor has been struck off the register in France, she has also been struck off throughout the EU. True, we can contrast the initial core intent: to reduce regulatory duplication in order to expand EU-wide trade, on the one hand, and to reduce regulatory duplication in order to reduce EU-wide asylum application processing, and presumably successful ones, on the other. Whether the transnational enforcement of state acts curbs or, on the contrary, empowers individuals or society against the state depends on the context. The management of mutual recognition will generally involve a division of labour between host and home states – an area where again the difference between the two realms should not be overstated. In judicial matters, for instance, the member state issuing the warrant delegates the act of arresting a suspect to another – unwilling host state – which therefore lends out its monopoly of force. In trade or establishment, the host state may similarly conduct investigations of foreign firms or professionals in order to enforce their home-state standards or codes of conduct. In both realms, the risks of 'collusion in state control' are real and need to be counterbalanced by enhanced individual rights – hence, the Commission proposal on procedural rights in criminal matters, and the right of appeal devised for service providers in the services directive. But then, such a need to embed mutual recognition in a system of rights may itself run counter to the queen of all objections: subsidiarity.

Indeed, the analogy between JHA and the single market is better served by using the single market in services rather than goods and considering the EU entry of third-country nationals. The asymmetry is clear. In principle, the licensing of a non-EU lawyer by a public authority can be seen as analogous to granting a 'licence to stay' to an asylum seeker. But the crucial difference here is that, in the case of asylum, EU states have not yet agreed on positive recognition, only negative recognition. Indeed, in both cases, state denial of the 'licence' will deny free movement – in the case of professionals, an inability to pursue their profession, either because of a lack of a diploma or for a breach of a professional code of conduct (Nicolaïdis 2005a). The bias towards the restrictive rather than the permissive side in the case of JHA is not due to a structural difference in the 'object of recognition' – always acts of states – but rather to the very nature of the acts being recognized (regulative versus coercive functions of the state) and the alternatives left on the table for the individuals concerned (consider where an 'unrecognized' lawyer versus a refugee will have to return to). In both cases too, lack of trust (of the binding kind) may mean that recognition is so 'managed' that it becomes meaningless, as Lavenex illustrates for JHA.

Thus here again recognition is predicated on binding trust. Both realms make clear that mutual recognition of state acts and harmonization or convergence of standards are not pure alternatives. In fact, recognition is predicated on convergence which may or may not require formal harmonization of the underlying standards, rules or criteria used by regulators, asylum law enforcers, diploma issuers to grant entry. But even the most adamant proponents of harmonization have to accept that recognition is a challenge that is posed above and beyond. The distinction between underlying laws and how such standards are interpreted applies across the board: given an existing level of convergence between asylum granting or professional training standards in different countries, should a host country recognize as valid the access granted by the home-country authority?

In JHA, recognition means that a 'member state not only recognizes a law as being equivalent but recognizes the judicial act in its interpretation of all relevant provisions in a given case' (Lavenex 2007: 765); under single market rules recognition means an ongoing acceptance of how a partner state interprets professional training standards when accrediting licence-granting bodies. In both cases ongoing recognition is predicated on trust that another state's enforcement of mutually compatible standards will result in mutually compatible decisions.

Recognition must remain embedded to remain sustainable. This was the message of the UK Court of Appeal which – after stating in 1998 that a discrepancy of approach between various member states to the criteria of refugee protection did not matter unless deemed 'outside the range of tolerance' – refused recognition of French and German asylum jurisdiction because it did not acknowledge persecution by agents other than the state as grounds for granting refugee status (see Lavenex 2007). It is little surprise that such a life-and-death difference in standards would fall outside the range of tolerance.

3. FROM ACTS OF STATES TO THE CONSTITUTION OF STATES: RECOGNITION AS CONSTITUTIVE

But recognition, of course, before involving the 'acts of states' actually concerned the constitution of states themselves and their becoming members of international society. Since the Treaty of Westphalia (1648) a vast body of legal thinking and state practice has developed to regulate the emergence of new actors, that is, states, in the international order. Here the coveted prize is *statehood*, defined as 'a claim of right, based on a certain legal and factual situation' (Crawford 1979), in practice, the requirements for statehood listed in the 1933 Montevideo Convention: a permanent population; a defined territory; government and capacity to enter into relations with other states. To be sure, it seems that at first sight 'diplomatic recognition' is a far cry from the kind of regulatory and legal recognition as a mode of governance that occupies us in this volume in that it is simply about bringing about sovereignty rather than the deeper horizontal sharing of sovereignty. And yet more profoundly, it can also be seen as the foundational interventionist act on the part of the community of state. Indeed, we could argue that the circumstances of diplomatic recognition demonstrate more vividly and tragically than with other realms the import of appropriately 'managing' such recognition.

Europe's Tocquevillean moment started with a struggle for recognition of this kind, at the edges of the Union, namely, that of the republics emerging from the ashes of Yugoslavia. In this context, the conditional granting of recognition of constituent states as fully sovereign members of international society was to be the foremost foreign policy instrument available to the EU. The story has often been told how the EU's recognition strategy, painstakingly designed in the course of 1991 to stall conflict, actually contributed to increasing it (Caplan 2005).

The basic assumptions made by European governments at the time were twofold. First, recognition would lead to a change of unit of interaction and would therefore externalize the conflict, making it more legitimate for outside actors like the EU to intervene, which in turn would deter Serbian aggression. Second, the EU could use the leverage of *conditional* recognition to enforce a change in the internal behaviour of its beneficiaries. Indeed, EU authorities, including the Badinter Commission of legal experts, went to considerable lengths to try to devise such conditions, relying on and adapting traditional criteria for statehood.

And here again, we see a balance between blind and binding trust, deferential and interventionist recognition. On the one hand, European states added to traditional Montevideo criteria for statehood – as with the requirement to hold a referendum on independence in Bosnia-Hercegovina, for instance. On the other hand, recognition itself is not supposed to introduce any *arbitrary* change in the subject which is recognized, namely the boundaries of the new states which, according to the legal principle of *uti possidetis juris*, can only reflect the territorial status quo of the former Yugoslav republics (at the time, Montenegro could be recognized but not Kosovo).

Our original distinction between blind versus binding trust as underpinning two very different kinds of recognition is reflected in the long-standing debate between the *declaratory* and the *constitutive* schools of diplomatic recognition (Caplan 2005). Advocates of the former argue that the role of recognition is simply to acknowledge that a territorial entity has satisfied the criteria of statehood but does not itself create states; those of the latter see a political or strategic role for recognition in that the very existence of a state depends on the political existence of other states and their acknowledgement of the attribute of sovereignty. Obviously, the reality is more subtle: Israel, Cyprus and Macedonia have existed as states short of universal recognition. But there is indeed what Caplan (2005) calls a recognition paradox: recognition provides the very evidence of statehood – and acknowledgement of the rights associated with it – that may be needed to attract recognition in the first place. It is only after the fact that what is recognized as (pre)existing, in fact, comes to exist.

Clearly, the consequences of diplomatic recognition, if not totally unpredictable, must be considered as at least unintended. To the extent that recognition constitutes a bet with regard to a future state of affairs, it is generally *irreversible* and can best be understood through the analogy of tipping models with changing dynamics of the system before and after the fact of recognition. However much recognition may be predicated on future monitoring of the emerging states, it constitutes an abdication, an acknowledgement that we will continue to interact in spite of our differences. As with 'single market recognition', the conditional ex-ante becomes conditional ex-post. Binding trust implies that what you do is now my business but even if I am not happy with it, it is difficult to revert to the status quo ante.

In the long run, of course, the recognition of the fledging republics by the EU both enshrined (and some would argue precipitated) the disintegration of

Yugoslavia and constituted the prelude to the integration of these new states in the broader continent. It can also be argued that many EU conditions for recognition did bite and that it is more the EU's failure to take them seriously than their effectiveness *per se* which is to blame for the lack of progress in the area of minority rights (Caplan 2005: 183).

In a more detailed account we would need to explore the historical cases of *mutual recognition* between two states which have hitherto co-existed in a state of war, often by being each other's significant others: the two Germanys before 1974, the two Koreas, Israel and Palestine. Here more than anywhere else, we see that the decision to interact means acknowledging the other in spite of fundamental political differences and in order to narrow them. In the case of the two Germanys, the binding recognition eventually led to merger in part because it kick-started a process which itself contributed to the end of the Cold War. As with IPE, diplomatic mutual recognition can only be a stable equilibrium if truly constitutive of the other side rather than a means of accelerating convergence.

Generalizing from these regional and bilateral cases, mutual recognition is the very foundation of the international society of states as we know it and the subject of a whole body of international law. The most elementary expression as well as the facilitating factor for the web of diplomatic mutual recognition was the exchange of embassies which took place in the seventeenth century creating islands of extraterritoriality. Of course, the exchange of rights and duties that ensued was not always symmetrical; witness the treaties of capitulation between the Ottoman Empire and the Western powers whereby European law was to be applied in Asia Minor for European citizens only. This was not, of course, recognition as we are discussing it here: the Ottomans were coerced into accepting the extraterritorial application of European law and such extraterritoriality was a one-way mechanism to protect the commercial interests and private property of foreign traders. Which brings us to our third realm of recognition and the core feature of the kind of recognition which occupies us here, namely mutuality.

4. FROM SACRED CONTRACTS TO SACRED SYMBOLS: RECOGNITION AS MUTUAL

To some extent, as Fukuyama reminds us in his *End of History*, the Enlightenment project can be seen as an attempt at taming the lethal thriving for recognition that drove so many individuals to the fight to death. If human intercourse could be organized around the politics of interest rather than the politics of identity, the violent struggle for honour would give way to the peaceful pursuit of mutually assured prosperity. We know what happened to the enlightenment project in the course of the twentieth century. But where are we today in Europe? From Sarajevo's no man's land to Paris's suburbs, even our Kantian island Europe seems more than ever caught up in struggles about identity and their recognition rather than simple bargains over interests. Perhaps the story of the Polish plumber is also a mix of pure interest-based corporatism and the fear of loss of identity in an expanding Europe, itself seen as serving as a 'Trojan horse for globalization'.

Indeed, we no longer understand 'European integration' as referring to what happens in and through Brussels but to the integration of citizens within their respective national polities – or 'integration across Europe'. As Paris burnt in the autumn of 2005 the flames licked the wounds of many beyond the hexagon. Social inclusion on the part of individuals and groups disenfranchised economically, ethnically or geographically is perhaps the foremost challenge of European politics today. Here, I argue, we need to understand the demands of these disparate actors – from *banlieusards* to strikers in the docks to illegal migrants – not only as struggles for recognition but as part of greater *mutual* recognition battles on the European scene.

The French philosopher Paul Ricoeur (2004) may be seen as one of the most inspired exponents of this vision of 'conflictual consensus' (*consensus conflictuel*) based on mutuality. While radical thinking about social recognition these days overlooks the importance of mutuality (Fraser and Honneth 2003), recognition, Ricoeur believed, speaks of the fundamental link uniting the members of a polity through Aristotle's 'political friendship', itself based on an even more fundamental relationship of an anthropological nature. Recognition takes us beyond the idea of politics as a simple game of redistribution between individuals well assured of their membership in society (Fraser 1995). Instead, the idea of mutuality exceeds the kind of reciprocity which underpins the liberal contract and this 'plus' is 'constitutive' (again) of the political body (Garapon 2006). Mutual recognition may acknowledge dissymmetry (between, say, a victim and the accused) but it serves to tame otherness, to mediate the risk of violence by literally creating Arendt's *inter-esse*, this transitional space in between individuals which makes for our politics. Recognizing the other cannot be solely a matter of positive law since it is based on 'an equivalence that can neither be measured nor calculated' (Ricoeur 2004: 251). And mutuality is about assessing such equivalence beyond the emotional poverty of procedures and rights.

The cartoon controversy which blew up in Europe in the spring of 2006 can be used as a test case here (Nicolaïdis 2006). We do not need to essentialize the relationship between Europe and Islam to acknowledge it as perhaps the most difficult *mutual* recognition challenge facing Europe today. If this is the case, there may be a common cause and common patterns to the denial of recognition with regard to the fate of our Polish plumbers and the fate of Mohammed cartoons on European soil. In both cases, passionate advocates saw grand principles pitted against one another: freedom of movement against sacred social laws when it comes to plumbers; freedom of speech against sacred symbols when it comes to cartoons; socialism versus neo-liberalism in one case; the West versus the rest in the other.

And yet in neither case can we accept the framing of the issue in such stark either–or terms. The real opposition is between self-righteousness on all sides and the difficult search for justice in a globalized world groping for ways to manage our increasingly conspicuous – if not actually greater – cultural and economic differences.

At the heart of both controversies lies the same paradox. If we want people from elsewhere to integrate better in our economies and our societies, we need to recognize the validity of at least *some* of their habits and rules from home. Only in the name of an old-fashioned defence of sovereignty and the absolute match between territorial, legal and administrative jurisdiction can we reject the multifaceted demand for recognition.

National treatment, or 'when in Rome do as the Romans do', will not do. If we want their countries to catch up, small businesses and people from east and central Europe cannot be asked to adapt all over again to each country's rule in a European space which is supposed to be borderless. Similarly, we cannot simply ignore the civic responsibilities that come with Europe's claim to primacy in the so-called dialogue of civilization with the Muslim world within and beyond our borders. Most Muslims cannot be expected to buy our hard-earned fondness of blasphemy wholesale, here and now. Recognition, be it of home regulations or identities, means some degree of internalizing the interests and beliefs of others, as a precondition for freedom of movement, on one hand, and freedom of speech, on the other.

This means, however, that recognition must not only be managed, as I have argued above; it must also be mutual. Managed mutual recognition implies that acceptance of other people's norms can and must be reciprocal, conditional, progressive, partial, negotiated, dynamic and predicated on critical safeguards, which in turn makes it progressive and flexible over time. Thus, the services directive enables governments to enforce local rules pursuing social, environmental, health, security and consumer protection objectives, but only to the extent that these are 'necessary' and 'proportional' to the goals pursued. If countries of origin do their job, they will see their laws recognized to the extent that the European court, the Commission and other associated interests remain keen to enforce non-discrimination to the fullest. The sphere of mutual recognition should expand in tandem with the requisite level of convergence and tolerance between social systems.

Which brings us back to the cartoon clash. For Europeans to be truly reconciled to recognizing Muslims sensitivities, mutuality will certainly help. Muslim societies do not have to become like ours – although more freedom of speech in many of their countries would be welcome – but they must understand that many of us hold sacred the right to express disrespect for religion. Here, as with the single market, the spirit of proportionality would help. Moderates ought to argue on the finer points – should limits to free speech be legal or moral questions, should bans be considered in the case of disrespect or only incitement to violence, etc? But surely, the hope is that with time, greater convergence, mutual knowledge and indeed healthy non-violent conflict, the scope for mutual recognition will expand here too.

This is the (idealized) European vision, if there is one: living with our differences and seeking to harmonize if, and only if, such differences are illegitimate in the eyes of either one of the parties involved. Recognition is a tough call on all sides of the political spectrum. The left fears social dumping when recognition means importing market rules; libertarians fear political dumping when recognition means importing curbs on free speech. Even if these fears can be exploited to demonize Polish plumbers or Muslim migrants, they must be assuaged. Ultimately, however, they must be transcended if we are to live in Europe and in the world as a community of others.

CONCLUSION

This article cannot do justice to the wide relevance of mutual recognition as a norm or to the many different meanings of the idea itself. It only suggests some benchmarks for exporting recognition across seemingly disparate areas – single market, JHA, diplomacy, multicultural dilemmas. And in doing so, it brings together a set of concepts that ought to accompany the quest for sustainable recognition: managed mutual recognition, binding trust and the accompanying features of recognition as embedded, constitutive and mutual.

The research agenda laid out here is to explore the commonalities between the various theatres where the struggle for recognition unfolds from at least three disciplinary standpoints: trade law and IPE; international relations and political philosophy. In each of these realms the resistance to mutual recognition and the preconditions for extending it are grounded in the same constraint of acceptable differences and necessary deference between the parties involved – in other words the double anchor of the needs for sameness (harmonization) and separateness (national treatment). And these very patterns of resistance are the key to designing sustainable recognition regimes.

Many would argue that demands for recognition are so prone to conflict that societies are better off ignoring them, especially when it comes to transnational affairs. The Hegelian project of playing out and eventually resolving the struggle of recognition echoed by Kojeve's (2005) universal state predicated on generalized mutual recognition continues to constitute a key political horizon in today's world. As a result, recognition holds an ever ambiguous ideological status. On the one hand, it can be seen as second best, limiting the need for more harmonious strategies such as equality of chances and solidarity. On the other hand, struggles for recognition are at the heart of a progressive agenda for world politics. Obviously, the themes touched on above are relevant well beyond the confines of the EU. Increasingly, global institutions are designed to reflect our need to interact in spite of our differences and our capacity to agree on the limits of our mutual trust. With greater interdependence comes a greater awareness of differentiation and the need to work out patterns of recognition that are conditional, partial and managed and as such the only game in town.

Biographical note: Kalaypso Nicolaïdis is Director of the European Studies Centre at the University of Oxford and Lecturer in International Relations.

ACKNOWLEDGEMENTS

I would like to thank Shachar Nativ and Susanne Schmidt for their comments.

NOTES

1　As an outcome, managed mutual recognition can be contrasted with 'pure' mutual recognition in the same sense as managed trade can be contrasted with free trade. It involves complex sets of rules and procedures that may serve to reduce, if not eliminate, the open-endedness of access rights. The four main dimensions along which mutual recognition can be fine-tuned are: (a) prior conditions for equivalence, from convergence to inter-institutional agreements; (b) degree of automaticity of access; (c) scope of activities or features covered by recognition; and (d) ex-post guarantees, including ultimately provisions for reversibility. Statically, variation along each of these dimensions can be seen to indicate how far parties have travelled down the road to full recognition. Dynamically, the management of mutual recognition can be viewed as a process involving evolving trade-offs between these dimensions.

2　For instance, Evelyne Gebhardt, of the Parti Socialiste Européen (PSE) rapporteur on the services directive, argued that the Socialist Party was proposing to 'establish the principle of mutual recognition instead of that of country of origin in the directive that is that if one enterprise was established in one country legally it should be able to establish services in the whole of the EU not having to apply all the relevant country of origin principles (*sic*) but operating under a principle of minimum standards applicable in the host country. The "country of origin" principle is not a European answer to the problem – but mutual recognition and harmonization are.'

REFERENCES

Calvino, I. (1983) *Palomar*, Torino: Giulio Einaudi.

Caplan, R. (2005) *Europe and the Recognition of New States in Yugoslavia*, Cambridge: Cambridge University Press.

Crawford, J. (1979) *The Creation of States in International Law*, Oxford: Clarendon Press, pp. 31, 119.

Fraser, N. (1995) 'From redistribution to recognition? Dilemmas of justice in a "post-socialist" age', *New Left Review* I/212: 68–93.

Fraser, N. and Honneth, A. (2003) *Redistribution or Recognition? A Political–Philosophical Exchange*, London: Verso.

Garapon, A. (2006) 'Justice et reconnaissance', *Esprit* 323: 231–248.

Hoffman, A. (2002) 'A conceptualization of trust in international relations', *European Journal of International Relations* 8(3): 375–401.

Honneth, A. (1996) *The Struggle for Recognition: The Moral Grammar of Social Conflicts*, Cambridge: Polity Press.

Kojéve, A. (2005) *Outline of a Phenomenology of Right*, Lanham, MD: Rowman & Littlefield Publishers, Inc.

Kostoris Padoa Schioppa, F. (2005) 'The cultural foundations of mutual recognition', in F. Kostoris Padoa Schioppa (ed.), *The Principle of Mutual Recognition in the European Integration Process*, Basingstoke: Palgrave Macmillan, pp. 224–31.

Lavenex, S. (2007) 'Mutual recognition and the monopoly of force: limits of the single market analogy', *Journal of European Public Policy* 14(5): 762–79.

Nicolaïdis, K. (1989) 'Mutual recognition: the next frontier of multilateralism?', *Project Promethee Perspectives*, Paris, July.

Nicolaïdis, K. (1993) 'Mutual recognition among nations: the European Community and trade in services', Ph.D. dissertation, Harvard, Cambridge, MA.

Nicolaïdis, K. (1997) 'Mutual recognition of regulatory regimes: some lessons and prospects', *Jean Monnet Paper Series*, Cambridge, MA: Harvard Law School.

Nicolaïdis, K. (2004) 'We, the peoples of Europe', *Foreign Affairs* 83(6): 97–110.

Nicolaïdis, K. (2005a) 'Globalization with human faces: managed mutual recognition and the free movement of professionals', in F. Kostoris Padoa Schioppa (ed.), *The Principle of Mutual Recognition in the European Integration Process*, Basingstoke: Palgrave Macmillan, pp. 129–89.

Nicolaïdis, K. (2005b) 'UE: Un Moment Tocquevilien', *Politique Etrangere*, 3 (September): 497–509.

Nicolaïdis, K. (2006) 'Europe and beyond: struggles for recognition', *Open Democracy*, February.

Nicolaïdis, K. and Egan, M. (2001) 'Transnational market governance and regional policy externality: why recognize foreign standards?', *Journal of European Public Policy* 8(3): 454–73.

Nicolaïdis, K. and Shaffer, G. (2005) 'Managed mutual recognition regimes: governance without global government', *Law and Contemporary Problems* 68: 267–322. <http://ssrn.com/abstract=728383>.

Nicolaïdis, K. and Schmidt, S.K. (2007) 'Mutual recognition "on trial": the long road to services liberalization', *Journal of European Public Policy* 14(5): 717–34.

Ricoeur, P. (2004) *Parcours de la Reconnaissance*, Trois Etudes, Paris: Stock.

Schmidt, S.K. (2007) 'Mutual recognition as a new mode of governance', *Journal of European Public Policy* 14(5): 667–81.

Seligman, A.B. (1997) *The Problem of Trust*, Princeton, NJ: Princeton University Press.

Taylor, C. (1994) 'The politics of recognition', in A. Gutman (ed.), *Multiculturalism: Examining the Politics of Recognition*, Princeton, NJ: Princeton University Press, pp. 25–73.

Weiler, J. (2005) 'Mutual recognition, functional equivalence and harmonization in the evolution of the European common market and the WTO', in F. Kostoris Padoa Schioppa (ed.), *The Principle of Mutual Recognition in the European Integration Process*, Basingstoke: Palgrave Macmillan, pp. 25–84.

Mutual recognition in goods.
On promises and disillusions

Jacques Pelkmans

1. INTRODUCTION

Mutual recognition (MR) is rightly applauded as an ingenious innovation by economists, lawyers and political scientists alike. Nevertheless, MR is very demanding in actual practice, both for authorities in the European Union (EU) and at member state levels of government and for business attempting to exploit opportunities in the internal goods market. This article addresses the pros and cons of MR in EU goods markets and seeks to find effective remedies to be applied by the authorities and, to some extent, by business. The analysis and the remedies accord well with the general notion that MR is a demanding form of 'governance'.

At the outset, we explore what exactly MR (in goods markets) is and is not. Not only should judicial MR be distinguished from regulatory MR (explained in section 1) but MR is best understood when placed in a context of alternative ways of accomplishing free movement in the internal market. Section 2 surveys the current MR regime in the EU 25. This regime combines judicial and regulatory aspects while also relying on (recognized) voluntary standards and conformity assessment. Section 3 surveys the regime in actual practice, making a critical distinction in the regime between tackling *existing* barriers to free movement (3.1) and *potential* barriers caused by new legislation in member states (3.2). Section 3.3 provides a benefit/cost analysis of the regime, starting from the presumption that it should serve the EU general interest as reflected in the Treaty of the European Community (TEC) while respecting diversity where possible and proportionate. It turns out that MR is associated with many substantial benefits and many types of costs at the same time, in particular for judicial MR. Section 4 explores several routes which would result in more and better MR. These better modes of dealing with MR can be conceived of as improvements of 'governance'. After all, MR can be regarded as one form of realizing governance functions for 'free movement', but this is best seen together with its alternatives such as harmonization and national treatment. Unlike much of the literature, however, the issue is not so much whether a race to the bottom results. As we emphasize, this is a non-issue because MR in the EU requires equivalence. Rather, the issue is how to minimize the costs of MR in markets and to shift the burden of effort largely to the importing member state. Section 5 concludes.

2. MUTUAL RECOGNITION: WHAT ARE WE TALKING ABOUT?

In order to keep the article within acceptable limits, the logic of MR in the EU is treated in its essentials.[1] Consider Figure 1, which attempts to familiarize the reader with the rigorous logic of MR. It should also help readers to appreciate the powerful role of free movement as well as the alternative of approximation (or harmonization).

The starting point is that free movement is much more compelling and far-reaching than 'free trade'. Under free trade, a country agrees not to impose (say) tariffs and quotas under an international treaty, so it is 'bound' in that respect but remains autonomous otherwise. Such autonomy can be further constrained (as it is in the World Trade Organization) in very limited degrees. Free movement, however, forces the country into a different position: the right of market access (here, inside the EU) is not negotiable but guaranteed as such, and the country can only deviate by explicit derogations as specified in the treaty or European Court of Justice (ECJ) case law. Thus, free movement needs to be ensured by stringent prohibitions of non-tariff measures such as quotas as well as the panoply of regulatory barriers. Without such prohibitions, the internal market would merely be a customs union. Art. 28, TEC prohibits 'measures having an equivalent effect' to quantitative restrictions. Initially, this article was legalistically interpreted. Hence, the term would not catch anywhere near the number and types of 'regulatory barriers' required to render free movement meaningful in the internal goods market. Once the ECJ understood that free movement requires an 'economic' interpretation of this prohibition (rather than a formal and too literal one), it ruled in *Dassonville* (C-8/74) that (what we call) regulatory barriers refer to trading rules 'capable of hindering, directly

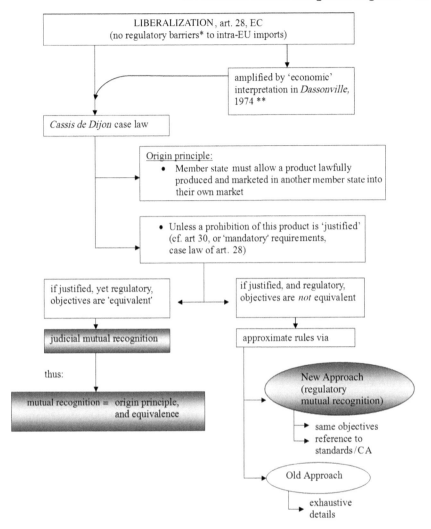

Figure 1 Logic of mutual recognition goods

Notes: *Art. 28 speaks of 'measures having an equivalent effect' to 'quantitative restrictions'. Since *Dassonville*, this is tantamount to regulatory barriers.

**What we call 'regulatory barriers' are defined by the ECJ as 'all trading rules enacted by member states which are capable of hindering, directly or indirectly, actually or potentially, intra-Community trade.'

CA = Confirming Assessment.

or indirectly, actually or potentially, intra-Community trade'. This strict prohibition is balanced by derogations, which need to be respected but also disciplined, otherwise they would undermine the accomplishment of free movement.

It is here that the *Cassis de Dijon* (C-120/78) case law comes in, leading to MR. Following logically from *Dassonville*, the ECJ first defines what has now come to be called the 'origin principle': 'Member States must allow a product lawfully produced and marketed in another Member State into their own market.' Member states can block imports or condition them but only if 'justified' (the derogations listed in art. 30, EC, and the case law, based on the rule of reason, on art. 28, TEC itself). As noted above, the issue is how to respect *and* discipline recourse to these derogations. Case law since *Cassis de Dijon* does both (!) by asking whether a formally justified recourse to derogations really matters for the risks that consumers or workers run in the internal market. The overwhelming majority of the exceptions invoked relate to what could be called 'SHEC' type regulation, that is, related to objectives of safety, health, environment or consumer protection.[2] SHEC regulation is in essence 'risk regulation'. If the risk reduction aimed for is similar, the regulatory objective is essentially the same, and a good can be freely imported. Note that, in actual practice, civil servants or inspectors may focus on the detailed specifics in their national laws, indeed, that is likely to be their routine instruction. The ECJ verifies whether the regulatory objectives in the origin and destination countries are 'equivalent'. If equivalent, the derogation cannot be invoked. The importing member state ought to 'recognize' that the regulatory regime of the exporting member state does not increase risks in an appreciable way. In so doing, the ECJ implies that MR amounts to the combination of the origin principle and equivalence. This is called 'judicial MR' in this article (bottom left boxes in Figure 1).

If not equivalent, the derogations do apply and the only way to restore free movement is 'approximation' as the treaty says. However, even here MR can lead (and did lead) to a highly significant simplification. After all, there is no reason why, in approximation, the issue of equivalence should not be a priority, too. Thus, the New Approach is based on directives where the joint definition of regulatory (SHEC) objectives is the heart of the matter. Once objectives are commonly defined, the lack of equivalence can no longer be a reason to hinder imports. The Old Approach (mainly developed before *Cassis de Dijon*), by contrast, harmonizes by attempting to unify almost all technical aspects of (SHEC) regulation, including extremely detailed technical specifications, testing, approvals and certification. It violates the respect for diversity.[3]

The Old Approach can only be justified economically in cases of extreme risks where uncertainty is potentially too costly: the high costs of extreme specification are overcompensated by the benefits of avoiding unacceptable risks.[4] The New Approach is much easier to negotiate since it is predominantly about regulatory objectives. There is, in addition, a learning process among the member states precisely because they cannot normally fall back on specific technical solutions, driven by engineers, but have to focus on risks, risk reduction and performance requirements. Thus, the market failures are addressed whilst the costs of EU regulation fall considerably. The New Approach is therefore not synonymous with MR but the underlying thinking is closely related, which is why it is often referred to as 'regulatory MR'. This phrase refers to the common definition of regulatory objectives in a light directive.[5] The absence of further technical details implies that different technical requirements are subject to MR. The sensitivity of this type of risk regulation is such that both member states and business are in need of greater practical guidance about what is 'recognized' in markets; after all, one light directive might refer to many thousands of quite distinct goods. Thus, in the New Approach, the common objectives in light directives are complemented by the 'reference to standards'. A carefully structured regime has been set up which develops (voluntary) European technical standards on the basis of 'mandates' issued by the European Commission, in turn derived from the SHEC objectives in the relevant directive(s). Market participants, and not Eurocrats or national civil servants, develop standards for the EU.[6] The Commission recognizes these standards and, after official publication, business can rely on them for intra-EU free movement.[7] This regime is much appreciated because it provides business with guidelines and certainty. European standards incorporated in a regulatory MR regime are also attractive because they do remain voluntary. In case a company is innovative and creates novel aspects or techniques or uses new materials not foreseen in a European standard, the new good can be tested directly on compliance with the SHEC objectives in the relevant directive(s).

In short, as Figure 1 sets out, judicial MR amounts to the origin principle in its pure formulation, together with equivalence of regulatory objectives of member states, whereas its main alternative, regulatory MR, consists of the common regulation of SHEC objectives, together with MR of all the specific technical requirements in national laws. In both approaches, therefore, the quite sensational result is that existing technical details in national laws, supposedly to be enforced by the responsible inspectors or civil servants, cannot be used to block intra-EU imports, except if that good does not comply with recognized European standards or clearly violates SHEC objectives themselves.

3. THE EU MUTUAL RECOGNITION REGIME IN PRACTICE

It is exceedingly hard to 'see' the MR regime in the Union. Business cannot readily 'observe' the law, nor is it immediately obvious for inspecting officers. By definition, MR is based on general judicial principles which have arisen from ECJ cases and not only on regulations that the officers are quite naturally asked to enforce, namely, their own. Where MR applies, there are also no EU laws. MR avoids centralization via approximation or common rules, yet protects free movement. In other words, in day-to-day practice in trade and transport, MR seems to be 'invisible', as it were. MR is therefore difficult to explain and even harder to apply in actual practice when goods enter markets of other member states. The EU institutions render it even more mysterious as they speak of goods falling under MR as if they are a 'residual'. The Eurospeak is: goods 'in the non-harmonized field' (*sic!*). Also, factually, MR is not easily studied. There is no effort to collect statistics or to set up a databank on all cases ever discussed at the national level. The upshot is that it becomes difficult to estimate the economic significance of MR in terms of value added or intra-EU trade affected (see Atkins 1997; Brenton *et al.* 2001). There is fragmented or selective evidence and there are business anecdotes, without much of a clue as to whether they are representative or not. It is possible, however, to set out the MR regime as it is supposed to work. The present section is devoted to an exposition of what one might denote as the official EU 'doctrine' of MR in goods. In section 3.3, where the costs of MR are discussed, it will become clear that actual EU practice deviates considerably from the doctrine.

One should first distinguish existing and future obstacles to free movement. The latter may arise from new legislation in member states and is tackled at the drafting stage. It will be discussed in section 3.2, after the exposition of how MR can overcome existing barriers.

3.1 Overcoming existing barriers through mutual recognition

When inspecting officers of member state A find an imported good from another member state[8] which does not comply literally with the requirements of the laws of A, they might not act differently from elsewhere in the world, that is, order the producer or seller to withdraw the good. Since many goods are subject to at least some form of risk regulation (in short, usually SHEC), numerous costly barriers would make a mockery of the internal market for goods. To understand whether and how MR might alter this conduct of national authorities, consider the following steps. First, judicial MR does not apply if the good falls under approximation directives. This can refer to both New and Old Approach directives and the conformity assessment systems related to them (including CE (*Communauté Européenne*) marking). It also refers to food law where a specific variant of New Approach thinking has been developed since the mid-1980s. Altogether, goods falling under approximated rules easily amount to 50 per cent of intra-EU trade. The practical problems arising under approximated rules have gradually been reduced to relatively few as the system has been improved and refined. Due to specifications in Old Approach directives or to European standards related to New Approach directives, there is a high degree of uniformity in the application at national level. Business is generally quite confident because of the exactitude of the EU-wide technical references and the related conformity assessment.[9]

Second, if the good does not fall under approximation directives, it should in principle be admitted on the basis of free movement, unless derogations apply (judicial MR). But if EU countries maintain SHEC type legislation which is not harmonized, their inclination will be to enforce their laws. This inclination is further strengthened by the fact that member states' responsibility for SHEC type objectives has always been retained. The EU level of government is not ultimately responsible and politically accountable for the health and safety, etc. of the citizens; national governments are. Thus, there can be no doubt about the right of member state A to verify conformity of imported goods with the protection (against risk) afforded in A. What is so special about the MR regime of the Union is that the exercise of this right is severely disciplined by a host of strict requirements emerging from case law and interpretations by the

European Commission. The point of these disciplines is to uphold free movement where possible and to avoid any disadvantage at any stage for the company introducing the good into A compared to companies inside A. The spirit behind much of these disciplines (since *Cassis de Dijon*) is that it cannot be assumed a priori that other member states do not care about the risks their citizens might be subjected to. That is why verification of the rules in the member state of origin is required with a view to an equivalent protection.

The central features of the regime are as follows: member state A should *not* start by ordering immediate withdrawal but contact the company and give it reasonable time to provide hard evidence (e.g. laws from the country of origin, standards, test reports, certificates, approvals) that the regulatory objectives of A have been satisfied, even if the technical details in A's law are not minutely followed.[10]

With data collected, A should verify whether the level of protection in the country of origin is *equivalent*. If so, market access should be granted. Thus, it is often unavoidable to go deeper into ways of verification. After establishing that the protection sought is recognized as legitimate under the treaty (art. 30, EC) or by the ECJ (the so-called mandatory requirements of the case law of art. 28, EC), the level of protection as expressed by technical rules has to be supported by risk assessment, including scientific justification. If there is no appreciable risk in this sense, consumers should be free to choose, possibly subject to a labelling requirement. In other words, the necessity of the technical rules can be challenged and, if not necessary, European case law considers it 'disproportionate'. Observe that MR applies irrespective of whether local goods in A remain subject to the restrictive provisions in A's law for that good. However, even if the necessity of the measure(s) is accepted, there may well be less restrictive alternatives to accomplish the objective pursued. In that event, either A must recognize a less restrictive measure in the country of origin or itself apply a least restrictive measure lowering the cost for companies exporting to A.[11]

Member states should make every effort to have proper communication with the company concerned, for reasons of clarity (the basis for appeal, for example), and notify the Commission in case of a negative decision.

The application of MR can be very intrusive. At the same time, MR is in need of a well-developed regime beyond the member state level, to protect all bona fide companies trying to exploit the internal market. The better developed the 'governance' of MR, backed up by hard case law and the role of the Commission as the guardian of the treaty, the more effective will be the function of MR and the lower its costs. Unfortunately, precisely the governance of MR for existing barriers leaves much to be desired even in a highly developed system like that of the Union, as we shall see in later sections.

3.2 Overcoming prospective barriers through mutual recognition

Interestingly, a well-developed form of 'governance' has already existed for some 20 years for *prospective* barriers in draft legislation of the member states. This is remarkable. At first sight, one would assume that it is easier to tackle existing barriers on the basis of complaints and reporting, or perhaps even 'screening', than presumed obstacles arising from ex-ante interpretation before a national law is even enacted. Stranger still, how can one possibly expect the Union to be *more* effective in preventing barriers that have not even manifested themselves than in overcoming existing obstacles in concrete cases with direct and observable consequences in the internal market? For a 'governance' of MR in the case of prospective barriers in the future, would not the Union have to intervene directly in the national legislative processes, the heart of sovereignty of the member states? Indeed, that is exactly what happened.

The EU regime preventing new regulatory barriers from arising has MR as its foundation. But this is topped by an intrusive and stringent notification system (with tough sanctions in the case of non-notification, emerging from firm rulings by the ECJ), close monitoring by the Commission of failures to notify, detailed scrutiny of draft laws of member states by a special committee chaired by the Commission, and – most remarkable of all – automatic or semi-automatic suspension of the national legislative process for periods varying from three months to as much as 18 months, depending on the need for remedies and their nature. This contribution is not the place to discuss all the features of the regime (Pelkmans *et al.* 2000). What matters for our present purposes is how central MR is to the remedies sought. The basic requirement for these national regulations is that there be explicit and clear clauses on MR or 'equivalence'. After all, regulations where member states still have regulatory autonomy (in goods) must be in the 'non-harmonized area' and that is where MR ought to apply.[12] Such clauses can be attached to the objectives or the technical standards referred to. This reference to standards becomes more effective over time as the European Committee for Standardization (CEN) and the European Committee for Electrotechnical Standardization (CENELEC)[13] increasingly write standards which, by definition, are valid for all European Economic Area (EEA) countries, Turkey (owing to the customs union with the EU), Switzerland and several other European countries. In a rising number of instances, such standards may be identical to world standards.[14] When world standards are used in such instances, MR extends to imports from third countries if adherence to these standards is ensured by credible conformity assessment. The large majority of national draft laws passing the 98/34 committee either contain equivalence clauses by now or have been adjusted after insistence by the committee (Pelkmans *et al.* 2000). If the enacted laws, later, do not have such clauses, they infringe EC law, and are unenforceable against intra-EC imports. The conclusion is that the regime, backed up by significant resources and efforts as well as by firm ECJ rulings, forms a powerful and credible agent for MR to be maintained and to become more 'visible' for business.

How important is this regime for free movement? Without prejudging the effectiveness of MR for existing barriers, which is assessed later, it should be underlined that the regime to prevent regulatory barriers (mainly) with MR is far more relevant in the longer run.

The reason is as simple as it is overwhelming: modern developed countries have turned into machines for risk regulation (SHEC). Without the regime to impose MR, the internal goods market of the EU would long have been lost! Pelkmans *et al.* (2000) show that total notifications over the 11 years between 1988 and 1998 were around 5,000 and the trend was upward. Note that this figure relates to a relatively limited range: only goods, and not those merely approximated in EC directives. The annual rate over 1995–98 was at a baffling 600 plus a year. Figure 2 shows that the average annual number of notifications before the Eastern enlargement is slightly below 600. With the new member states, the EU total increases by some 30 per cent (2005 over 2004). Figure 2 can also be interpreted as evidence about the *degree* of 'pre-emption' of potential barriers and their substitution by MR. One reasonable assumption could be that the responses given in the 98/34 committee indicate when national drafts would have led to potential barriers.[15] One glance at Figure 2 makes clear that, with a crude annual average of about 300 comments, perhaps up to 2,100 or so national laws in just seven years would have led to potential regulatory barriers. Indeed, after two decades of the 98/34 committee (formerly the 83/189 committee), it is unlikely that this permanent scrutiny has no positive influence on the way national (technical) regulation is drafted. In view of these figures, how could the internal goods market – in so far as it is not governed by harmonization–possibly have been safeguarded without the 'pre-emption machinery'? It goes without saying that infringement procedures and judicial review can never be expected to resolve more than a tiny fraction of this regulatory avalanche.

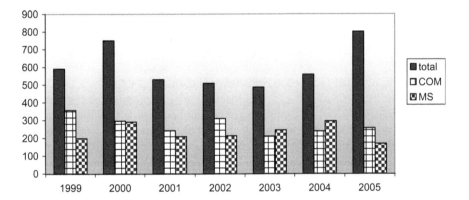

Figure 2 Searching for potential regulatory barriers
Notes: 1. total = number of 98/34 notifications of draft regulations of EU member states and the European Fee Trade Association (EFTA); 2. COM = written responses by the Commission on the member state draft regulations; and 3. MS = member states' written responses on member state draft regulations. Own calculations.
Source: <http://europa.eu.int/comm/enterprise/tris/index_en.htm>

3.3 Assessing the EU mutual recognition regime

It is insightful to subject MR in goods to a benefit/cost analysis. This is done in Table 1 and briefly elaborated in the text of this section.[16] There are many benefits to MR, whether judicial or regulatory. Table 1 suggests three categories of benefits. First, regulatory benefits, in the sense of better regulation. If MR is purely judicial, member states' autonomy with respect to regulatory objectives is retained owing to their 'equivalence', even though free movement prevails. If MR is regulatory, the treaty prescribes a high level of protection (typically, in SHEC type risk regulation), so that there can be no race to the bottom via bargaining. Moreover, there will be a bias against regulatory failure of member states because technical specifications (which might lead to over-regulation) are no longer in directives, whilst the technical standards referred to are based on performance criteria rather than design (i.e. prescriptive detail).

Second, strategic benefits relate to the deepening and quality of the internal market. If MR is judiciary, the breakthrough was, and is, that free movement prevails whereas it was hindered or blocked before. It accomplishes this without adding any EU regulation, that is, it avoids centralization. Moreover, judicial MR disciplines member states' over-regulation, since their rules cannot stop intra-EU imports originating from regimes with lighter rules (as long as the objectives are equivalent). Finally, judicial MR forms the basis for 'regulatory competition' without a race to the bottom which goes further than MR in a static sense (see Sun and Pelkmans 1995). If MR is regulatory, the deepening of the internal market is accelerated because lengthy negotiations can be avoided (including blockages on technical details) and agreement on goals is easier. Furthermore, it disciplines over-regulation at both levels of government, since the focus is on objectives and the reliance on European performance standards reduces considerably the scope for idiosyncratic (or protectionist?) specifics. Regulatory MR does add EU rules but minimally so, compared to the Old Approach.

The third benefit concerns economic welfare which is what the internal market is all about: MR is pro-competitive (Pelkmans 2005a).

With this litany of advantages, MR seems almost too good to be true. Indeed, this is how, naively, MR is often portrayed among economists. In European law, however, and even in political science, there is also an inclination to neglect the considerable drawbacks of MR in actual practice, both for business and the authorities, whether EU or national. It is important to appreciate the costs of MR for business and authorities.

Table 1 distinguishes three types of costs. First, information costs, which are especially large for judicial MR. After all, MR is 'invisible' to economic agents, unless specific laws contain clear equivalence clauses, be it on objectives or standards. What economic agents 'see' are the requirements in local laws. Since judicial MR is developed in ECJ case law, numerous businesses have no idea about MR or that it might matter to them, let alone that companies might know how to verify whether it is applied to their goods.[17] One costly consequence of this

Table 1 Benefits and costs of mutual recognition

Types of benefits	Judicial MR	Regulatory MR	Types of costs	Judicial MR	Regulatory MR
Regulatory	autonomy MS retained for objectives	common SHEC objectives ensured bias against 'regulatory failure'	**Information**	MR 'invisible' for economic agents, except at high costs (without clear MR clauses) even if information is collected, many 'grey areas'; uncertainty (e.g. case law) for business and MSAU no rule book imposed on MSAU	some modest uncertainty, if European standards are lacking or innovation is used
Strategic	free movement prevails over-regulation of MS disciplined basis for regulatory competition without race to the bottom no (additional) EU rules	internal market deepening accelerated over-regulation MS and EU disciplined only minimal (extra) EU rules	**Transaction**	monitoring extremely costly, evidence anecdotal at best when MSAU refuse, reputation and waiting costs, little (EU) help (except SOLVIT) assuring rights for business unattractive, costly and slow	regulatory and standardizers' networks monitor and solve, partly (with delays) (*idem*, but rare)
Economic welfare	pro-competitive	pro-competitive	**Compliance**	unknown, possibly serious costs for existing rules	

Notes: MS = member states; MSAU = member state authorities.
NB This table merely assesses the MR of *existing* rules (see section 3.1).

ignorance is that many small and medium-sized enterprises (SMEs) fail to consider MR and thus either refrain from exporting to countries, or do export but
after adaptations, which is exactly what MR aims to avoid. For companies which
do know about MR, the costs of verifying whether MR would apply to their
goods can be high and/or lead to uncertainty. In addition, there are costs
because of 'grey areas' about when 'equivalence' applies, both for business
and the authorities, even when national authorities do act in the spirit of
MR. Unfortunately, the lack of a 'rule book' for MR, in particular for national
inspecting agencies or other officials, causes most civil servants not to act in that
spirit; rather, they often attempt to enforce local rules. The Commission has
gradually come to realize the down-side of judicial MR and issued reports
and soft guidelines; it has also greatly improved the information on its
(TRIS) website,[18] promoted seminars and launched a special campaign for
the new member states. *Vis-à-vis*, business, this is unlikely to help much
because many SMEs tend to ignore such general campaigns. For officials, the
usefulness is greater. For regulatory MR, information costs are far lower.

Second, transaction costs are also substantial for judicial MR. However, hard
evidence about transaction costs is scattered and/or anecdotal, and gives little
idea of how representative these data are, as the Commission cannot monitor
judicial MR. Case studies indicate that SMEs in particular are deterred by
actual transaction costs as well as by uncertainty. The deterrent effect is greatest
when member state authorities routinely refuse market access if a good does not
match local technical requirements. Imposing withdrawal implies a loss of reputation. This is followed by waiting costs, which can only be reduced drastically if
bilateral co-operation between member states is quasi-automatic or the Commission intervenes. The recent SOLVIT voluntary co-operation procedures[19]
are beginning to help fill this gap. Furthermore, business is often hesitant to
ensure its rights under Community law, one reason being that future business
in the destination country ought not to be jeopardized. Besides, the pursuit
of one's rights under Community law is very slow and costly. Business often
rightly notes that legal progress about free movement should not be conquered
by it but reasonably guaranteed by the system. It is striking that these costs
largely arise from the absence of networking and sound investment in bilateral
co-operation inside the Union. The contrast with regulatory MR is significant.
In sectors covered by the New Approach, regulatory and standardizers' networks
broadly monitor the situation, contacts are not anonymous, irregular network
meetings take place and some problem-solving does occur, be it with delays.
As a result, assuring one's rights is rarely necessary.

Third, compliance costs typically exist when judicial MR fails; under regulatory MR they are exceptional. However, there is no reliable evidence on compliance costs.

MR in the EU goods market is thus characterized by multiple and substantial
benefits and a number of costs which, for business, tend to accumulate to possibly deterrent levels. There are also costs for national authorities, but only when
they enforce rules in the spirit of MR. The disturbing conclusion, at least for

judicial MR, is that the very companies relying on MR in the internal market are hardly 'protected' by its regime. The incentives are therefore perverse and they will have to be altered into positive ones for judicial MR to engender the much wanted benefits for the Union. The picture for regulatory MR is far brighter.

4. MORE AND BETTER MUTUAL RECOGNITION?

It is important to insist on more and better MR in the internal goods market. I shall propose several routes for improvement which can be pursued simultaneously. The problem of better governance of MR in the Union relates to the incentive and discipline structure for the authorities and business, minimizing the costs (including uncertainty) and developing a multi-layered 'MR culture'. There are four issues here.

First, the contrast between the governance of MR in dealing with *potential* barriers in goods markets and the weak, haphazard, unreliable and slow 'governance' of MR when encountering *existing* differences in technical specifications between member states is very stark indeed. This contrast is a function of the path dependency of goods regulation once it is in force. Member states are very hesitant, if not manifestly unwilling, to adapt existing laws outside of an approximation process. And even if they would be prepared to adapt, the question would be: adapt to what example, given the many bilateral relationships among member states? This leads to a choice between two very different routes to improvement of MR: either a set of enforceable and clear disciplines are imposed on the member state authorities, which sufficiently 'protect' business claiming market access so as to drastically reduce the costs of judicial MR, or the very reasons for costs and uncertainty are removed via some light form of regulatory MR. Both are probably perceived as costly by member states and will thus be resisted.

The disciplines currently applying to member states are both weak and fuzzy, as they arise from selected pronouncements by the ECJ.[20] In essence they boil down to the following. Once a good to be imported from another member state appears not to comply with national rules, the national authorities must do something that they are not easily inclined to do; namely, rather than ordering withdrawal right away, they should analyse their own rules (!) in the light of art. 30, TEC and the rule of reason (about 'mandatory requirements') applied by the ECJ to art. 28, TEC. This counter-intuitive act may well result in discovering that the provision conflicts with the treaty or case law. They must then apply MR. If they are convinced that the provision is not incorrect under Community law, the authorities should demonstrate to the exporter concerned (a) the reason in the public interest leading to that provision, (b) the necessity of the restriction and (c) its proportionality (e.g. no less restrictive means available). However, this ambitious (self-) governance does not work, is also not enforceable, and is not monitored. Few companies, often not aware of MR, realize that such disciplines for the authorities have been pronounced by EU institutions, and even fewer would dare to assure their rights formally.

These disciplines should therefore be tightened and made compulsory, strengthening the governance of MR. In 2006, the Commission discussed with the member states, at senior officials level, some procedural guarantees, including the obligation to provide a written and reasoned reply to enterprises based on conformity with Community law. The stick behind such a set-up is not so much a legal measure as such at EU level, but the 'inapplicability' of national provisions (hence automatic market access) if the disciplines have not been properly executed. Such an incentive would reverse the burden of effort and proof away from companies (at least in destination markets) to member states inclined not to allow free movement. Another point of discussion is the strengthening of administrative co-operation between the member states, for which there is not a good track record. An Internal Market Information System has been set up and this should provide ample scope to create a network of (single or otherwise relevant) contact points, tied to minimum endeavours and deadlines. In effect, what administrative co-operation could accomplish is, first, to gradually foster some sense of an MR 'culture', and, second, at least faintly mimic the kind of more specialized networks so common in New Approach directives. The latter will never be achieved for judicial MR because of its horizontal nature but monitoring, experience and data could greatly assist.

Second, a better appreciation of how business exploits the internal goods market, or fails to do so, is required. The unawareness problem could be countered by providing far greater exactitude and transparency about what categories of goods fall under judicial MR, either fully (i.e. there are no sectoral or horizontal directives) or partially (owing to aspects of goods regulated by approximation). Such a list cannot pretend to be exhaustive but is likely to reduce initial uncertainty. One should expect it to be rapidly diffused via websites and trade associations and so reach SMEs as well. Companies typically operating throughout the internal market or the EEA are aware of MR and of their rights. Nowadays, however, their strategies voluntarily mimic a kind of regulatory MR when judicial MR would legally apply. A typical company following such a strategy is IKEA. The strategy consists of screening national requirements and, if at all possible, designing the product in such a way that a high level of SHEC protection is guaranteed, satisfying all national provisions. The good is thus sold in countries with lower requirements in an identical form as it is in countries with more ambitious legislation. The reasons are economies of scale in distribution, marketing and (sometimes) production itself, as well as a powerful drive to avoid costs to reputation following withdrawal. The upshot is tantamount to what David Vogel (1995) has called 'trading up', be it here by market forces.

Third, it is interesting to consider practical solutions to refusals of MR (see Atkins 1997; Pelkmans 2005a). Solutions tend to go some way in the direction of regulatory MR, thereby reducing uncertainty. One example is bicycles, where the safety and consumer protection objectives themselves were not 'harmonized' but a newly developed CEN standard came to be accepted on the basis of which de facto market access emerged. At the more general level of lobbying by European business, the disenchantment of MR is explicit since the UNICE (Industrial and Employees' Confederations of Europe) report on regulation (UNICE 1995, 2004; see also Molitor *et al.* 1995). Regulatory MR is much appreciated by companies, not only because of greater certainty about objectives and standards but also because of the procedural obligations of member states, thus avoiding most of the costs of judicial MR. In the light of 'better regulation', however, which ought to minimize EU regulation to what is indispensable, it seems that firm 'governance' of judicial MR would be preferable.

Fourth, one should not forget that the more ambitious regime preventing potential barriers will gradually reduce the remaining problems of judicial MR. It is unclear how fast this process works. However, in the last few decades, technical progress has caused almost all laws and decrees to be revisited sooner or later. This is one explanation of the enormous number of notifications to the 98/34 committee. Also, CEN/CENELEC/the European Telecommunications Standards Institute (ETSI) standards and sometimes world standards rapidly multiply in areas not governed by 'mandates' from the Commission. These trends provide many occasions to insert explicit MR or equivalence clauses into such national laws and, when relevant, refer to European standards as a basis for compliance.

5. CONCLUSIONS

MR in EU goods markets is well developed and has helped to realize free movement while respecting diversity and some national regulatory autonomy. But it has proved to be far more successful in its regulatory variant than in the 'pure' judicial form. The 300 odd ECJ cases on MR in goods might give the impression of a monumental edifice, governing and safeguarding free movement in the 'non-harmonized area' of the internal goods market. Undoubtedly, the case law has helped us to explore and better appreciate the complexities of MR. But the manifold and non-trivial costs of judicial MR are not fully appreciated by EU institutions. The costs of judicial MR matter a great deal to business, in particular SMEs. True, EU governance, with strict judicial review and the assurance of 'equivalence' of regulatory objectives (sometimes complemented by the application of 'proportionality'), is sophisticated. Nevertheless, the lack of enforceable disciplines for member states' authorities, as well as the lack of credible incentives, have been shown to be a serious obstacle to the effectiveness of judicial MR. In addition, governance can be further improved by other efforts such as reducing information costs via detailed product lists and a duty to engage in active administrative co-operation between member states.

In the longer run, however, the problem will gradually be reduced in view of the ambitious scrutiny of national draft laws possibly containing prospective regulatory barriers, coupled with a duty to insert equivalence clauses in new laws. The 98/34 committee doing this work has, over the last two decades, uncovered many thousands of laws and decrees which would have incorporated provisions restricting free movement, short of the committee's insistence on corrections and equivalence clauses. Without this ex-ante kind of governance, the internal market would have been a mockery!

Altogether, the inference is that, for MR to be effective in guaranteeing market access, a very rich and powerful regime as well as considerable and permanent efforts at both levels of government are necessary. However, that should not be interpreted as an inevitable drift to either harmonization or national treatment (i.e. a great deal of fragmentation). MR in goods is at work today and, as noted above, will gradually gain significance. The disillusions of business are concerned, first, with the great under-utilization of the potential of MR (at their peril) and, second, the problem of MR creating uncertainty, longer time to market and potentially high image costs. Opportunities in the internal goods market should not come with such high costs. The remedies in section 4 would greatly lower such costs while not reducing the benefits of MR.

Biographical note: Jacques Pelkmans holds the Jan Tinbergen Chair and is Director of the Department of European Economic Studies at the College of Europe, Campus Bruges. He is a member of the WRR (PM's think-tank) in The Hague.

ACKNOWLEDGEMENTS

I would like to thank Susanne Schmidt for her helpful comments on earlier drafts of this article.

NOTES

1 For more elaborate treatment, see the contributions by, respectively, Mattera, Weiler and Pelkmans in Kostoris Padoa Schioppa (2005), all mainly referring to goods markets. See also Pelkmans *et al.* (2000).

2 The notion of SHEC is a simplification but it catches the large bulk of regulatory issues related to MR. In art. 30, EC the key references are to health and safety and possibly elements of environmental policy. As far as the 'rule of reason' case law of art. 28, EC is concerned, it underpins environmental and consumer protection. In addition, some other justifications can be found here, all of marginal importance. For legal analysis, see, for example, Barnard (2004), chapters 6 and 18, as well as Weiler (2005).

3 For details, see for example, Atkins (1997), also Pelkmans (1987) for the many drawbacks of the Old Approach. A good example is tractor safety regulation. There are 23 tractor directives.

4 See, for instance, directive 94/9/EC on equipment and protective systems intended for use in explosive atmospheres (ATEX dir.) <http://ec.europa.eu/comm/ enterprises/atex/guide/index.htm> or the entire debate on detailed testing requirements for some 30,000 long known chemicals in the framework of REACH; see Pelkmans (2005b).

5 A typical case being the toys directive 88/378/EEC. An extremely broad application is the machines directive 98/37/EC, covering more than 40,000 types of 'machines'.

6 Indeed, often for the European Economic Area (EEA) – the EU plus Norway, Liechtenstein and Iceland – and even wider.

7 This is referred to as the 'presumption' of compliance.

8 Or from other EEA countries or Turkey, the latter because of the 'deep' customs union with the EU 25.

9 Of course, the New Approach is also subject to further improvements. See COM (2003) 240 of 7 May 2003 and the suggestions in the twentieth anniversary conference of the New Approach, 30 November 2005, at <http://europa.eu.int/comm/ enterprise/newapproach/new_approach_conference_en.htm>

10 The Commission's interpretative communication on the practical application of MR, 2003/C 265 of 4 November 2003. It specifies, furthermore, undue translation requirements, no duplication of tests, recognition of testing and certification based on EN 45,000 standards of quality and independence, and no additional tests not required for domestic companies.

11 A famous example is the Beer Purity Law in Germany where the ECJ held that the pursuit of consumer protection should be conducted with measures such as labelling rather than an import ban. Case 274/87 *Commission* vs. *Germany*, [1989] ECR 229.

12 It is possible, though rare, that national regulations are drafted for SHEC objectives where approximation failed, say, because of a split in the Council or because of extreme uncertainty in science, hence risk assessment. In such instances, MR would also fail because of a lack of equivalence. One such case is that of so-called 'fortified foods', where sharp differences between the member states and at times contrasting views by scholars pre-empted Commission proposals. See Atkins (1997), chapter 17, for details. After a struggle lasting decades, the Commission proposed a partial remedy in COM (2003) 424 of 16 July 2003 on nutrition and health claims made for foods. In May 2006 the draft was in its second reading and likely to be adopted.

13 The EU standards bodies are CEN, CENELEC and ETSI. See <http:// www.cenorm.be>, <http://www.cenelec.org> and <http://www.etsi.org>.

14 World standards are written by the International Organization Standarlization (ISO) and the International Electrotechnical Committee (IEC) and for telecoms by a special committee of the International Telecommunication Union (ITU). All three European bodies have formal agreements with the world bodies about procedures which facilitate the fullest possible use of world standards (where they exist; for goods, rather than processes, testing or for information, world standards are often absent) as European standards.

15 Member states and the Commission can give observations (also called 'comments'), besides so-called 'detailed opinions', which reflect serious concerns about prospective barriers. Both are included in Figure 2. If a member state does not adjust drafts after 'detailed opinions', it risks an infringement procedure, or the Commission might regard the matter as so problematic that it proposes a directive.

16 The following is adapted from Pelkmans (2005a) and Pelkmans (2006: section 4.4.3.).

17 See COM (1999) 299 of 16 June 1999 on MR in the internal market, COM (2002) 419 of 23 July 2002 (second biannual report on MR), The Internal Market Scoreboard no. 10 of May 2002.

18 Since July 2006, the new address of the TRIS (technical regulation information system) website is: <http://ec.europe.eu/enterprise/tris/index_en.htm>; it collects information on the removal or prevention of regulatory (mainly technical) barriers to free movement.

19 SOLVIT is an on-line problem-solving network of national officials, co-ordinated by the Commission. It tackles complaints about the misapplication of internal market law by public (and also local) authorities, but without legal proceedings, in a period of a maximum of ten weeks. SOLVIT claims (September 2006) a success rate of 75 per cent of cases solved, a clear incentive to use it. Some 16 per

cent of the cases are about market access of goods (i.e. often MR). See <http://ec.europa.eu/solvit/site/about/index_en.htm>.
20 For a recent overview, see the Commission's 2003 interpretative communication on ... the practical application of MR, as in note 15.

REFERENCES

Atkins, W. (1997) 'Technical barriers to trade', study for the *Single Market Review* 3(1), Luxembourg: Office for Official Publications of the EU/London: Kogan Page.

Barnard, C. (2004) *The Substantive Law of the EU: The Four Freedoms*, Oxford: Oxford University Press.

Brenton, P., Sheehy, J. and Vancauteren, M. (2001) 'Technical barriers to trade in the EU', *Journal of Common Market Studies* 39(2): 265–85.

Kostoris Padoa Schioppa, F. (ed.) (2005) *The Principle of Mutual Recognition in the European Integration Process*, Basingstoke: Palgrave-Macmillan.

Mattera, A. (2005) 'The principle of mutual recognition and respect for national, regional and local identities and traditions', in F. Kostoris Padoa Schioppa (ed.), *The Principle of Mutual Recognition in the European Integration Process*, Basingstoke: Palgrave Macmillan, pp. 1–24.

Molitor, B. *et al.* (1995) 'Report of the group of independent experts on legislation and administrative simplification', *COM(95) 228* of 21 May 1995.

Pelkmans, J. (1987) 'The new approach to technical harmonisation and standardisation', *Journal of Common Market Studies* 25(3): 249–69.

Pelkmans, J. (2005a) 'Mutual recognition in goods and services, an economic perspective', in F. Kosteris Padoa Schioppa (ed.), *The Principle of Mutual Recognition in the European Integration Process*, Basingstoke: Palgrave Macmillan, pp. 85–128.

Pelkmans J. (2005b) 'REACH: getting the chemistry right in Europe', in D.S. Hamilton and J.P. Quinlan (eds), *Deep Integration, How Transatlantic Markets are Leading Globalization*, Center for Transatlantic Relations, Johns Hopkins University, Paul H. Nitze School of Advanced International Studies, and Centre for European Policy Studies (CEPS), pp. 221–35.

Pelkmans, J. (2006) *European Integration, Methods and Economic Analysis*, 3rd revised edn, Harlow: Pearson Education.

Pelkmans, J., Vos, E. and di Mauro, L. (2000) 'Reforming product market regulation in the EU: a painstaking, iterative two-level game', in G. Galli and J. Pelkmans (eds), *Regulatory Reform and Competitiveness in Europe*, Cheltenham: Edward Elgar, Vol. I, pp. 238–91.

Sun, J.M. and Pelkmans, J. (1995) 'Regulatory competition in the internal market', *Journal of Common Market Studies* 33(1): 67–90.

UNICE (1995) *Releasing Europe's Potential Through Targeted Reform*, Brussels: UNICE.

UNICE (2004) *It is the Internal Market, Stupid!*, a company survey on trade barriers in the EU, Brussels: UNICE Internal Market Working Group.

Vogel, D. (1995) *Trading Up: Consumer and Environmental Regulation in a Global Economy*, Cambridge, MA: Harvard University Press.

Weiler, J. (2005) 'Mutual recognition, functional equivalence and harmonization in the evolution of the European common market and the WTO', in F. Kostoris Padoa Schioppa (ed.), *The Principle of Mutual Recognition in the European Integration Process*, Basingstoke: Palgrave Macmillan, pp. 25–84.

Mutual recognition 'on trial': the long road to services liberalization

Kalypso Nicolaïdis and Susanne K. Schmidt

INTRODUCTION

The trial of mutual recognition in the European Union (EU) in the years 2004–06 is a fascinating story, full of personal and political drama, false accusations and genuine resentment, aggressive grandstanding and painstaking attempts at amicable settlement. The trial was run as much outside as inside the court-room in Brussels, with crowds gathering in ever greater numbers to await the final verdict. The trial meant different things to different people: a crucial test for the Commission's liberal agenda as well as for the left's 'social Europe'; the promise of a better life for service workers from the East, the threat to a way of life for unions in the West.

Crucially, the first exhibit in the trial was a usurpation of identity: mutual reco-nition, stripped down to its bare bones, under the label of the 'country-of-origin' principle. Paradoxically, this principle would be the source of redemption for some, the source of all evils for others. Supporters of the 'country-of-origin' principle conjured up abstruse examples of hindrances to cross-border services deliveries. For example, are long, cumbersome administrative procedures in order to fix an elevator across borders proportionate to the task? Is it right for a Slovak tourist guide working in Prague to be arrested? By the same token, opponents depicted doomsday scenarios where Polish butchers and plumbers would be let loose in western European markets disregarding the social *acquis* of beleaguered trade unions, with phantom firms escaping all regulatory control thanks to a letter-box in the East.

Such polarization came as a surprise to the Commission, for whom the application of mutual recognition to services had long been a technocratic tale of trial and error. While it had appeared in the Treaty of Rome only with regard to the professions, Lord Cockfield had hailed mutual recognition in his 1986 White Paper as the miracle formula for the much needed liberalization of services markets across Europe. Twenty years later, however, such liberalization was still wanting even though it had become ever more crucial to foster economic growth in the ailing economies of the old member states.

This article analyses the problems associated with integrating services markets via mutual recognition, with particular emphasis on the 2004–06 negotiations concerning the horizontal, non-sector specific services directive and its progressive evolution away from its original incarnation as the 'Bolkenstein directive'. We make three interrelated arguments.

First, we argue that in the initial phase of the debate, both sides misrepresented the EU's prior experience in this area: the ardent proponents of the country-of-origin principle who argued that this had been the EU approach all along, and its ardent opponents who argued that it was completely new. By failing to admit that the EU had consistently practised a form of 'managed' mutual recognition in the past, in which home-country control is conditioned, partial and monitored, the Commission and the member state governments contributed to an extremely polarized situation in which agreement seemed impossible (Nicolaïdis 1993, 1996, 2004).

Second, we argue that the political context had changed significantly in the intervening years, with the politicization of the single market and the greater differences between member state regulatory and economic development associated with eastern enlargement. Fears of regulatory competition and social dumping in the richer member states, which had previously been invoked only to 'manage' mutual recognition, now led to a political veto.

The emblematic figure of the 'Polish plumber' captures the challenge faced by the attempt to liberalize in such a context. Given the distributional consequences of the services directive, it was no surprise that unconditional mutual recognition proved unacceptable for many of the 'old' member states. While the discussion focused predominantly on economic gains and losses, behind these stood significant political repercussions for governments given the uncertain implications of the directive for a variety of domestic regulatory bargains. We take the case of Germany to illustrate our argument.

Third, we analyse the final compromise and argue that it succeeded precisely because it recovers the spirit of managed mutual recognition. Nevertheless, the great irony is that it did so by eradicating mutual recognition altogether from the legislative text. By bringing host-country jurisdiction back in – even if in a constrained form – the directive has understandably disappointed the most liberal constituency in the EU, especially in the new member states.

In the following, we start with a discussion of the services freedom laid down in the Treaty, which the services directive aims to realize, as well as a discussion of the contrast between trade in services and trade of goods. This is necessary as many of the confusions surrounding the services directive relate to it.

SPECIFICS OF SERVICES TRADE, REGULATION AND LAW

Mutual recognition as a means of creating a common market was first associated with services in the Treaty of Rome where it was mentioned with regard to professional services and the mutual recognition of diplomas. In spite of this, mutual recognition was only applied to a couple of professions in the 1970s, on the basis of significant prior harmonization. And while the case law concerning judicial recognition of equivalence was developed with regard to goods (*Dassonville, Cassis*), the European Court of Justice (ECJ) balked at apply-ing it to services. Indeed, services are considered a 'harder case' for liberalization than goods, not only because they are generally more regulated, but because of their mode of delivery, which often involves the movement of either service pro-viders or consumers across borders – unless the service is provided electroni-cally. It is often said that services are intangible and invisible – recall *The Economist's* famous definition that services are that which cannot fall on your foot. One implication is that it can be difficult to separate their production from their consumption, in that value is produced for the consumer at the moment of interaction with the provider. We can draw an analytical distinction between the service delivery and the product itself in the same way that process and product standard are distinguished for goods. But for services almost all regulations have to do with processes, themselves bound up with home-country rules whether concerning market access (e.g. training requirements for ski instructors), operation (e.g. certain solvency requirements, speed limits), acceptable products (e.g. types of insurance), and their distribution (cf. Roth 2002: 16). Thus, host countries usually need to apply their regulations to process standards if they want to affect the quality of the service; but such application may in turn impede delivery of the service altogether.

This reasoning holds, provided that free movement of services can be distin-guished from free movement of labour or establishment since the latter two naturally call for host-country control. The core test here – as stated in the Treaties – is temporariness. If a cabinet-maker offers particularly tailored repair services across borders, he profits from the freedom of services, and, at least theoretically, from home-country rule; if he does it on a continuous basis with some sort of establishment, it is the freedom of establishment that applies, and thus host-country rule. According to this reasoning, workers posted temporarily would deliver services according to the working conditions (pay, training) of their home countries, side by side with the very differently regulated workers of the host country. It is easy to see how such an inference could be resisted.

Since freedom of services targets temporary activities, it required constraints on the application of host-country regulations to avoid a prohibitive burden, but it also generously provided for exceptions – allowing the host country to invoke general interest and the like in order to justify the application of its own rules (Hailbronner and Nachbaur 1992: 112). As with goods, such allowance would, of course, be subject to the rule of reason (necessity and proportionality test), but services restrictions always seemed to be based on good reason. When it came to labour standards, working conditions and pay, the court clearly allowed 'the general interest' to justify host-country control (*Rush Portuguesa* ruling, C-113/89).

The question becomes, therefore, to what extent is it desirable and feasible to move from a situation of constrained host-state jurisdiction, as is currently the case for all services not covered by sector-specific directives, to a situation closer to mutual recognition, as has been the case for trade in goods? Given the prevalence of process standards, it is no surprise that the prospect of generalized mutual recognition raised fears of uncontrolled regulatory arbitrage, even though regulatory competition and the downgrading of standards does not seem to occur in sectors where recognition has already been adopted.

RECURRENT PATTERN: FROM THE 1986 WHITE PAPER TO THE 2006 SERVICES DIRECTIVE

At a time when the 'new' character of the current services agenda has been stressed so relentlessly by the media, it seems fascinating to highlight the parallels between Frits Bolkestein and Lord Cockfield in their respective crusade on behalf of mutual recognition. One English, one Dutch, the two Commissioners in charge of the single market were both outspoken liberals. Like Bolkestein 20 years later, Cockfield took to its ultimate logic the single market imperative. In his White Paper – endorsed by member states through Delors' Single Act – he picked up on the approach worked out by the Commission since *Cassis de Dijon*, which was to generalize the philosophy of 'recognition of equivalence' to the whole of services. But many services fell outside the net of the Single Act.

Then and now: three interrelated logics

By 2000, in spite of the dynamic set in motion by Delors and Cockfield, and while almost every type of services had been touched by one directive or another, the Commission continued to identify numerous barriers and even still nationality requirements. At the turn of the century, the single market was far from complete, calling – again! – for a more radical approach. The familiar pattern can be summed up as an interaction between three logics.

First, the *jurisprudence* of the ECJ which, instead of an injunction to recognize, provided a 'road map' for future legislation. The distinctions made in the insurance directives between types of consumer that could or could not withstand the logic of mutual recognition or the 1996 directive on the posting of workers are prominent examples of the political translation of the Court's jurisprudence. The Court might have become slightly bolder in the early 2000s than in the early 1980s – proportionality was to be taken seriously – but the same limitations applied (Hatzopoulos and Do 2006).

The second logic is broadly *integrationist* whereby, usually for exogenous reasons, Heads of States assert the teleological credo of the need to complete the single market, instructing the Commission to make it happen (demand side). As they had instructed Delors in 1984, they repeated more or less the same message at their 2000 meeting in Lisbon, where they set out a strategy for 2010, to make the Union the most competitive region in the world. In both cases, completing the single market was at the core of the agenda. 'In 2001 intra-EU exports of services ... only represented around 20% of trade in the Internal Market, compared with services' 53.6% share of GDP' (European Commission 2004: 9). The Commission (supply side) then takes the politicians at their word, in fact 'upping the ante' by proposing a radical generalization of the Court's approach in pursuit of the completion of the single market for services, which is after all what the political masters are asking for.

But then a third logic kicks in, the properly political process of bargaining, whereby a winning coalition of member states succeeds in watering down the extent of transfer of sovereignty through recognition in order to make liberalization politically acceptable.

The difference between the two periods lies both in the salience of such political bargains and in the Commission's capacity to anticipate them. While Bolkestein sought to implement his 'pure' philosophy directly through a single horizontal directive, Cockfield's was spelled out separately in the 1986 White Paper and then translated through several dozen sectoral directives (including communication, transport, finance and the professions) which did not simply enforce mutual recognition. Instead, they reflected subtle and complex bargains struck among regulators, who sought to please their political masters by liberalizing for the headlines but complemented recognition with all sorts of caveats (Nicolaïdis 1993, 1996, 2004). Mutual recognition was managed to ensure that regulatory competition did not lead to consumer confusion and a general downgrading of standards. Managed recognition involved minimum prior harmonization or convergence of standards as with goods, but also other attributes, such as diminishing the automaticity of access to host-country markets by granting residual host-country control, reducing its scope in various ways and setting up mechanisms of ex-post guarantees and monitoring (indeed, such 'tricks' to attenuate the import of mutual recognition had been used since the 1960s). In short, in 1986–92, the monopoly of initiative of the

Commission was not used to carry out the radical agenda as such but to fine-tune its limits.

In contrast, oblivious to the political nature of services regulation even when responding to the mandate of politicians, the Prodi Commission refused to make concessions to political expediency. In December 2000 it proposed a comprehensive strategy to complete the single market, including seven new directives. Most importantly, Directorate-General (DG) Single Market was charged with drawing up an inventory of all remaining barriers to services, delivered in 2002 to the Council which then requested action. More than happy to oblige, Frits Bolkestein drafted the most radical directive ever to address the single market for services, in all those areas where specific measures had not yet been taken. Given that sector-specific attempts at building the single market for services had had their limitations, such a horizontal approach was in fact consensual across EU institutions and member states. Bolkestein consulted with national ministries over a period of two years and national bureaucrats seemed to be more or less on his wavelength.

So by early 2004 the draft 'Bolkestein directive' was born. Little did its creator suspect that it would achieve such fame and disrepute. What was so different this time around? To what extent did the directive depart from the previous step-by-step logic of managed mutual recognition adopted earlier by the Commission?

A bold directive

To start with, the *scope* of the draft directive was extremely broad, targeting both the freedom of establishment and the freedom of services for those not previously covered by other directives. The directive exempted only lotteries for commercial services. Critically, the directive covered services of a *general economic interest*, including health and social services outside direct state provisions – while genuinely *general interest services*, which are delivered without any profit interest (e.g. education, cultural activities), were left out.

Moreover, the scope was also made ambiguous with regard to the relationship between the draft directive and *existing European law for services*, concerning financial services, utilities, services of general economic interest, posted workers, professions. The draft did not apply to these sectors, nor did it exempt them; instead it 'complements existing services laws', leaving room for all sorts of forecasts concerning potential conflicts.

Most importantly, the very core of the directive is the idea that the only way to remedy the petty bureaucratic impediments imposed by host countries is to make access to markets across borders as easy and *automatic* as possible, which in turn would require fully enforcing the principle of 'country-of-origin' or home-country control. As a result, the host country would be restricted from enforcing its own laws or practices to justifications linked to 'public order, public health, and public safety' – in other words a narrowly defined public-interest rule which did not even encompass the 'rule of reason exceptions' recognized by the Court (Drijber 2004: 3).

Relatedly, the directive also tackled the issue of *applicable contract law*. Home-country rules were only relevant for business rather than consumers, for whom international private law would remain applicable. Such introduction of home-country control without detailed specifications as to its scope and prior conditions led to much criticism as serious conflicts with Rome I and II were feared (Basedow 2004).

To be fair, the directive did not call for jurisdiction of the country-of-origin across the board. Obviously, greater *freedom of establishment* will always allow for host-state territorial control; but at least the directive required host states to create a one-stop shop with exclusive administrative responsibility (Art. 6) in order to do away with restrictions on establishment which cannot be justified by the principle of proportionality.

More to the point, the most controversial aspects of the directive had to do with the conditions under which workers providing cross-border services – such as butchers, plumbers or construction workers – would be treated. Theoretically, such movement falls under the *1996 posted workers directive* (96/71/ EC) and its application of host labour law and wages. However, the draft foresaw the easing of some restrictions, such as the need to carry papers for local controls in the host country and the obligation to appoint a national representative (Art. 24). Such provisions would make it more difficult for host countries to know whether posted workers complied with their legal provisions, thus bringing even the area of labour movement in to the ambit of recognition through the back door.

Open questions related also to the precise definition of the *temporary* nature of service provision which determines in turn whether a worker is a service provider or a migrant. The directive left this open as it is difficult to set limits which are relevant across the board. For instance, seasonal services such as skiing instruction would need to be treated differently from other activities.[1] Given the planned extent of pure recognition, a precise definition of temporariness would have been key to preventing a situation of 'anything goes'.

Finally, while no concession was made to *prior harmonization*, the directive did include the obligation of national authorities to co-operate with each other, thus including *ex-post safeguards*. Thereby, since freedom of services often leads to situations where host countries have to verify the actual respect of home rule, the directive sought to improve their capacity to do so by requiring information from home-country authorities as to the legality of companies posting workers, for instance.

Perhaps such a sweeping horizontal directive, targeting different conditions in different services sectors, was bound to be contentious in the traditional political economy of the EU where constituencies naturally resist reforms which may question their economic rents. However, to understand the unprecedented escalation observed in the opposition to it, we need to examine more closely the changing context and frames of liberalization in the late 1990s and early 2000s.

CHANGING CONTEXT AND CHANGING FRAMES FOR LIBERALIZATION

There is little doubt that the EU's biggest enlargement since its inception conditioned the reactions to the services proposal. Simply put, the level of differences in national regulatory and legal settings was becoming too great to sustain the permissive consensus on liberalization that had (more or less) prevailed until then. The German case can help us understand how this general state of affairs translated into specific resistance to the directive. As the largest member state, neighbouring the new member states, and plagued with high unemployment, high wages but no minimum wage, Germany is bound to be a special target for low-cost services exports. Perhaps Germany could be considered an outlier. But while especially vulnerable, it was also a harbinger of things to come.

Changed context: an influx of Eastern Europeans

A few months after the 2004 enlargement, Germany was surprised by the extent to which East Europeans put pressure on its national job market. This was unexpected as it had joined most of the other member states (with the exception of the UK, Ireland and Sweden) in using the transitory arrangement $(2 + 3 + 2$ years) to restrict freedom of labour for the new member states (excluding Cyprus and Malta). In addition, Germany had negotiated a transitory regime for freedom of services, exempting construction services, cleaning and interior decoration. Arguably, these exemptions are precisely in those areas where East Europeans could profit least from existing wage differentials as construction is a sector where a minimum wage applies. In all other sectors, workers can come in temporarily under the freedom of services arrangement – interpreted by the German authorities as up to one year – and replace German workers and receive the wages of their home country, given that there is no general minimum wage (Christen 2004; Temming 2005).

As a result, enlargement has turned public opinion against the *existing* freedom of services provisions. Germans have been laid off on a large scale from slaughterhouses which brought in personnel 'from the East', working for little money under deplorable conditions (in some cases, wages are only two to three euros per hour and daily working time is up to 16 hours). The responsible trade union spoke of 26,000 job losses, or one third of all employees in the sector being replaced by East Europeans.[2] The legal situation is complicated as East Europeans can come in under a combination of host and home provisions, to which illegal activities can be added. Moreover, under the freedom of establishment, East Europeans with lower expectations of labour standards face no restrictions (FAZ 10.9.2005, p. 16). No wonder the prospect of further liberalization through the services directive was unwelcome (Hamburger Abendblatt 26.2.2005, p. 23).

To make matters worse, domestic reforms had increased Germany's vulnerability after significant liberalization in 2004 of the crafts law which made it easier to set up a company even with one self-employed person. Until then, the 1953 crafts law restricted such set-up to individuals with a 'Meisterbrief', i.e. a master craftsman's diploma involving expensive and long-term training. East Europeans constituted the bulk of those taking advantage of the new law (265 out of 391 new tilers after the reform in Munich). This is not surprising since there were no specific wage and social security obligations for the self-employed. At the same time, stories started to emerge of East European craftsmen getting round the requirement for a 'permanent establishment with sufficient space' by sharing a single address, or illegally claiming establishment while exclusively or predominantly working for a single customer (Stuttgarter Zeitung 12.4.2005, p. 1; General-Anzeiger 14.5.2005, p. 3).

Short of establishment, the posted workers directive prescribes German labour conditions for all branches. However, with no general minimum wage, there are no wage restrictions on posted workers. The posting company is only required by law to discharge social security expenses and be active in the home country – a safeguard against mere 'letter-box companies'. Moreover, posted workers cannot be integrated fully in the German company's work process; otherwise social security would have to be paid in Germany (Fleischwirtschaft 12.5.2005, p. 10).

Consequently, a host of opportunities arise for illegal activities: are workers really temporary? What does it mean to apply the working conditions of the host country? What is reasonable pay when there is no host-state minimum wage? Is the home company real and active or merely established for posting workers? What is the criterion; for example, what percentage of company employers must actually work in Poland, representing what percentage of the annual turnover? And does the company really pay social security? How would the host country know? Can it trust controls carried out in the home country? Indeed, if the home country itself suffers from high unemployment rates, what is its incentive to play by the rules?

Changing frames: anti-globalization ... Europe's way

By the time the services directive came to the attention of the European media, such questions had not been resolved in Germany or in the rest of Europe. With slow growth in Europe and the gross domestic product (GDP) share of services, the renewed attempt of the Commission to tackle services liberalization could have been seen as an imperative. Indeed, supporters of the draft directive easily produced numerous examples of abstruse hindrances to the freedom of services, which were clear violations of Treaty obligations. But the arguments of their opponents were put in even starker terms. There seemed to be no meeting point between the two worldviews.

To put matters simply, we could argue that two broad trends in Europe provided a backdrop for the mounting resistance against what came to be called the 'Frankenstein directive'. The first was part of a more global *politicization* of trade, the European version of anti- or alter-globalization, or the idea of

Europeanization as globalization. The mobilization of fears in the broader public was based on the now familiar notion that sources of comparative advantage across countries are not uniform and that to extend liberalization to countries with significantly lower GDP per capita allowed them to exploit their 'unfair' advantage. This move from free trade to 'fair trade' reached a critical point with the 2005 bra war against Chinese imports.

This argument took on a special force in the case of the services directive where instead of social dumping *at a distance*, we have what could be called *face-to-face* social dumping. Thus a principle that had been widely used in the EU to complete the single market – namely, that of country of origin – now made a reappearance in the European public sphere as the Trojan horse of 'unfair competition' and 'social dumping', in a way that the public could indeed comprehend: people coming to work here will carry their home rule on their shoulders, so to speak, like double agents operating in the European social space. Citizens from the new member states were not fellow Europeans but *strangers within*, objectified as a group through the very real metaphor of the *Polish plumber* (or butcher in Germany). No matter that Polish plumbers on French soil were very few and far between.

The case for the defence argued that social dumping should not be a concern given that the posting of workers directive largely prescribed host-country rules. But as the German case illustrates, the truth is more ambiguous as only minimum wages – but not collective wage agreements – can be made mandatory. Like Germany, Scandinavian countries had come under pressure, as the ECJ does not treat minimum wages and collective agreements in the same way, although they are institutional equivalents (Woolfson and Sommers 2006).

The second general trend associated with the resistance to the draft directive and its core suspect, the country-of-origin principle, has to do with *ideologization*. While there had been debate for a long time about the liberal bias of the single market and the need for social flanking measures, only in recent times had free trade come to be associated with deregulation and a 'neo-liberal agenda'. It may be true that the prior phases of building the single market had demonstrated that liberalization most often went with re-regulation, but there is no denying that the draft directive was likely to have a significant deregulatory impact, as Commissioner Bolkestein himself stressed: 'Some of the national restrictions are archaic, overly burdensome and break EU law. Those have simply got to go. A much longer list of differing national rules needs sweeping regulatory reform.'[3]

This kind of statement, of course, reinforced social resistance to what was seen as the disembeddedness of global markets. Opposition to the directive became a rallying cry for the left, for unions and groups like the Association pour la Taxation des Transactions pour l'Aide aux Citoyens (ATTAC). It was widely used in the French referendum campaign to illustrate the drift to a neo-liberal Europe, regardless of the fact that the directive could be passed under the existing Treaties. In this ideological context, host-country rules were defended not as *protectionist*, nor even as social *protection* for the workers of the West, but as an extended hand to the workers of the East in a grand gesture of solidarity to guarantee better working conditions for them too. The Polish plumber should be denied home-country rule for his own good, as otherwise Poland would soon suffer from wage differentials with Ukraine, a reason invoked by Solidarność to oppose the services directive.

In other words, opponents stressed the unique qualities of services trade and denied the analogy to goods. Services trade has to do with the movement of people, they stressed. It is less objectionable to sell shoes which were made under different conditions in Europe and in East Asia in the same shop than to have service providers from different countries working alongside each other while subject to different rules and pay. Whereas a person working in a shoe factory in the Far East can at least – however poor – live on her wages there, posted workers delivering services on a temporary basis could not easily live where they worked under home-country wages (cf. Streeck 2000).

Moreover, the old arguments against mutual recognition as a burden for consumers and not just as a guarantee of choice reappeared in this context. The legal certainty obtained for service providers when operating under home-country rules would be at the cost of legal uncertainty for host-country consumers, who might not be aware that a service was provided for them under an unfamiliar set of rules. The transaction costs of adapting to several legal systems would be shifted from service providers to consumers.

In sum, after the liberalization of utilities and financial markets as well as changes in corporate governance with the takeover directive, the services directive was perceived as the final blow to the European social model and the advent of pure Anglo-Saxon capitalism (Höpner and Schäfer 2007). Much of the contention was caused by the uncertain implications of the directive. Would mutual recognition imply that a Dutch architect planning and building a house in Germany would do so according to Dutch building laws? Could a Polish cleaning woman working in Germany use detergents not certified on the German market (Hamburger Abendblatt 26.2.2005, p. 23)? Would a British bus driver working in Germany drive on the left? While the last question is obviously absurd, it illustrates *a contrario* the logic of the prosecution.

In contrast, those for the defence were at pains to stress analogies with goods and the long history of transferring mutual recognition from goods to services. The Commission's impact assessment stressed the cost of non-'services Europe' in terms of growth and employment potential and reiterated the absurdity of the barriers targeted by the directive (European Commission 2004). Proponents referred to France, where service workers from other member states have to register eight days in advance, making it impossible to cross the border and repair an elevator; to Belgium, where a painter has to transport his ladder in a special car, usually not owned by EU foreigners; to southern European member states, where tourist guides have to take special training, making it difficult for tourist groups to enter with their own guide; or the need for service providers everywhere in Europe to present officially translated documents and certificates.

Moreover, supporters stressed that small and medium-sized enterprises suffer most from the status quo, while large companies can acquire the necessary legal assistance to adapt to host-country rules. And since cross-border services delivery was often a necessary first step for a cross-border establishment, allowing for demand to be tested, such investment was also impeded. Against the fears of social dumping, they argued that all would benefit in letting uncompetitive service sectors disappear – especially low-cost service sectors in high-wage countries. Liberalization would ease the export of highly specialized services to Eastern members whose markets were growing fast. In addition, the pressure on low-skill services jobs in countries like Germany was not due to European but to domestic political processes. Germany could affect face-to-face social dumping simply by opting for a minimum wage. But could it have its cake and eat it too? No one seemed to complain about the meat companies from the Netherlands and Denmark relocating to Germany in order to profit from East European wages.[4]

More generally, supporters responded to the views of Europeanization as globalization with a vision of Europeanization as 'non-discrimination'. They stressed the desirability of globalization 'with a human face' (even that of a Polish plumber!), the desire of most human beings to return to 'home sweet home' and the need to convey solidarity through open markets rather than harmonization.

Supporters of the directive, however, failed to mobilize on a par with its opponents. While the unions mounted protest after protest, consumers or employers' associations did not emphasize their interest in liberalization. In the Commission, single market Commissioner McCreevy similarly opted for a low profile, leaving it largely to President Barroso to argue in favour of the directive. The centrality of the directive for the Lisbon Agenda was thus not sufficiently underlined (FTD 17.2.2006, p. 29). Perhaps, in any case, the directive in its original form was doomed once its opponents had successfully reframed the issues at stake.

NEGOTIATION AND COMPROMISE: MUTUAL RECOGNITION SACRIFICED

Opposition to the directive mounted throughout 2004–05, coinciding with the ratification campaign for the constitutional Treaty. In view of the calls for 'death to the services directive', it may seem like a miracle that the European Parliament (EP) voted with an overwhelming majority for a revised draft, after which the Council issued its common position in July 2006. Indeed, for the first time so visibly in the context of the single market, the locus where political bargains were struck had changed from the Council to the EP. However, in order to reach a compromise the letter, if not unambiguously the spirit, of mutual recognition had been sacrificed.

How did Member of the European Parliament (MEP) Evelyn Gebhardt, a German social democrat and rapporteur of the single market committee, succeed? In a nutshell, through politicization, or the self-conscious adaptation of a hitherto technical exercise to the new political context in which it was taking place. In view of the contention surrounding the home-country principle, this meant finding a compromise between the two largest political parties of the parliament, the European Socialists (PES) and the European People's Party (EPP). At first, the compromise came in the form of a safety clause allowing member states in certain cases not to apply the principle. But one week before the plenary vote, the EP protagonists decided to abolish the home-country principle altogether.

To be sure, Evelyn Gebhardt and her colleagues had tried for a while to replace the country-of-origin principle with mutual recognition as the core principle for the directive. She was at pains to explain that the two had to be differentiated radically. *Cassis*, she stressed, was also about allowing the host country to impose its own mandatory requirements. Mutual recognition was a conditional process and did not have the either–or character of the country-of-origin principle. In Drijber's words:

> Under the Court's rulings, the law of the host state must be 'disapplied' to incoming services in so far as its application would give rise to an unjustified restriction of free trade. In other words, mutual recognition is a conditional obligation because the host state may always try to justify a restrictive means. By contrast, the country-of-origin principle works like a rule of conflict. It sets aside the law of the host state, including rules that are compatible with the Treaty. Mutual recognition becomes an unconditional obligation. The Directive therefore goes much further than the case law.
>
> (Drijber 2004: 3f.)

Thus, by prescribing home-country control, the draft had gone way beyond services freedom and its interpretation (Albath and Giesler 2006: 38f.; Schlichting and Spelten 2005: 239). In contrast, mutual recognition as understood by Gebhardt was above all an ongoing *process* of political negotiations where the burden of proof would still be on the home state to show the equivalence of its rules.

In other words, the contrast was between the unconditional and systematic adoption of the country-of-origin principle, on the one hand, and what we described above as managed mutual recognition, on the other hand. Perhaps by insisting on the virtues of mutual recognition as opposed to the (unconditional) country-of-origin principle, the MEPs believed for a while that semantics matter and that the connotation of 'recognition' would be more politically correct from the perspective of the broader public. But given the extent of opposition, the term 'mutual recognition' could not be rescued.

Instead, the final compromise of November 2006 (Directive 2006/123/EC), which built on the Parliament's first reading of February and a Council compromise of May, refrained from moving beyond the jurisprudence of the Court. Depending on expectations, it can be read alternatively as an insignificant gloss on the *status quo ante* or as putting in place the first steps of a highly managed form of mutual recognition.

Accordingly, where is the balance struck on *automaticity* of access? The compromise focuses on the obligation to enable freedom of services through *non-discrimination* – a minimalist approach which, of course, in its extreme interpretation could eventually be regarded as an injunction of recognition. For now, the host country has to ensure that service providers have 'free access to and free exercise of the service activity within its territory' (Art. 16) but it remains in control of what happens on its territory. For instance, recital 87 reads 'this Directive should not affect the right for the Member State where the service is provided to determine the existence of an employment relationship and the distinction between self-employed persons and employed persons, including "false self-employed persons"'. The burden of proof clearly remains in favour of host-country rule.

However, the move back to the host country's jurisdiction is coupled with a long list of restrictions on the measures they can impose, which, in good ECJ parlance, must be necessary and proportional. It is prohibited to request authorization, registration, identification or establishment as well as to prescribe certain materials and tools for service provision (Art. 16). And the socialists failed to allow for host-state measures justified by 'consumer interests and social policy reasons' (FTD 17.2.2006, p. 9). Under the 'managed recognition' reading, the prohibition to impose these types of host-country rules does imply that home-country rules are valid *in such cases*, and that the directive helps the authorities of both host and home countries to control enforcement of their own rules wherever the service provision takes place.

As to applicable *scope*, the directive remains horizontal in nature. But Art. 2 excludes many of the services which were particularly contentious, such as all health services, public transport, social and security services, temporary work agencies, gambling and lotteries, postal services, electricity, gas, water, waste, audiovisual services, electronic communication, financial and legal services. Moreover, facilitations foreseen for the posted workers directive were deleted. This was very much against the interest of the East European member states, who had felt discriminated against by the requirements of this directive. In order to compensate, the Commission began an assessment of the implementation of the directive in the member states (FTD 9.2.2006, p. 9; 10.2.2006, p. 11).

Moreover, the parliament introduced in the directive a call for the Commission to propose further *harmonization* measures. Other original provisions were kept, such as the requirement of host countries to create a one-stop shop to facilitate freedom of establishment, the need to abolish rules implying disproportionate burdens, and the requirement for home- and host-country authorities to improve co-operation and information flows.

The House of Lords European Union Committee spoke in favour of the directive:

> We are persuaded that the list of exclusions and derogations are less daunting than they might seem and that the revised draft Directive covers a substantial part of the services sector such that it can make a useful contribution to the growth of cross-border services provision within the EU.
>
> (House of Lords 2006: 19).

The Commission had come to accept that the services market would have to be liberalized by less radical means and made clear that it would back a compromise rather than use its right to withdraw the proposal. Commissioner McCreevy also noted in this context that criticism of the compromise was hypocrisy, given that the employers' associations had hardly supported the directive when the unions mounted their protests (FAZ 22.2.2006, p. 12). In proposing small amendments, the Commission's philosophy seemed to be to try to save whatever was possible from the spirit of recognition. It resisted the parliament's attempt to get rid of the mutual evaluation scheme between regulators which would increase the scrutiny on host states seeking to retain arbitrary measures. Hence the Commission used a communication published just before the passing of the Directive ('Guidance on the posting of workers in the framework of the provision of services'[5]) to reintroduce the provision of two of the administrative means often used by host states and prohibited in the early draft under Art. 24 (obtaining an authorization form, having a representative in the territory of the host state). In terms of scope, it insisted on keeping notaries under the directive, at least for some of their activities – a classic disaggregation technique familiar to prior managed mutual recognition exercises. These were, on the whole, minor points, as the Commission ultimately rallied to the EP's sacrifice of mutual recognition.

The final version of the directive was adopted by the Council in December 2006 with abstentions from Lithuania and Belgium, thus avoiding a persistent conflict pitting new and (a majority of) old member states. Such a conflict had seemed likely after parliament's first reading, since many East European MEPs had voted against the initial compromise. Moreover, there had been rumours that their governments were trying to organize a blocking minority in the Council, encouraged by the fact that the UK, Spain, Poland, the Czech Republic, the Netherlands and Hungary had spoken out for a more liberal solution (FAZ 11.3.2006, pp. 1, 11).

CONCLUSION

If recourse to mutual recognition has long been considered the path of least resistance, 'easier than harmonization', we can no longer doubt its contentious character. While European integration is often criticized for taking place behind the public's back, the Court – like the drama which surrounded the infamous Bolkestein directive between 2004 and 2006 – demonstrates mutual recognition's highly political nature, if at least occasionally. We made three interrelated arguments: on the radical strategies of the respective actors, the changing political context, and the character of the final compromise. The first two concern the disconnection between chosen institutional strategies and a changing political context, which led to an extreme polarization of the issue. With hindsight, we believe that the Commission made a political mistake in departing from its experience with managed mutual recognition and pressing for a rather radical form of recognition across the board. Given the lack of progress in the targeted sectors and the economic benefits at stake, such a change in strategy was understandable. But given public unease surrounding both enlargement and globalization (or simply 'competition'), the Commission might have anticipated resistance.

The case for the defence is compelling. Services are indeed a challenging object of trade liberalization, often involving as they do the movement of people as well as highly regulated sectors of the economy. Extraterritorial tensions are bound to accompany the kind of recognition necessary to ensure a market 'without borders': clients unfamiliar with the foreign rules governing their service providers; employees in the same workplace in companies regulated in different countries; authorities of the host country having to verify the application of home rules but constrained in doing so; host-country rules which still apply but need to be enforced by home-country authorities where companies are located. The original directive would have cut the Gordian knot.

The last part of our argument concerns the compromise that was finally struck in the autumn of 2006. First and foremost, we must highlight a fundamental political shift, namely the new role of the EP in serving as the locus for such compromise-crafting politics. We have shown how, unfortunately, the EP had to formally sacrifice mutual recognition at the altar of crude criticism which failed to understand that such recognition could be managed to address the extraterritorial tensions inherent in trade in services. To some extent, this minimalist result can be seen as the inevitable consequence of the trust dilemma associated with recognition (Nicolaïdis 2007). The compromise eases fears stemming from lack of trust but its sustainability is nevertheless predicated on some level of trust.

This dilemma in turn will affect the impact of the services directive. Many observers in the EU legal community believe that, by emphasizing the rights of the host country, the directive falls behind the case law of the ECJ (Editorial Comments 2006). Others say that, by strictly circumscribing such rights, the directive will allow for a comprehensive assessment of all domestic rules concerning access to, or exercise of, services activities across the EU. In fact, we argue, the actual impact of the directive on the ground will depend on three concurrent factors – for each trust plays a crucial role, whether between regulators, courts or indeed the citizens of Europe.

First, it will depend on whether there will be a genuine commitment on the part of the regulatory authorities of member states – acting as host states – to refrain from exploiting their remaining authority under the directive and to abide by the spirit of the 'rule of reason'. This commitment in turn will depend on whether they learn to trust their home-state counterparts, whether 'fraud stories' continue to make the headlines and whether labour market pressures remain politically manageable.

Second, there is no doubt that the directive leaves the door wide open for judicial activism on the part of the ECJ, an opening that can be used more or less wisely. Thus, the impact of the directive will depend on adequate enforcement of both host- and home-country obligations by the Commission and the Court, including soft enforcement through the mutual evaluation process. In doing so, these actors need to engage with great political sensitivity in the determination of which host-state requirements are legitimate – such as whether collective agreements can be considered as functional equivalents to minimum wages.

Finally, the fate of liberalization in the EU will depend on the evolution of the political culture of activists, unions and the broader public towards a greater understanding of the spirit of mutual recognition as a process of managing ongoing differences and negotiating their tolerable limit. Mutual recognition is a demanding form of transnational governance which seems more acceptable to states and their publics when they perceive it as a form of co-operation rather than competition (Nicolaïdis and Shaffer 2005; Schmidt 2007). And yet, if today's challenge for Europeans is no longer just about the single market, but also about the kind of political union they want to share, the latter must build on the former and the link long established in the Union – albeit still contested – between free movement, borderlessness, extraterritorial law, trust and recognition.

Biographical notes: Kalypso Nicolaïdis is Director of the European Studies Centre at the University of Oxford and Lecturer in International Relations. Susanne K. Schmidt is Professor of Political Science at the University of Bremen, Germany.

ACKNOWLEDGEMENTS

We would like to thank Anand Menon, Gabrielle Krapels, and an anonymous referee as well as the participants at the workshop for their comments, in particular Fiorella Kostoris and Wendy van den Nouland. Susanne Schmidt acknowledges support under the 6th framework programme of the European Union (Contract No. CIT1-CT-2004-506-392).

NOTES

1 Interview information, DG Internal Market, September 2005.
2 FTD 9.2.2005, p. 27. Der Spiegel 7. 2005, pp. 32–5.
3 Rapid press release IP/04/37, 13.1.2004.
4 Lebensmittel Zeitung 1.7.2005, p. 37; 22.4.2005.
5 COM/2006/0159 final.

REFERENCES

Albath, L. and Giesler, M. (2006) 'Das Herkunftslandprinzip in der Dienstleistungs-richtlinie – eine Kodifizierung der Rechtsprechung', *Europäische Zeitschrift für Wirtschaftsrecht* 17(2): 38–42.
Basedow, J. (2004) 'Dienstleistungsrichtlinie, Herkunftslandprinzip und Internatio-nales Privatrecht', *Europäische Zeitschrift für Wirtschaftsrecht* 15(14): 423–26.
Christen, T. (2004) 'Der Zugang zum deutschen Arbeitsmarkt nach der EU-Erweiter-ung', *Bundesarbeitsblatt* 3: 4–16.
Drijber, B. (2004) 'The country of origin principle'. Hearing before the Committee Internal Market and Consumer Protection on the Proposed Directive on Services in the Internal Market, 11 November 2004, http://www.europarl.europa.eu/hear-ings/20041111/imco/contributions_en.htm.

Editorial Comments (2006) 'The services directive proposal: striking a balance between the promotion of the internal market and preserving the European social model?', *Common Market Law Review* 43(2): 307–11.

European Commission (2004) 'Extended Impact Assessment of Proposal for a Directive on Services in the Internal Market', SEC(2004) 21, 13.1.2004; available under: http://ec.europa.eu/internal_market/services/docs/services-dir/impact/2004-imp act-assessment_en.pdf (accessed March 2007).

Hailbronner, K. and Nachbaur, A. (1992) 'Die Dienstleistungsfreiheit in der Rechtsprechung des EuGH', *Europäische Zeitschrift für Wirtschaftsrecht* 3(6): 105–13.

Hatzopoulos, V. and Do, T.U. (2006) 'The case law of the ECJ concerning the free provision of services', *Common Market Law Review* 43(4): 923–91.

Höpner, M. and Schäfer, A. (2007): 'A new phase of European integration: organized capitalisms in post-Ricardian Europe', *MPIfG Discussion Paper 07/4*, Cologne: Max Planck Institute for the Study of Societies.

House of Lords (2006) *The Services Directive Revisited.* Report with evidence by the European Union Committee, London: The Stationery Office.

Nicolaïdis, K. (1993) 'Mutual recognition among nations: the European Community and trade in services', Ph.D. dissertation, Harvard, Cambridge, MA.

Nicolaïdis, K. (1996) 'Mutual recognition of regulatory regimes: some lessons and prospects', in *Regulatory Reform and International Market Openness*, Paris: OECD Publications. Reprinted in 1997 as *Jean Monnet Paper Series*, Cambridge, MA: Harvard Law School.

Nicolaïdis, K. (2004) 'Globalization with human faces: managed mutual recognition and the free movement of professionals', in F. Kostoris Padoa Schioppa (ed.), *The Principle of Mutual Recognition in the European Integration Process*, Basingstoke: Palgrave Macmillan, pp. 129–89.

Nicolaïdis, K. (2007) 'Trusting the Poles? Constructing Europe through mutual recognition', *Journal of European Public Policy* 14(5): 682–98.

Nicolaïdis, K. and Shaffer, G. (2005) 'Transnational mutual recognition regimes: governance without global government', *Michigan Review of International Law* 68: 267–322.

Roth, W. (2002) 'The European Court of Justice's case law on freedom to provide services: is Keck relevant?', in M. Andenas and W. Roth (eds), *Services and Free Movement in EU Law.* Oxford: Oxford University Press, pp. 1–24.

Schlichting, J. and Spelten, W. (2005) 'Die Dienstleistungsrichtlinie', *Europäische Zeitschrift für Wirtschaftsrecht* 16(8): 238–43.

Schmidt, S.K. (2007) 'Mutual recognition as a new mode of governance', *Journal of European Public Policy* 14(5): 667–81.

Streeck, W. (2000) 'Vorwort: Europäische? Sozialpolitik?', in W. Eichhorst (ed.), *Europäische Sozialpolitik zwischen nationaler Autonomie und Marktfreiheit. Die Entsendung von Arbeitnehmern in der EU*, Frankfurt/Main: Campus Verlag, pp. 19–35.

Temming, F. (2005) 'EU-Osterweiterung: Wie beschränkt ist die Dienstleistungsfreiheit?', *Recht der Arbeit* 58(3): 186–92.

Woolfson, C. and Sommers, J. (2006) 'Labour mobility in construction: European implications of the Laval un Partneri dispute with Swedish labour', *European Journal of Industrial Relations* 12(1): 49–68.

Dominant losers: a comment on the services directive from an economic perspective

Fiorella Kostoris Padoa Schioppa

It is a pleasure for me to comment on the paper by Kalypso Nicolaïdis and Susanne Schmidt (2007) on mutual recognition and the services directive within the framework offered in the introduction to the volume on 'Mutual Recognition as a New Mode of Governance' by Susanne Schmidt (2007).

In these two complementary texts three critical questions on mutual recognition in services arise. I will not examine other questions where the authors' answers and my own appear to coincide, focusing on the contrary on the few cases where my viewpoint seems to differ from theirs.

QUESTION 1: WHAT IS SPECIFIC TO SERVICES THAT MAKES IT LESS STRAIGHTFORWARD TO APPLY MUTUAL RECOGNITION TO SERVICES THAN TO COMMODITIES IN THE EU?

Nicolaïdis and Schmidt's (2007) answer is quite articulate, but essentially they state that 'services are considered a "harder case" for liberalization than goods, not only because they are generally more regulated, but because of their mode of delivery, which often involves the movement of either service providers or consumers across borders' (Nicolaïdis and Schmidt 2007: 719). Indeed, unlike with commodities, there is no separation in services between the process and the product delivery phases, and this sometimes implies that the alternative of simply mutually recognizing different national regulations may not be an option; a good illustration would be driving according to the speed limit of the home country. In other cases, mutual recognition is possible but not satisfactory, as 'for instance it may be desirable to have uniform technical standards in electronics and in telecommunications in order to enable interconnection' (Gatsios and Seabright 1989: 43). More generally, since it is difficult in services to separate production from consumption, mutual recognition risks becoming, even when possible and economically satisfactory, socially less acceptable than in the commodity market. While in the latter sector different standards followed by various suppliers are not obvious, as producers of a good sold in a given place operate quite separately, in the former the different production conditions set up for various providers of a similar service are more evident, as producers operate nearby, all being close to the consumers of an identical country or region.

In my opinion, such an explanation is ingenious but it is partial. Moreover, one can argue about why it is unacceptable in Western Europe to observe heterogeneous standards which maintain for homogeneous productive factors. And why it is considered politically correct to state that it is socially unacceptable that a Polish plumber receives a lower price than her French colleague for an equally good plumbing job. The classical alibi put forward in Western Europe – namely, that the Polish service provider would in fact be exploited in France under these circumstances – is a nonsense because nobody obliges her to cross the border and offer her labour in France; by doing this, she shows that she is interested in the French market. At the other ethical extreme, the often-quoted principle of European cohesion and solidarity should allow the less well-off Polish citizen to earn her money in France.

Even purely economic reasons should induce French society to welcome the Polish lady, as she would accept a lower income not only if she meant to spend part of it in her cheaper home country, but also if she spent all of it in the host country, as this is always the case with recent immigrants. She would be equally capable in plumbing, and yet she would cost less than the French incumbent. This form of higher efficiency should be good news for French firms seeking to lower labour costs, and for French households looking to widen their purchasing power through better prices. Only French plumbers should oppose the newcomers, as they would be less expensive while being equally productive: indeed, the resident plumbers know that they are less competitive than their Polish colleagues, precisely because the latter are less costly than them. And yet, why does this understandable fear of inefficient French plumbers dominate the whole debate in a society which seems to forget the efficiency and the equity arguments about welcoming the Poles, and why does France overall behave as if it consisted only of plumbers? Mancur Olson (1982) would answer that, since the benefits in France of a virtual barrier to entry regarding the Poles would be huge and concentrated among few individuals (the French plumbers), while the costs for the rest of the population would be diffused and therefore relatively small, there is little public resistance to the needs of the former group. My own answer is somewhat different. International trade theory predicts that the European integration process obtained through factor mobility between two different countries (like France and Poland) or two groups of countries (like Western and Central Eastern Europe), differently endowed with skilled and unskilled labour, allows us to internalize the comparative advantages, benefiting all member states if the compensation principle is adopted. But in the short term there would be losers and winners in Western Europe, even though in the long term society as a whole would be better off: and, in the absence of compensations, the Western attitude typically takes the position of the losers, presumably because the welfare function is of a Rawlsian type (see Rawls 1971). On the contrary, this conflict of interest does not exist equally within Central Eastern Europe, where unskilled workers, in particular, would be immediately better off, thanks to labour mobility across the borders, and skilled workers would not be disadvantaged. In fact, in the short term, there is a double conflict of interests: first, within Western Europe, between consumers, producers and skilled labour, on the one hand, and unskilled labour, on the other, the latter being threatened by excellent foreign competitors; second, between Western and Central Eastern European societies. Practically everybody benefits in the latter, because they have a much higher percentage of unskilled workers and their skilled workers are not threatened by an equally large comparative advantage of highly skilled Western colleagues, given that they are unwilling to move East or there is still an insufficient demand for them across the border, as the Central Eastern European stage of development is lagging behind.

QUESTION 2: WOULD IT BE POSSIBLE TO ADOPT MUTUAL RECOGNITION IN SERVICES WITHOUT AFFECTING THE (DEPENDENT) LABOUR MARKET IN THE EU?

Up to now the discussion has focused on self-employed service workers. Notice that they include not only non-regulated and unskilled services but also regulated and skilled ones, which are usually subject to professional rules and public or semi-public regulations in most European countries. For example, minimum salaries or set fees for notaries, lawyers, dentists, auditors, etc. often apply. But the argument is also valid for employees. And indeed, another way of saying that Nicolaïdis and Schmidt's (2007) answer to Question 1, in my view, is incomplete is the following: it is harder to apply mutual recognition to services than to goods, as in the former market not only can production not be separated from consumption, but the worker cannot be separated from his own product, and furthermore the worker himself combines two means of production – labour and capital. Thus, all the four freedoms are to some extent integrated in the service market. That makes utilizing mutual recognition and the home-country principle particularly difficult, because in the (dependent) labour market mutual recognition is considered a form of social dumping in the European Union (EU). For European employees, the exact opposite principle holds true, and is called parity of treatment, and is itself identical to the host-country principle (see Kostoris Padoa Schioppa 2005). Competition in the (dependent) labour market is limited by the national insiders who understandably want to maintain their privileges, and consequently impose the host-country principle rather than the home-country one. Therefore, a French firm can hire a Polish plumber as an employee but can only use French standards and regulations and only offer a French wage, French holidays, French working hours; hence, the incentives for a French firm to hire a Pole are reduced to zero and any Polish unemployed individual is reluctant to move to France in his job search. Indeed, assuming, as is unfortunately the empirical case, that there is classic unemployment both in France and Poland, French firms are hindered by French wage and regulatory rigidities and, if they do not find it profitable under those conditions to hire from the French labour force, they certainly do not want to hire Poles (on the same conditions as required by the host-country principle). But they would be ready to hire them under the Polish conditions, which presumably are not as costly and as rigid. Hence, labour mobility from Central Eastern Europe is almost annulled, labour rigidity in continental Western Europe is confirmed, and unemployment rises everywhere. A much better social outcome would be obtained for both countries if French firms were allowed to hire Polish plumbers as employees on home- (Polish) rather than host-country (French) conditions. But, given the clear connections between self-employed individuals and employees in the plumbing trade, the adoption of the mutual recognition principle in either of the two cases would represent a terrible threat to the other. Mutual recognition has therefore to be avoided in both.

The question then becomes: how are services to be precisely defined in this context? The answer is not clear in Nicolaïdis and Schmidt (2007) and the problem is not discussed in depth in their paper. My last example shows that it is difficult to conceptualize the service market, because, as mentioned by Pelkmans (2006), it has 'an extremely diversified nature'. On the one hand, it may be defined according to the intrinsic characteristics of the *object* produced (plumbing, for example), which is often intangible, sometimes non-tradable, in any case always belonging to a '*tertium genus*' besides agriculture (the 'primary' sector) and industry (the 'secondary' sector), following the well-known methodology common to all modern national account systems. This is the way utilized, for example, in the Cockfield Report prepared for President Delors (see Commission of the European Communities 1985). By contrast, services are often defined, on the other hand, particularly in the Treaty Establishing the European Communities (TEC), in the context of the single market, according to the characteristics of the *subject* who produces them, alternative to what concerns the 'free movement of goods', of 'workers', of 'capital'. Indeed, Chapter 3 of the Title III of Part 3 of the TEC states in Art. 50:

Services shall be considered to be 'services' within the meaning of this Treaty where they are normally provided for remuneration in so far as they are not governed by the provisions relating to freedom of movement for goods, capital and persons. 'Services' shall in particular include: (a) activities of an industrial character; (b) activities of a commercial character; (c) activities of craftsmen; (d) activities of the professions.

In this respect, the European services directive adds some further confusion: Art. 1 refers to 'the exercise of the freedom of establishment for service providers and the free movement of services', where, in this context, 'service means any self-employed economic activity' (Art. 4) or 'any activity which a person performs outside a relationship of subordination' (Council of the European Union 2006).

QUESTION 3: ARE THE FREEDOM OF ESTABLISHMENT AND THE FREE MOVEMENT OF SERVICES BOTH NECESSARY AND SUFFICIENT CONCEPTS TO COVER THE FREEDOM OF SERVICES TO BE ESTABLISHED IN THE EUROPEAN SINGLE MARKET?

Nicolaïdis and Schmidt's (2007) answer seems to be positive, as they appear to believe that there are only two ways to supply services in the internal market, the distinction between the two depending on the temporariness of the corresponding activities: 'The core test here – as stated in the Treaties – is temporariness. If a cabinet-maker offers particularly tailored repair services across borders, he profits from the freedom of services ... if he does it on a continuous basis with some sort of establishment, it is the freedom of establishment that applies' (Nicolaïdis and Schmidt 2007: 719–20). This almost entirely corresponds to what is written in the Council of the European Union (2006), reporting on the European services directive. Nicolaïdis and Schmidt (2007) add that, unlike in freedom of establishment, in freedom of services the home-country rule is at least theoretically adopted. I do not share this view, as I do not think that it corresponds to the current version of the services directive.

In my opinion, moreover, freedom of establishment and free movement of services are, on the one hand, concepts which are too large to concern only the self-employed – to which the European services directive refers – but, on the other hand, too limited to describe the complete set of possibilities to be offered to grant freedom of services in the European single market. Freedom of establishment in the TEC regards all kinds of firms of one Member State setting up a new location 'in the territory of any Member State' (Art. 43). Thus, it includes individual companies made up of one or a few self-employed individuals, but also larger companies 'including co-operative societies, and other legal persons governed by public or private law' (Art. 48). It then becomes perfectly conceivable that the permanent services offered outside the home country are supplied, rather than by the self-employed, by employees of firms established in the host country. By a similar reasoning, services in a destination Member State may be produced by posted dependent workers of an enterprise set up in a different EU-origin country. Altogether it seems to me that, taking into consideration the primary laws of the Treaties, which can never be overcome by the secondary norms of a directive, there are essentially three and not two ways of granting freedom of services in the EU single market. As noted also by Daniel Gros (2005), these three ways correspond to the temporary posting in a host country of workers employed by an enterprise of another Member State, to the permanent establishment of a foreign EU firm in the destination country (using independent or dependent workers to provide its services), and to the movement of self-employed individuals coming from another country of origin and temporarily crossing their national borders.

It is important to distinguish between these three cases because the original European services directive (the one drafted by Commissioner Bolkestein, circulated in 2004, and much hated) did not try to introduce competitive innovations in the fields where strong insiders and protected employees or firms were involved; therefore, it maintained the host-country principle both for posted workers and for newly established firms, but it aimed at eliminating all barriers to entry in services supplied by self-employed persons temporarily crossing national borders. Indeed, limiting my comment to the comparison between temporary posted employees and the self-employed temporarily crossing national borders, I recall that the Bolkestein draft explicitly indicated the prevalence of the old directive 96/71/EC for posted workers over the new norms. And the current version of the European services directive confirms that it

should not affect terms and conditions of employment which, pursuant to Directive 96/71/EC of the European Parliament and of the Council of 16 December 1996 concerning the posting of workers in the framework of the provision of services, apply to workers posted to provide a service in the territory of another Member State. In such cases, Directive 96/71/EC stipulates that providers have to comply with terms and conditions of employment in a listed number of areas applicable in the Member State where the service is provided. These are: maximum work periods and minimum rest periods, minimum paid annual holidays, minimum rates of pay, including overtime rates, the conditions of hiring out of workers, in particular the protection of workers hired out by temporary employment undertakings, health, safety and hygiene at work, protective measures with regard to the terms and conditions of employment of pregnant women or women who have recently given birth and of children and young people and equality of treatment between men and women and other provisions on non-discrimination. (Council of the European Union 2006: 38)

Hence, host-country conditions are always imposed on posted workers, except for social security contributions during a period which is shorter than a year:

the posting duration is important as, if the period of posting abroad does not exceed 12 months, it creates a situation which derogates to the general rule whereby, with regard to social protection, employees and the self-employed are subject to the legislation of the Member State where they carry out their activities. In fact, posted employees are insured in their home Member State and continue to pay their mandatory social security contributions to their home State; however, they are entitled to all health-care benefits in kind in the country where they work irrespective of their transferring their residence or not, and to receive the family allowances in the country where they are insured irrespective of their families' place of residence. (Kostoris Padoa Schioppa 2005: 198)

By contrast, Art. 16 of the original 2004 Bolkestein draft stated that, in order to grant free movement of services to self-employed individuals temporarily crossing their national borders in the EU, 'Member States shall ensure that providers are subject only to the national provisions of their Member State of origin.' This sentence by itself, if adopted, would have implied a true revolution. That was so well understood by trade unions, by protected employees and by their parties in continental Western Europe that they aimed only at its cancellation, after massive demonstrations where they pretended to represent social Europe. Central Eastern European governments unsuccessfully opposed this outcome and so did the liberal Europe of the Anglo-Saxon and some of the Nordic countries. Central Eastern trade unions remained silent, on the one hand, because they felt, and still feel, weaker than their Western colleagues and, on the other hand, because the host-country rule limits the access of Central Eastern workers to Western labour markets but offers better conditions to the happy few who are accepted in the West. In any case, the Central Eastern relative failure should have been expected because, as we should know from the sixteenth-century *Prince* by Machiavelli (see Machiavelli 2003), the potential losers of a new policy always become more vocal and aggressive than the potential winners, even though the latter may be more numerous. In the end, the EU as a whole has lost, as the host-country rule now prevails in all self-employed and employees' labour markets.

Biographical note: Fiorella Kostoris Padoa Schioppa is Professor of Economics at the University of Rome '*La Sapienza*' and at the College of Europe, Bruges.

ACKNOWLEDGEMENTS

I would like to thank Susanne Schmidt for her helpful comments on earlier drafts of this article.

REFERENCES

Commission of the European Communities (1985) *Completing the Internal Market. White Paper from the Commission to the European Council (Milan, 28–29 June 1985)*, COM(85) 310 final, 14 June.

Council of the European Union (2006) *Common Position Adopted by the Council with a View to the Adoption of the Directive of the European Parliament and of the Council on Services in the Internal Market*, 17 July.

Gatsios, K. and Seabright, P. (1989) 'Regulation in the European Community', *Oxford Review of Economic Policy* 5(2): 37–60.

Gros, D. (2005) 'Europe needs the single market in services', *Financial Times*, 7 April.

Kostoris Padoa Schioppa, F. (2005) 'Mutual recognition, unemployment and the welfare state', in F. Kostoris Padoa Schioppa (ed.), *The Principle of Mutual Recognition in the European Integration Process*, Basingstoke: Palgrave Macmillan, pp. 190–223.

Machiavelli, N. (2003) *The Prince*, London: Penguin Books; reissue with revision.

Nicolaïdis, K. and Schmidt, S.K. (2007) 'Mutual recognition "on trial": the long road to services liberalization', *Journal of European Public Policy* 14(5): 717–34.

Olson, M. (1982) *The Rise and Decline of Nations: Economic Growth, Stagflation and Social Rigidities*, New Haven, CT: Yale University Press.

Pelkmans, J. (2006) *European Integration: Methods and Economic Analysis*, 3rd edn, London: Pearson Education.

Rawls, J. (1971) *A Theory of Justice*, Cambridge, MA: The Belknap Press of Harvard University Press.

Schmidt, S.K. (2007) 'Mutual recognition as a new mode of governance', *Journal of European Public Policy* 14(5): 667–81.

Why no mutual recognition of VAT? Regulation, taxation and the integration of the EU's internal market for goods

Philipp Genschel

1. INTRODUCTION: ONE MARKET – TWO PRINCIPLES OF MARKET INTEGRATION

Trade is hindered by regulatory and tax barriers in the European Union's (EU's) internal market for goods. Surprisingly, however, both types of barriers are dealt with under different rules. While mutual recognition is the standard approach to removing regulatory barriers (see Pelkmans 2007), national treatment applies to indirect taxation. Usually it is the country of origin which regulates (origin principle) but the country of destination which collects the value added tax (VAT) (destination principle). Why this difference in approach? Why isn't mutual recognition also applied to VAT?[1] It is clearly not for lack of proposals for an origin-based VAT system, i.e. for mutual recognition in taxation. A switch to an origin-based system was discussed during the negotiations of the Treaty of Rome. The Council formally accepted its desirability in 1967; the Commission tabled proposals for a 'definitive' origin-based VAT system in 1987 and 1996, but to no avail: VAT remains to this day a destination-based tax.

In this paper, I argue that three factors explain the lack of mutual recognition of VAT. First, it is economically less beneficial to abandon national treatment in turnover taxation than in product regulation. Second, it is politically more difficult to introduce mutual recognition because it is more likely to lead to problems of systems competition, harmonization and joint administration in taxation than in regulation. Finally, there is less judicial pressure towards mutual recognition of VAT than of product regulations.

In view of these factors, the explanation why national treatment still prevails in VAT may appear to be overly obvious. VAT, it seems, is simply a least likely case for mutual recognition to work. However, while this may be clear now, it was by no means clear in the early days of European integration. Indeed, it was in turnover taxation, not in product regulation, that a switch to the principle of mutual recognition was first called for in the EU, and the thrust of much of the VAT policy of the EU was to implement this change. Only the continuous failure to achieve this goal gradually revealed the high obstacles to mutual recognition of VAT. In this paper, I review the major steps of this collective learning process and the lessons it teaches about the specific problems of mutual recognition of VAT and the general problems of tax integration in the internal market.

The paper is organized as follows. Section 2 compares the costs of national treatment in product regulation and turnover taxation in order to assess the 'demand' for mutual recognition. Section 3 turns to the 'supply side' and examines the early plans of the Commission on how to move beyond national treatment in both policy fields in the 1960s and 1970s. Section 4 briefly reviews the role of the European Court of Justice (ECJ) as a sponsor of mutual recognition for product regulations in the 1970s and 1980s, and asks why it cannot play the same role in VAT. Section 5 analyses the reasons why the Council of Ministers rejected all Commission proposals for an origin-based VAT system in the 1980s and 1990s, despite its commitment to the single market programme. Section 6 summarizes the main findings and concludes that in turnover taxation, at least, it may be beneficial to maintain some 'barriers' among the member states.

2.   THE COSTS OF NATIONAL TREATMENT

If mutual recognition is not applied to VAT, this might be simply because there is less demand for it than in product regulation. However, as I will show in this section, this is not the case. In the 1960s there was already a perceived need to go beyond national treatment in both policy fields.

Discriminatory barriers

The principle of national treatment shaped the Community's original approach to market integration in the 1950s and 1960s. The main objective during this period was Customs Union, i.e. the elimination of tariff barriers and quotas between the member states. The major concern was that member states could sabotage this goal by replacing tariff barriers with tax barriers. While Article 90 (former 95) of the European Community (EC) Treaty outlawed the protectionist abuse of indirect taxes in principle, in practice this was impossible to monitor because five of the six member states levied so-called 'cumulative' turnover taxes. Cumulative taxes produce cascading tax burdens that are extremely difficult to measure and compare across different products. This made it impractical to establish whether member states imposed similar taxes on imports and domestic goods, thus encouraging protectionist abuse. To remedy this problem, in 1962 the Commission proposed switching collectively to a non-cascading tax system. The Council responded by adopting the common VAT system in 1967. VAT is a completely transparent tax: the effective VAT burden always equals the nominal VAT rate, thus the introduction of VAT made it technically possible to impose equivalent tax burdens on imports and domestic goods, and consequently, to enforce national treatment in taxation (Genschel 2002: 70–5).

Of course, regulatory barriers also posed a potential threat to customs union. In 1962, the Commission sent out questionnaires to survey the extent of discriminatory regulations in the member states, and in 1969 the Council passed a directive banning all regulations which imposed additional costs or restrictions on imports (Egan 2001: 67–9). However, compared with turnover taxation, discriminatory regulations were a secondary issue that received much less political attention.

Non-discriminatory barriers

While in the 1960s the Community was still working towards the goal of ensuring national treatment of taxes and regulations, the Commission had already embarked on higher goals. National treatment, Commission officials argued, was not sufficient to guarantee the completion of the internal market (see e.g. Groeben 1962, 1967). While the consistent application of this principle would put an end to protectionism, and level the playing field for imports and domestic goods, it would do so separately within each member state and not uniformly across all of them. In a Community of six, it would create six self-contained level playing fields rather than a single integrated one. The internal market would remain jurisdictionally fragmented, and this fragmentation would continue to constitute an obstacle to trade among the member states.

In product regulation the major trade impediment was considered to be regulatory diversity. The principle of national treatment leaves member states with complete freedom to define their own idiosyncratic product standards – as long as they are non-discriminatory. The ensuing diversity of standards forces producers to make different products for each national market. This deters market entry and keeps market integration at less than optimal levels. Production runs remain smaller than they would be if producers were able to market similar products across the entire internal market. Potential economies of scale are lost, decreasing the competitiveness of European companies (Egan 2001: 40–1).

In turnover taxation, on the contrary, diversity was not a problem. While national treatment (i.e. the destination principle) allows member states to charge VAT at different rates, these differences do not affect the structure of production: companies do not have to make a different product in order to gain access to the markets of another member state with a different VAT rate. Hence, national treatment poses much less of a threat to production efficiency in taxation than in regulation. Nevertheless, it inhibits cross-border trade through so-called border tax adjustments. Border tax adjustments are necessary in order to ensure that imports and domestic goods compete on an equal VAT footing: exports have to receive a refund for VAT paid to the exporting country (country of origin) and imports have to pay VAT to the importing country (destination country) in order to ensure that they are taxed at the same level as products originating from the import country. In other words, border tax adjustments prevent exports from a country with a high VAT rate like Denmark from being at a disadvantage in a country with a low VAT rate like Luxembourg, by relieving them of Danish VAT and submitting them to Luxembourg VAT. This way, they also ensure that the revenue goes to the country of destination, Luxembourg, and not to the country of origin, Denmark. The perceived problem with border tax adjustments was that they imposed extra compliance costs on international trade but also, perhaps even more importantly, that they were administered by customs officials at the border: truckers had to stop, have their goods checked and fill in tax forms. In the eyes of the Commission, this undermined the Community's greatest achievement of the 1960s: customs union. 'Customs borders are eliminated but tax borders remain' (Groeben 1962: 10).

To summarize: in the 1960s the Commission had perceived a need to go beyond national treatment in order to create an internal market with 'conditions similar to that of a domestic market' (Groeben 1962: 10). In product regulation, this perceived need was based more on economic considerations, while in turnover taxation symbolic concerns also played a role.

3.   ALTERNATIVES TO NATIONAL TREATMENT: EARLY COMMISSION PROPOSALS

There are two basic alternatives to national treatment: harmonization and mutual recognition (see Schmidt 2007). The Commission studied both of them in the 1960s and recommended mutual recognition as the preferred approach in turnover taxation and harmonization in product regulation. In this section, I briefly review the reasons for the two different approaches.

Mutual recognition of turnover taxes

The Commission opted for the mutual recognition of turnover taxes because it offered the *only* solution to the problem of border tax adjustments. Harmonization was not a solution because, as long as the destination principle applied, even a total harmonization of VAT would not eliminate the need for border tax adjustments. It would still be necessary to give a VAT refund to exports and impose VAT on imports in order to ensure that the revenue went to the 'right' country, i.e. the country of destination. For VAT purposes cross-border sales would continue to be treated differently from domestic sales. Only a switch to mutual recognition could ensure equal tax treatment for domestic and cross-border trade and, thus, create tax conditions in the internal market similar to those of a domestic market.

In 1962, the Commission formally proposed that the Community should switch to an origin-based system of turnover taxation. In 1967, the Council endorsed this proposal in principle and asked the Commission to prepare draft legislation for the abolition of border tax adjustments in the internal market (European Community 1967: article 4). By the late 1960s, both the Commission and the Council officially acknowledged the need for an origin-based VAT system, i.e. for mutual recognition in turnover taxation.

(Total) harmonization of product regulations
The Commission also assessed the potential of mutual recognition to solve the problem of regulatory fragmentation. The verdict was negative. As Commissioner von der Groeben explained:

> At first, the key word of 'mutual recognition of controls' seemed to guide a way out. . . . If each member state accepted that a product approved by the authorities of another member state is also fit for its own citizens, the problem of trade obstacles and economies of scale would be solved. . . . [Unfortunately, however, this solution encounters] almost insurmountable difficulties. . . . There is the legal argument that the mutual recognition of controls implies the creation of new institutional mechanisms and, therefore, is not covered by the harmonization provisions of the Treaty. Also, some member states have already signalled their unwillingness to accept the loss of sovereignty implied in giving foreign controls, i.e. acts of foreign sovereignty, domestic effect, and this even if the foreign controls are based on material and procedural regulations that are identical to domestic regulation.
> (Groeben 1967: 137)

The Commission's misgivings reflected doubts about the feasibility and effectiveness of mutual recognition but also, and perhaps more importantly, that a seemingly superior alternative was available: harmonization. Harmonization was perceived as a more effective means of regulatory integration because it aimed straight at the root cause of the problem of regulatory diversity. Harmonization also appeared to be more feasible politically because it left the member states in control of regulatory policy. In case of doubt, a government could always veto the adoption of a particular harmonization directive in the Council of Ministers, thereby preventing its application in the domestic market. Finally, harmonization promised to foster a sense of commonality and shared identity that mutual recognition, by highlighting differences, did not. Harmonization, therefore, became the standard approach to regulatory integration. The Commission specified the harmonization needs in a 'General Programme for the removal of technical obstacles to trade' in 1968 and the Council set about its work (Egan 2001).

To summarize, the concept of mutual recognition enjoyed a head start in turnover taxation. The Commission thought of mutual recognition for VAT before the ECJ 'invented' it for product regulation, and the Council acknowledged the need for a mutual recognition-based system of VAT when (total) harmonization was still the undisputed norm of regulatory integration.

4.   THE EUROPEAN COURT OF JUSTICE AS A SPONSOR OF MUTUAL RECOGNITION

The Commission's enthusiasm for (total) regulatory harmonization waned quickly during the 1970s. The negotiations of large parts of the 'General Programme' came to a standstill in the Council of Ministers, and Commission officials started to search for alternatives. They were greatly helped by the ECJ. Its rulings prepared the legal ground for the paradigm shift to mutual recognition, epitomized by the Commission's White Paper on 'Completing the internal market' in 1985 (European Commission 1985). In this section, I explore why the ECJ cannot bring about a similar shift to mutual recognition of VAT.

Article 28 and the mutual recognition of product regulations

It is well known that the ECJ played a crucial role in the rise to prominence of mutual recognition (Alter and Meunier-Aitsahalia 1994). By reading the logic of mutual recognition into the text of the Treaty, it prepared the legal basis for mutual recognition's final political triumph. Two landmark decisions were especially important in this respect: *Dassonville* and *Cassis de Dijon*. Both decisions concerned the scope of Article 28's prohibition of 'measures having equivalent effect' to quantitative restrictions. There had been considerable uncertainty about the precise meaning of this concept in the 1960s. Did it apply only to discriminatory measures or did it also cover non-discriminatory regulations?

In *Dassonville* the Court ruled in 1974 that any measure 'capable of hindering, directly or indirectly, actually or potentially intra-Community trade' is equivalent to a quantitative restriction. This implied that Article 28 applies to both discriminatory and non-discriminatory measures. In its famous *Cassis de Dijon* formula, the Court spelled out one important implication of this interpretation in 1979: member states cannot deny market access to goods produced according to foreign standards. This, of course, is the doctrine of mutual recognition. However, the *Cassis* formula also established a so-called *rule of reason*, which limits the scope of mutual recognition. The rule of reason allows member states to deny recognition to foreign regulations if these regulations pose a threat to essential goals of public policy such as public safety, health, environmental and consumer protection, etc. In other words, if foreign regulations are not 'functionally equivalent' to domestic regulations, governments are not obliged to grant unrestricted market access to goods produced under these foreign regulations (Weiler 2005).

In short, the *Cassis* judgment established a general presumption in favour of mutual recognition tempered by a derogation, the rule of reason, for those special cases in which, in the judgment of the Court, the mandatory requirements of public safety, health, environmental and consumer protection differ so much across member states that national regulations cannot be considered as equivalent. The Commission, disenchanted by the slow pace of regulatory harmonization during the 1970s, quickly seized the opportunity offered by this judgment to promote mutual recognition as the new paradigm of regulatory integration (just see European Commission 1985).

Article 90 and the mutual recognition of indirect taxes

The *Cassis* judgment had little bearing on VAT because indirect taxes fall under the purview of Article 90 (former 95) rather than 28 (Weiler 2005). Article 90 maintains that: 'No Member State shall impose, directly or indirectly, on the products of other Member States any internal taxation of any kind in excess of that imposed directly or indirectly on similar domestic products.' This provides a legal basis for subjecting national tax policy to very strict tests of national treatment. However, it provides no basis to compel member states to mutually recognize their (indirect) taxes as equivalent, i.e. to force member states to grant market access to imports without border tax adjustment. Stating explicitly that taxes on imports should not be discriminatory, it implicitly allows for imports to be taxed. This is the crucial difference between Article 90 and Article 28. While individuals, corporations and the Commission can rely on Article 28 to force governments to accept origin-based regulation (within the bounds of the rule of reason), they cannot rely on Article 90 to force governments to accept origin-based taxation.

To conclude, the ECJ prepared the legal ground for mutual recognition in product regulation by reading an obligation to grant market access to goods lawfully marketed in other member states into Article 28 of the EC Treaty. However, the ECJ cannot, in the same way, prepare the legal ground for the mutual recognition of VAT because Article 90 explicitly allows the (non-discriminatory) taxation of imports and, hence, border tax adjustments.

5.   COUNCIL RESISTANCE TO MUTUAL RECOGNITION

Even if the ECJ lacks the power to impose the mutual recognition of VAT by judicial fiat, the Council clearly has the power to impose mutual recognition by political fiat. As I have pointed out in section 3, the Council had already made a commitment to abandon the destination-based VAT in 1967. This commitment was further reinforced by the single market project and its calls for an abolition of 'fiscal barriers' in the mid-1980s (European Commission 1985). However, when the Commission presented a proposal for a definitive, origin-based VAT system in 1987 (European Commission 1987), the Council postponed its adoption and opted instead for a so-called transitional system (European Community 1991). The transitional system preserves the destination principle basically intact. Border tax adjustments continue to exist but were moved from customs posts at the border to tax offices behind the border, in order to allow the abolition of tax-related frontier controls. The only change of economic substance concerned cross-border purchases of final consumers.[2] They were now taxed on an origin basis, simply because the abolition of border controls made it impractical to subject the purchases of, for example, a Danish traveller to Germany to border tax adjustments on his return home.[3] In 1996, the Commission presented yet another plan on how to move to a definitive, origin-based VAT system (European Commission 1996). The Council did not even bother to discuss it.

In the next sub-sections, I explore three possible explanations for the Council's failure to introduce an origin-based VAT: fear of tax competition, conflict over tax harmonization and the administrative implications of mutual recognition.

Systems competition

Mutual recognition exposes states to systems competition because it allows economic agents to choose among different national tax and regulatory regimes. Companies can avoid high taxes or strict regulations by taking up residence in a foreign country with lower taxes or less stringent regulations. As a consequence, governments can no longer set taxes and regulations exclusively with an eye to domestic revenue needs or regulatory preferences. They have to take the level of foreign taxes and regulations into account in order to avoid an outflow, or trigger an inflow, of business. The result, as is often feared, would be a race to the bottom and an under-provision of risk protection and tax-financed public goods (e.g. Sinn 1997). As I will show next, this fear is more justified in taxation than in regulation.

Regulatory competition

Most observers now agree that the single market programme and the advent of mutual recognition have not had any major deregulatory effect (e.g. Radaelli 2004; Schmidt 2007). Three related factors help to explain this: the rule of reason, the high transaction costs of proving equivalence, and the 'certification effect' (Scharpf 1999: 93) of stringent product regulations.

The rule of reason provides a safety net against competitive deregulation because it allows member states to deny market access to imports produced under foreign regulations not equivalent to domestic regulations in terms of safety, health, environmental and consumer protection or the protection of other essential goals of public policy. Since the member states are entitled, by the Treaty (Article 95) as well as by the case law of the ECJ, to insist on a high level of protection, there is little competitive advantage to be gained for governments and companies by undercutting other member states' safety standards. On the contrary, tough regulations may be a competitive advantage not only because they are a prerequisite for unrestricted market access, but also because consumers often show a preference for products manufactured according to high standards, since they regard them as a guarantee of high quality – the certification effect. Therefore, even intense competitive pressure is unlikely to undermine essential regulatory objectives in the Community.

Moreover, the high transaction costs of proving equivalence make it unlikely for competitive pressure to ever become intense. The source of these transaction costs is, again, the rule of reason. It makes mutual recognition contingent on functional equivalence – no recognition of foreign regulations without equivalence of regulatory objectives or effects. This forces importers to prove and national administrations to ensure that imports were produced according to specifications equivalent to domestic regulations in objective and in effect. This is difficult for both sides. Since national administrations are politically responsible for all cases of regulatory failure within their national territory, they tend to take a very cautious attitude towards functional equivalence. Before taking a risk with foreign regulations they do not know, they often insist that imports conform to national rules they do know (Pelkmans 2007). Companies, of course, can challenge this attitude in court. But this takes time and effort and makes little commercial sense. 'One cannot plan, produce and market product lines hoping that eventually a court decision will vindicate a claim of mutual recognition' (Weiler 2005: 49). Hence, companies often voluntarily comply with the regulations of the host country: they waive their right to unrestricted movement under mutual recognition because the transaction costs of using this right are too high.[4]

Tax competition
The fear of a race to the bottom in turnover taxation appears better justified by comparison. There are three reasons for this. First, the ECJ does not consider tax revenue as an essential requirement of public policy and, consequently, does not protect it under the rule of reason. Second, the transaction costs of proving equivalence are likely to be lower than in regulation. Finally, taxes do not have a certification effect.

On the rule of reason: tax revenue is not among the accepted public policy justifications for restrictive state measures. There is no Treaty provision that would entitle member states to deny market access to imports from member states with significantly lower taxes, and the ECJ has consistently refused to consider tax revenue as a mandatory requirement of public policy that can justify trade restrictions (e.g. Terra and Wattel 2001: 81).[5] Essential revenue objectives simply do not enjoy the same protection under EU law as essential regulatory objectives, which leaves member states without legal safeguard against competitive detaxation. This has important implications for the transaction costs of tax arbitrage under mutual recognition. Since revenue requirements are not accepted as justifications for restrictive policy measures, a switch to an origin-based VAT system would imply an *unconditional* obligation for member states to mutually recognize their VATs as equivalent. In other words, no matter how high or low the VAT burden is in the origin country, the destination country would have to accept it as 'equivalent' to its own VAT burden. This would reduce the transaction costs of proving equivalence almost to zero and, thus, facilitate tax arbitrage between national VAT systems, i.e. cross-border shopping by final consumers and transfer pricing by multinational business firms.[6] Finally, VAT is not a quality mark: products sold at high VAT rates are simply expensive but not in any way 'better' than products sold at low rates. Even consumers with a preference for high product standards will opt for lower VAT rates if offered the choice. Hence, if there is any tax competition at all, it is likely to induce rate cuts.

To conclude, there is no safety net against competitive detaxation, the transaction costs of cross-border arbitrage are likely to be lower than in product regulation, and economic agents have no incentive to stop a downward spiral of VAT rates. Hence, a switch to an origin-based system may cause a potentially very intense race to the bottom. This conclusion is corroborated by evidence from corporate taxation. Corporate taxation comes close to being an origin-based (source-based) system (see Sørensen 2001: 159). It is subject to significant tax rate competition (Ganghof and Genschel 2007), and the ECJ has done little so far to protect member states from arbitrage pressures and revenue losses. On the contrary, its case law was instrumental in establishing '"tax jurisdiction shopping" [as] a legitimate activity' in the internal market (Terra and Wattel 2001: 81).

Harmonization

The obvious way to mitigate tax-rate competition is tax-rate harmonization. In fact, in 1992 the Council agreed on a common minimum standard rate of 15 per cent for VAT, in order to reduce incentives for cross-border shopping under the transitional system (European Community 1992). However, according to the Commission, much more is required in order to prevent excessive tax competition under a fully-fledged origin-based tax system. In the 1996 programme for a definitive VAT system, the Commission even envisaged an (almost) uniform standard rate of VAT (European Commission 1996). The Council refused even to contemplate such an idea.

In this section, I argue that three factors concur in making *tax-rate harmonization* particularly difficult[7]: first, the unanimity requirement in the Council of Ministers; second, problems of distributive justice and democratic accountability; and, third, the adjustment costs of tax harmonization.

Unanimity
There is widespread agreement that the unanimity requirement in tax matters (see Articles 93, 94, 95 II EC Treaty) is the single most important obstacle to agreement on tax harmonization (e.g. Radaelli 1995: 160–1; European Commission 2001). This view is highly intuitive but raises the question of why

the unanimity requirement is not simply abandoned for taxation as it was gradually abandoned for most areas of regulation, starting with the Single European Act in the mid-1980s.

Redistribution, efficiency and democracy

One obstacle to majority voting on tax harmonization is that taxation is usually conceived as a redistributive policy instrument. The redistributive implications of tax policy choices make them prone to zero-sum conflict, and, by implication, dependent on majoritarian modes of collective decision-making, because where there is conflict, consensual decision-making easily leads to deadlock. Majoritarian decisions, in turn, need democratic accountability in order to be acceptable for the minority and, hence, legitimate. This creates a dilemma for tax harmonization. On the one hand, the political feasibility of VAT-rate harmonization depends crucially on majority voting in the Council, since it is likely to stir up conflict between high- and low-VAT member states. On the other hand, the legitimacy of tax harmonization depends crucially on the unanimity rule. Given the EU's real or perceived democratic deficit, tax harmonization cannot rely on legitimation via direct democratic control at the European level but has to rely on indirect democratic control via democratically accountable governments at the national level. This requires, however, that national governments have individual veto power in the Council, since otherwise national electorates could not hold them accountable for Council decisions (Scharpf 2003). Some governments, most prominently the British, therefore refuse to consider any relaxation of majority voting in taxation.

Majority voting on regulatory harmonization is easier to legitimize because product regulations purportedly aim at the correction of market failure rather than at redistribution (Majone 1996). The goal is to prevent price competition from lowering product quality to the point where public health and safety or environmental and consumer protection are at risk. To the extent that these safety risks affect everybody, their regulation is in everybody's interest. In this sense, regulation improves efficiency – it makes some (or all) actors better off without making anybody worse off. Of course, this still leaves room for secondary distributive conflicts as to how much and what type of regulation is required (Héritier 1996). Fundamentally, however, everybody agrees that, *all else being equal*, higher levels of regulation and risk protection are better than lower levels. This basic consensus is reflected, most visibly, in the Treaty obligation to aim at 'a high level of protection' in regulatory harmonization (Article 95 III EC Treaty). A similar Treaty obligation to aim at 'a high level of revenue' in tax harmonization is difficult to imagine because, even if all else were equal (which it hardly ever is), there is no consensus that more taxation is better than less taxation.[8] Therefore, majority voting is less likely to be prejudicial to legitimate regulatory interests than to legitimate taxing interests. To the extent that harmonized regulations are efficiency enhancing, they are self-legitimating and do not need democratic approval.[9]

Provided that risk regulation is efficiency enhancing while taxation is redistributive, cross-national differences in regulations are less likely to reflect a fundamental difference in policy objective than differences in tax rate. Different national regulations will often be only different means to an equivalent regulatory end. Different tax rates, by contrast, will often be means to different redistributive ends. This makes tax-rate harmonization potentially more conflictual and more dependent on democratic legitimacy than regulatory harmonization. Given the current state of democracy in the EU, many argue that this legitimacy can only be achieved indirectly via democratically accountable national governments – and this requires unanimity voting on tax matters in the Council of Ministers (e.g. Scharpf 2003).

Adjustment costs

A second obstacle to majority voting on tax matters is that the adjustment costs of tax harmonization fall mostly on governments. To be sure, regulatory harmonization also implies adjustment costs. But these costs are borne primarily by private companies which have to adjust product designs and production processes to harmonized standards. The government remains one step removed from the pains of adjustment (e.g. Héritier 1996). Not so in tax harmonization. The budgetary costs of a VAT-rate alignment would have to be borne directly and exclusively by the government – and these costs are potentially substantial. Calculations by Bernd Genser suggest, for example, that the introduction of a harmonized EU standard VAT rate as suggested by the Commission in 1996 (European Commission 1996) would cause a revenue loss of 2.4 per cent of gross domestic product (GDP) or 4.7 per cent of total tax revenue in high-VAT Denmark and a revenue gain of 1.5 per cent of GDP or 3.7 per cent of total tax revenue in low-VAT Luxembourg (Genser 2003: 742). Revenue changes of this magnitude are difficult to absorb, and no government would like to see them imposed on itself by a majority of other member states.

To conclude, the resilience of the unanimity requirement is a reflection of the special problems of tax harmonization rather than their cause. Tax harmonization is more difficult than regulatory harmonization because it is more dependent on democratic legitimacy and because it can cause substantial adjustment costs for governments.

Administration

Some observers maintain that the main stumbling block to an origin-based VAT system has not been fear of tax competition or conflict over VAT-rate harmonization but 'the perceived need for a "clearing system" to rebate VAT collected to the countries of final consumption' (e.g. Patterson and Serrano 1998: 20). In this section I explore where this perceived need comes from and why it causes so much unease among national governments.

Tax enforcement

A switch from a destination-based to an origin-based VAT system tends to redistribute tax revenue from destination states to origin states.[10] This is problematic for fiscal reasons – destination countries lose revenue – but also on conceptual grounds. The VAT is a tax on consumption. Therefore, it is commonly assumed that the revenue 'rightfully' belongs to the state of consumption, i.e. the destination country. Under an origin-based system this pattern of revenue allocation can only be achieved through cross-border revenue sharing among the member states. As a consequence, 'revenue clearing systems' featured prominently in all Commission proposals for a definitive VAT system (see European Commission 1987, 1996).

Despite considerable differences in architecture and technical detail, all proposed clearing systems share one fundamental similarity: they tend to transform the VAT from a national tax administered individually by each member state into a 'Community tax' which all member states administer jointly and share (European Commission 1996: 3). This is because, under a system of cross-national revenue clearing, the level of national revenue no longer depends on the enforcement efforts of the national tax administration alone but also on the enforcement activities of foreign administrations. During the negotiations of the 1987 Commission proposal for a definitive VAT system, many member states expressed concern that this mutual dependence in tax administration would fatally undermine the transparency, timeliness and reliability of VAT collections (Genschel 2002: 106). These concerns were substantiated by economic analyses highlighting the adverse incentive effects of revenue clearing. Revenue clearing turns tax collection from an individual good of each member state into a Community collective good of all member states and, thus, discourages enforcement efforts, encourages a free riding attitude, and erodes the level of collective revenue (e.g. Smith 1997; Genser 2003).

Regulatory enforcement
However, the problems in product regulation are not fundamentally different. The switch from destination-based to origin-based regulation, i.e. from national treatment to mutual recognition, turns risk prevention into a Community collective good as well. The safety of goods traded in a national market no longer depends on the reliability and effectiveness of national enforcement activities – testing, certification and policing – but also on the effectiveness of foreign enforcement activities. The individual regulatory responsibility of each member state is replaced by the joint responsibility of all member states (Holzinger and Knill 2004: 26) – with the same detrimental effect on enforcement incentives as in the VAT case. Most observers agree, therefore, that mutual recognition is a very demanding mode of integration, since it crucially depends on a high level of trust among the member states and/or an extensive involvement of the European level in regulatory policy – whether *ex ante* through prior harmonization and notification schemes, or *ex post* through extensive destination country safeguards, increased rights of regulatory oversight among the member states or the development of co-operative networks among national regulators (e.g. Nicolaïdis 1993).

The difference between enforcement problems in turnover taxation and product regulation seems to be a matter of degree rather than principle. The crucial point is that in product regulation, mutual recognition can be applied selectively, whereas in the case of VAT it is an 'all or nothing' proposition. As we have seen, the rule of reason premises the mutual recognition of product regulations on their functional equivalence. This facilitates a gradual phasing-in of mutual recognition. The process can start with 'easy' cases, where the equivalence of regulations is more or less obvious because no serious health and safety risks are at stake, and then extend gradually to more difficult cases. The member states can build up and test the administrative support infrastructure step by step. Mutual trust can grow slowly. The risks involved are limited because the member states can always take recourse in national treatment, i.e. home-country control in cases where host-country control does not seem to guarantee an adequate level of risk regulation. This is different in taxation. As we have also seen, the rule of reason provides little protection for revenue requirements. This implies that the transition towards an origin-based VAT system cannot be organized gradually but has to happen in a big bang. States cannot simply restrict the application of the principle of mutual recognition only to trade with member states with truly 'equivalent' tax levels but have to apply it indiscriminately to all trade with all other member states. This makes it impossible to develop and test, step by step, the administrative infrastructure of mutual recognition, including, most importantly, the reliability of the revenue-sharing mechanism. Hence, a switch to mutual recognition involves bigger risks and requires more trust than in product regulation.

In conclusion, mutual recognition puts an end to the separate, operationally independent national administration of taxes and regulations. However, while in product regulation this is a gradual process, in turnover taxation it involves a more or less dichotomous choice between national and joint European administration.

6. CONCLUSION: IN PRAISE OF NATIONAL TREATMENT

While the Commission still hails 'a definitive system of taxation in the Member State of origin ... as a long-term Community goal' (European Commission 2000, 2003), the old fervour is gone. The focus of recent policy initiative is to improve and modernize the transitional system, not to replace it. In light of the analysis of this paper, this development should be welcomed. Indeed, the Commission should go one step further and give up the idea of an origin-based VAT system altogether.

To be sure, an origin-based VAT would bring some benefits. By ensuring that 'sales and purchases across borders would be treated in exactly the same way as similar sales and purchases within the borders of the member states' (European Commission 1985: 45) it would perfectly symbolize the idea of an internal, border-free market. By making border tax adjustments redundant, it would also eliminate one source of tax compliance costs. At the same time, however, an origin-based system would introduce new administrative complexities such as, most importantly, cross-border revenue clearing. There is no guarantee, therefore, that the administrative workload would decrease overall.

There is also no guarantee that an origin-based VAT system would enhance economic efficiency. In fact, there are two reasons to suppose that it might not. First, national treatment of VAT is less detrimental to production efficiency than national treatment of product regulations because the key efficiency problem in product regulation, cross-national diversity, is not a problem in VAT. While companies may have to redesign products in order to market them according to foreign product standards, they do not have to redesign anything in order to market their goods at foreign VAT rates. Second, mutual recognition of VAT may introduce more inefficiencies than mutual recognition of product regulations because, as we have seen, wasteful tax arbitrage is less constrained by EU law and potentially more gainful for economic agents than regulatory arbitrage.

Finally, the political costs of an origin-based VAT system are high. The elimination of border tax adjustments would constrain national VAT-rate autonomy – *de facto* by tax competition and/or *de jure* by tax harmonization – and would reduce national independence in VAT administration. The member states would lose a substantial amount of political and administrative control over one major source of revenue to the EU level, which, however, has neither the decision-making capacity, nor the democratic credence or administrative machinery to take on this control effectively and legitimately.

In conclusion, there is little to be said in favour of mutual recognition of VAT. The EU should stick to the principle of national treatment in turnover taxation and give up plans for an origin-based definitive system. The symbolic, administrative and economic costs would be minor. The political benefit would be substantial. An explicit commitment to the destination principle would not only safeguard a high degree of national autonomy in VAT-rate setting and administration. It would even allow an increase in national autonomy by giving back to the member states control over those aspects of the VAT base and rate structure which had been harmonized in the past in anticipation of a definitive origin-based system, but which require no harmonization for the proper functioning of the destination principle. For example, the Byzantine system, by which national governments have to seek EU approval before they apply a reduced VAT rate to, say, district heating, restaurant services or bicycle repair (see e.g. European Community 2006), could be scrapped or at least substantially streamlined.

National treatment is sometimes portrayed as a principle of 'isolation, ghettoization' and 'separateness' that compares rather unfavourably to the more open-minded concept of mutual recognition (Nicolaïdis 2007; see also Kostoris Padoa Schioppa 2005). This portrayal has a certain appeal if the problem at hand is to achieve integration despite diversity, as in the case of product regulation. It is much less appealing, however, if the problem is to protect diversity from entropy, as in the case of VAT. National treatment is not only a protective reflex of national parochialism but also a repository of diversity for the Union. Even in the promised land of European integration it may be advisable to maintain some 'barriers' among the member states. Diversity requires not only recognition, but also protection.

Biographical note: Philipp Genschel is Professor of Political Science at Jacobs University, Bremen, Germany.

ACKNOWLEDGEMENTS

I would like to thank Barbara Dooley, Sandra Lavenex, Adrienne Héritier, Armin Schäfer, Susanne Schmidt, Dana Trif and the participants of the mutual recognition workshop in Bielefeld for their useful comments, discussions, and suggestions. Funding by the German Science Foundation (CRC 597 'Transformations of the State') is gratefully acknowledged.

NOTES

1 In the following I use the terms national treatment and destination principle interchangeably. National treatment refers to a system of destination-based taxation or regulation. In this system the power to define and enforce product regulations and to impose and collect VAT rests with the member state of final sale. Mutual recognition, by contrast, means origin-based taxation or regulation: the power to tax and regulate rests with the member state of production or business residence.

2 Note, however, that the transitional system brought some change of administrative substance by making, as many observers complained, the VAT system more complicated and susceptible to fraud.

3 The transitional system ensures, however, that large-scale cross-border sales to private individuals (cars, direct mail shopping, etc.) and sales to VAT-exempt firms continue to be taxed on a destination basis. In other words, all cross-border sales with high potential for tax arbitrage remain subject to national treatment. As a consequence, there is hardly any VAT competition in the internal market (e.g. Cnossen 2001: 499–500).

4 The 'New Approach' to technical harmonization greatly reduces the transaction costs of proving equivalence (Pelkmans 2007). Combining the harmonization of essential regulatory objectives with the 'reference to European standards' method to proving conformity, it helps companies to demonstrate the functional equivalence of regulations and insures governments against the risk of a race to the bottom.

5 To be sure, the ECJ has accepted tax-related essential requirements such as effective 'fiscal supervision' and the 'coherence of national tax systems'. However, the Court has tended to construe these justifications narrowly. Their practical significance has remained very limited so far (Terra and Wattel 2001; Sedemund 2007).

6 Note that the volume of tax arbitrage under an origin-based VAT system will depend crucially on how origin is defined for VAT purposes. If origin is defined as the country in which the sales outlet resides (as implied in European Commission 1987), arbitrage pressures are likely to be lower than if origin is defined as the country in which the company owning the sales outlet resides (as implied in European Commission 1996). In the former case, a consumer would actually have to travel to a low VAT country in order to take advantage of low VAT rates there.

In the latter case, he could simply go to a shop owned by a company from a low VAT country in his hometown.

7 Note, however, that the VAT system and base are highly harmonized (Uhl 2007).

8 Another way to see the difference between efficiency-enhancing regulation and redistributive taxation is to note that regulatory failure due to low levels of regulation scandalizes people easily, whereas revenue shortfalls due to low levels of taxation do not. In the former case, the public instinct is often that the government should have regulated and policed more, in the latter that it should have spent less.

9 Incidentally, this may also explain why the alleged 'majoritarian activism' of the ECJ decisions on potentially restrictive product regulations (see Maduro 1998) is, according to some observers, largely absent in its decisions on potentially restrictive direct tax rules (see Graetz and Warren 2006). The 'judicial harmonization' (Maduro) of product regulations is simply less likely to leave legitimate safety interests aggrieved whereas judicial harmonization of tax rules may harm legitimate distributive interests.

10 This is true even if tax rates and bases are fully harmonized, unless trade relations are completely balanced throughout the EU.

REFERENCES

Alter, K.J. and Meunier-Aitsahalia, S. (1994) 'Judicial politics in the European Community. European integration and the pathbreaking "Cassis de Dijon" decision', *Comparative Political Studies* 26(4): 535–61.

Cnossen, S. (2001) 'Tax policy in the European Union. A review of issues and options', *Finanzarchiv* 58(4): 466–558.

Egan, M.P. (2001) *Constructing a European Market. Standards, Regulation, and Governance*, Oxford: Oxford University Press.

European Commission (1985) *Completing the Internal Market. COM (85) 310 final*, Brussels: European Commission.

European Commission (1987) *Completion of the Internal Market: Approximation of Indirect Tax Rates and Harmonization of Indirect Tax Structure. COM (87) 320 final/2*, Brussels: European Commission.

European Commission (1996) *A Common System of VAT. A Programme for the Single Market. COM (96) 328 final*, Brussels: European Commission.

European Commission (2000) *A Strategy to Improve the Operation of the VAT System within the Context of the Internal Market. COM (2000) 348 final*, Brussels: European Commission.

European Commission (2001) *Tax Policy in the European Union – Priorities for the Years Ahead. COM (2001) 260 final*, Brussels: European Commission.

European Commission (2003) *Review and Update of VAT Strategy Priorities. COM (2003) 614 final*, Brussels: European Commission.

European Community (1967) 'First Council Directive 67/227/EEC of 11 April 1967 on the harmonisation of legislation of member states concerning turnover taxes', *Official Journal* P 071: 1301–3.

European Community (1991) 'Council Directive 91/680/EEC of 16 December 1991 supplementing the common system of value added tax and amending Directive 77/388/EEC with a view to the abolition of fiscal frontiers', *Official Journal* L 376: 0001–19.

European Community (1992) 'Council Directive 92/77/EEC of 19 October 1992 supplementing the common system of value added tax and amending Directive 77/388/EEC (approximation of VAT rates)', *Official Journal* L 316: 0001–4.

European Community (2006) 'Council Directive 2006/18/EC of 14 February 2006 amending Directive 77/388/EEC with regard to reduced rates of value added tax', *Official Journal* L 51: 12–13.

Ganghof, S. and Genschel, P. (2007) *Taxation and Democracy in the EU*, Cologne: Max Planck Institute for the Study of Societies DP 07/2.

Genschel, P. (2002) *Steuerharmonisierung und Steuerwettbewerb in der Europäischen Union*, Frankfurt a.M.: Campus.

Genser, B. (2003) 'Coordinating VATs between EU member states', *International Tax and Public Finance* 10(6): 735–52.

Graetz, M.J. and Warren, A.C. (2006) 'Income tax discrimination and the political and economic integration of Europe', *Yale Law Journal* 115(6): 1186–1255.

Groeben, H. v. d. (1962) 'Nationale Steuersysteme und Gemeinsamer Markt', *Europäische Steuerzeitung* 1: 6–14.

Groeben, H. v. d. (1967) 'Zur Politik der Rechtsangleichung in der Europäischen Wirtschaftsgemeinschaft', *Zeitschrift für Rechtsvergleichung* 8(3): 129–40.

Héritier, A. (1996) 'The accommodation of diversity in European policy-making and its outcomes: regulatory policy as a patchwork', *Journal of European Public Policy* 3(2): 149–67.

Holzinger, K. and Knill, C. (2004) 'Competition and cooperation in environmental policy: individual and interaction effects', *Journal of Public Policy* 24(1): 25–47.

Kostoris Padoa Schioppa, F. (2005) 'The cultural foundations of mutual recognition', in F. Kostoris Padoa Schioppa (ed.), *The Principle of Mutual Recognition in the European Integration Process*, Basingstoke: Palgrave Macmillan, pp. 224–31.

Maduro, M.P. (1998) *We the Court. The European Court of Justice and the European Economic Constitution*, Oxford: Hart.

Majone, G. (1996) 'The European Community as a regulatory state', *Collected Courses of the Academy of European Law* 5(1): 321–419.

Nicolaïdis, K. (1993) 'Mutual recognition among nations: the European Community and trade in services', Ph.D. dissertation, Harvard, Cambridge, MA.

Nicolaïdis, K. (2007) 'Trusting the Poles? Constructing Europe through mutual recognition', *Journal of European Public Policy* 14(5): 682–98.

Patterson, B. and Serrano, A.M. (1998) *Tax Competition in the European Union*, Luxembourg: European Parliament Working Paper ECON-105.

Pelkmans, J. (2007) 'Mutual recognition in goods. On promises and disillusions', *Journal of European Public Policy* 14(5): 699–716.

Radaelli, C.M. (1995) 'Corporate direct taxation in the European Union: explaining the policy process', *Journal of Public Policy* 15(2): 153–81.

Radaelli, C.M. (2004) 'The puzzle of regulatory competition', *Journal of Public Policy* 24(1): 1–24.

Scharpf, F.W. (1999) *Governing in Europe. Effective and Democratic?*, Oxford: Oxford University Press.

Scharpf, F.W. (2003) 'Problem-solving effectiveness and democratic accountability in the EU', *MPIfG Working Paper 03/1*, Cologne: Max Planck Institute for the Study of Societies.

Schmidt, S.K. (2007) 'Mutual recognition as a new mode of governance', *Journal of European Public Policy* 14(5): 667–81.

Sedemund, J. (2007) *Europäisches Ertragsteuerrecht*, Baden-Baden: Nomos.

Sinn, H.-W. (1997) 'The selection principle and market failure in systems competition', *Journal of Public Economics* 66(2): 247–74.

Smith, S. (1997) *The Definitive Regime for VAT*, London: Institute for Fiscal Studies Commentary 63.

Sørensen, P.B. (2001) 'Tax coordination in the European Union: what are the issues?', *Swedish Economic Policy Review* 8: 143–95.

Terra, B. and Wattel, P. (2001) *European Tax Law*, London: Kluwer Law International.
Uhl, S. (2007) 'Steuerstaatlichkeit in Europa'. Unpublished manuscript, School of Humanities and Social Science, Jacobs University, Bremen.
Weiler, J.H.H. (2005) 'Mutual recognition, functional equivalence and harmonization in the evolution of the European common market and the WTO', in F. Kostoris Padoa Schioppa (ed.), *The Principle of Mutual Recognition in the European Integration Process*, Basingstoke: Palgrave Macmillan, pp. 25–84.

Mutual recognition and the monopoly of force: limits of the single market analogy

Sandra Lavenex

INTRODUCTION

The adoption of the principle of mutual recognition in European Union (EU) justice and home affairs (JHA) co-operation can be seen as a typical case of institutional isomorphism where a policy concept that has proved useful in promoting integration in one area, the single market, has been borrowed to realize another area of integration, the 'area of freedom, security and justice' (AFSJ). With the Tampere European Council of 1999, it was decided that the principle of mutual recognition should become a cornerstone of judicial co-operation in both civil and criminal matters within the EU. Before, this principle had been realized in the system of state responsibility for the examination of asylum claims, the 1990 Dublin Convention, and later turned into a European Community (EC) Regulation. In a nutshell, the implementation of this principle removes a major obstacle to cross-border law enforcement because different national standards with regard to refugee law or criminal codes no longer obstruct judicial co-operation and extraditions between member states. At a first glance, the motives for adopting the principle in market integration and the AFSJ are similar: it allows for co-ordination despite the impossibility of agreeing on the harmonization of rules and a fully supranational integration. This perspective, together with the ambitions to turn JHA co-operation into a genuine European public order (Kaunert 2005; Lavenex and Wallace 2005) have led observers to compare the dynamism implied with that of the single market project.

These developments have not only induced an increasing number of scholars to work on the topic, but have also raised a number of concerns regarding the substance and potential effects of this deepening area of co-operation on both the balance between human rights and security considerations (e.g. Albrecht 2004; Guild 2004; Lavenex and Wagner 2005; Mitsilegas *et al.* 2003; Wagner 2007) and notions of sovereignty (Jachtenfuchs *et al.* 2006; Kaunert 2005). Although these two dimensions are crucial for any discussion of the principle of mutual recognition in JHA, the scope and limits of the single market analogy implied in this process have hitherto remained largely unreflected upon, so have the more structural preconditions for applying this principle in this area.

This article starts with a discussion on the viability of the single market analogy, that is, how far the principle of mutual recognition that we know from market integration retains the same meaning when transferred to the sphere of internal security. In other words, what is the purpose of mutual recognition, what is its object, and what are the effects on inter-state relations? There is a fundamental difference between the mutual recognition of regulations regarding trade products and the mutual recognition of judgments and judicial decisions that strike a balance between the interests of the issuing state and a person's rights and liberty. It will be argued that what serves as an instrument of liberalization in one sector, expanding the societal *vis-à-vis* governmental sphere, may work exactly in the opposite direction in another sector. The second section turns to the preconditions for an efficient and legitimate application of this principle in the various fields of the AFSJ (asylum policy and judicial co-operation in criminal matters) and its relations with other principles of integration such as harmonization and approximation. Introducing the main legal arguments of the debate, it will be argued that these preconditions may best be understood by adopting a governance perspective on co-operation that emphasizes the need for a strong institutional (decision-making rules) and normative (trust) embedding. The limits of the current framework of co-operation are then exemplified using evidence from the first practical experiences with mutual recognition in JHA, with an emphasis on the European Arrest Warrant (EAW). The conclusion situates this analysis in the context of the relationship between states' sovereignty and integration and discusses the prospects for mutual recognition in the context of an open constitutional future.

THE LIMITS OF THE SINGLE MARKET ANALOGY

The justification of the introduction of the principle of mutual recognition in JHA draws on the analogy with single market integration, its dynamism and success. Noting the slowness and intricateness of traditional forms of judicial co-operation, the Commission argued in its first Communication on the introduction of the principle that 'borrowing from concepts that have worked very well in the creation of the Single Market, the idea was born that judicial co-operation might also benefit from the concept of mutual recognition' (Commission 2000: 2). The simple analogy would be that 'a decision taken by an authority in one state could be accepted as such in another state, even though a comparable authority may not even exist in that state, or could not take such decisions, or would have taken an entirely different decision in a comparable case' (Commission 2000: 4). The limits of the single market analogy have to be sought at three levels: first, the question as to who benefits from mutual recognition, that is, the wider purpose of applying this principle; second, the scope of state regulations, structures and activities affected when applying mutual recognition; and third, the implications of mutual recognition in terms of its functional equivalence to other, alternative modes of integration.

Who benefits from mutual recognition and for what purpose?

The first set of questions relates to the subjects whose cross-border interactions benefit from mutual recognition, and the implications of adopting this principle for the relationship between sovereignty and liberalization in the process of European integration. In the single market, mutual recognition facilitates the cross-border flows of economic goods and services. It is an instrument to facilitate economic transactions between societal actors in spite of partly differing state regulations. In the AFSJ, mutual recognition promotes the free movement of judgments and judicial decisions; that is, state acts. In asylum matters, the member states agree to recognize the outcome of the asylum determination procedure issued in the state responsible for the examination of the claim under the Dublin Convention/Regulation. In criminal law, the member states accept final judicial decisions, e.g. an arrest warrant or other decisions laying down sanctions issued under the law of that state. Those benefiting from mutual recognition are hence not societal actors but state representatives. As stated in a recent JHA discussion paper by the Finnish Presidency: 'The advantages of mutual recognition over traditional forms of international co-operation are considerable ... As a result of the application of the principle of mutual recognition, judicial decisions can be enforced much more quickly and with greater certainty. The amount of discretion is reduced, as is the scope of grounds for refusal' (Finnish Presidency 2006: 1).

There is thus a fundamental difference in the nature of the flows addressed: in the first case, single market integration, mutual recognition eases the cross-border movement of societal interaction, thus contributing to processes of liberalization and socialization. The private sphere and the rights of individuals engaged in trade and consumption are enhanced while the regulatory scope of the member states is reduced. In the case of judicial co-operation in JHA, in contrast, the introduction of mutual recognition does not expand the rights of individuals *vis-à-vis* the state. On the contrary, it facilitates the cross-border movement of sovereign acts exercised by states' executives and judicial organs. The relationship between the principle of mutual recognition and the balance between state and society, liberalization and sovereignty is thus reversed. Fritz Scharpf's well-known criticism of the detrimental effects of mutual recognition and, more broadly, 'negative integration' on states' regulatory capacities and the dangers of a race to the bottom in the level of regulations (Scharpf 1999) thus needs to be revised in relation to the AFSJ. Instead of increasing individual freedoms in relation to the regulatory scope of government, in the AFSJ, mutual recognition boosts the transnational enforcement capacity of governmental actors. As will be argued below, in the absence of a complementary approximation of minimum standards, the application of this principle may also engender a race to the bottom, not with regard to regulation but to human rights and legal procedural guarantees. At this stage it shall suffice to point out that what used to be a tool of liberalization in one sector may become an instrument of governmentalization in another one.[1]

What is being mutually recognized?

The second important difference concerns the 'object' that governments agree to mutually recognize and its scope in terms of sovereignty implications for the participating states. In the economic sphere, the object of recognition are another country's rules on products and production methods. In its landmark *Cassis de Dijon* decision, the European Court of Justice (ECJ) ruled that all member state regulations, whatever their differences in detail, should be deemed equivalent in effect. Consequently, products produced legally in one member state should be considered equally safe, environmentally friendly, etc. as those produced legally in any other member state. If one member government prohibits the sale of a product produced legally in another member state, the producing firm can challenge that prohibition under European law. The issue at stake are hence member states' laws that enshrine regulatory standards; these are clearly discernible legal texts that can be easily accessed by other member states and, if necessary, courts. In JHA, by contrast, the object of recognition reaches much further as it applies to sovereign acts of the judiciary in their interpretation and application of a whole set of material and procedural laws. By applying mutual recognition, another member state not only recognizes a law as being equivalent but recognizes the judicial act in its interpretation of all relevant provisions in a given case. In other words, mutual recognition not only implies that member states recognize other norms as equivalent to their own but that they accept the need to co-operate in the enforcement of other states' systems of law. For instance, under the EAW (see below), the member state issuing the warrant delegates the act of arresting a suspect to another. The latter, by arresting the suspect, puts its monopoly of force into the service of the former (Jachtenfuchs *et al.* 2006: 24). The underlying assumption is that the requesting states' judicial decisions are both legal and legitimate in the light of shared standards of human rights and procedural safeguards. The object of recognition is extended to another country's legal and political system as such in its function as both warrant of internal security and protector of individual rights.[2] This, of course, requires a much higher degree of mutual trust than in the area of economic integration (see below).

The lure of sovereignty

The third problem with the single market analogy concerns the relationship between mutual recognition and other mechanisms of integration. At this functional level, the analogy suggests that mutual recognition would fulfil the same function as in the single market: it would allow for policy co-ordination and sectoral integration without the need for uniform legal and institutional standards. The apparent safeguarding of national sovereignty under the principle of mutual recognition in contrast to supranational harmonization was a major motive in the eyes of its promoters in the run-up to the Tampere summit, in particular the UK government. The idea that mutual recognition would allow for co-operation despite the many obstacles to harmonization, and thus would represent a more realistic and easily achievable alternative to the latter, permeates the earliest to the latest documents dealing with the issue. Although not completely denying the interplay between the two modes of co-ordination, the Commission, in its 2000 Communication, noted that

> Not always, but often, the concept of mutual recognition goes hand in hand with a certain degree of standardization of the way states do things. Such standardization indeed often makes it easier to accept results reached in another state. On the other hand, mutual recognition *can to some degree make standardization unnecessary.*
>
> (Commission 2000: 4; emphasis added)

In a similar vein, the relevant article of the (stalled) Constitutional Treaty reads: 'The Union shall endeavour to ensure a high level of security through ... the mutual recognition of judgments in criminal matters and, *if necessary,* through the approximation of criminal laws' (Art. III-257(3); emphasis added). On the surface, the adoption of mutual recognition appears easier than harmonization or the adoption of minimum standards since it does not imply the creation of supranational rules and thus appears less compromising for state sovereignty.

Yet, as Kalypso Nicolaïdis suggests, mutual recognition 'is both about respecting sovereignty' (by forgoing the option of total harmonization and centralization) 'and radically reconfiguring it – by delinking the exercise of sovereign power from its territorial anchor" (Nicolaïdis 2007: 685). From this perspective, the exercise of mutual recognition constitutes a reciprocal allocation of jurisdictional authority to prescribe and to enforce, or a horizontal transfer of sovereignty (see also Schmidt 2005: 190). Jurisdiction is disjoined from national territory, and hence also from the people and their democratic polity.

The framing of mutual recognition as the 'easier' and less demanding way to achieve co-ordination not only underestimates the importance of legal harmonization and approximation for the realization of mutual recognition in the single market as complementary mechanisms of integration (Majone 1994: 83; Nicolaïdis 1993; Schmidt 2005: 192), it also fails to see that for a number of institutional and normative reasons, these complementary mechanisms are much more difficult to achieve in JHA than in economic co-operation. These barriers are discussed in the next section.

PRECONDITIONS FOR MUTUAL RECOGNITION IN THE AFSJ

The temptation to regard mutual recognition as an alternative to harmonization neglects the fact that the application of mutual recognition never occurs in an institutional void but is always managed (Nicolaïdis 1993). This 'management' concerns first its relation with other, more formal principles of integration, along with the institutional prerequisites for their realization. The second dimension is more informal, and refers to the societal prerequisites of mutual recognition as trust and confidence in each other's legal systems. This section first summarizes the state of the art of the academic debate on mutual recognition in the AFSJ, which has a predominantly legal focus. Questioning this literature's expectations in the positive effects of a widening of the Union's legislative mandate the following sections emphasize from a governance perspective the institutional and normative preconditions for mutual recognition.

The legal argument: mutual recognition versus approximation and harmonization

Most discussions of mutual recognition in the AFSJ existing so far take a legal perspective and concentrate on its legal basis. This literature converges in an important observation, namely that the competences for facilitating law enforcement measures between member states, and thus the 'security' element of the AFSJ, are much stronger than that for approximating 'freedoms' or 'justice', especially human and procedural rights in criminal proceedings (i.e. Alegre and Leaf 2004; Guild 2004; Lööf 2006; Weyembergh 2005). Whereas Article 31 (1) a and b, Treaty on the European Union (TEU) provides an explicit legal basis for 'facilitating and accelerating co-operation between competent ministries and judicial or equivalent authorities of the Member States in relation to ... the enforcement of decisions' and 'facilitating extradition between Member States', the Commission has had to appeal to a (contested) logic of implied competences for action in the area of procedural rights.

A look at official documents introducing mutual recognition in the AFSJ shows that despite the principle's framing as an alternative to approximation or harmonization (see above), the need for certain common minimum standards on the suspects' rights has been recognized. The Tampere European Council argued, without further specification, that 'enhanced mutual recognition of judicial decisions and judgments and the necessary approximation of legislation would facilitate co-operation between authorities and the judicial protection of individual rights.' The common ground for this assumption is the European Convention on Human Rights (ECHR) to which all member states abide and in particular its Articles 5, 6 and 7. However, the Commission argued already in 2000 that 'Some specific aspects of procedural law could nevertheless be spelled out in more detail, for instance the conditions under which legal advice and interpretation are provided. The same can be said for particular types of procedures' (Commission 2000: 16). Another objection relates to procedural guarantees contained in Protocol 7 of the ECHR which is unevenly ratified amongst the member states. As Elspeth Guild notes, the Draft Constitutional Treaty, which would have made some progress in this direction, contains numerous weaknesses. It only partially incorporates the due process rights contained in the ECHR, and does not mention its seventh Protocol. What is more, the list of areas where minimum standards should be agreed according to Article III-166(2) is flawed because it misses key questions related to the implementation and exercise of law enforcement (Guild 2004: 231).

Despite differences in the exact motivation for their claims, both the Commission and most legal scholars converge in their conclusions that mutual recognition has unbalanced effects and that it requires a stronger level of legal approximation. Analysing the modes of governance predominant in JHA co-operation, and drawing parallels with other existing examples of 'positive' integration in this area, the next section argues that the effects of such exclusively legal reforms should not be over-estimated.

The governance perspective: institutional and normative embeddedness of mutual recognition

From a governance perspective, the scope for mutual recognition in JHA is constrained by a range of institutional and ideational factors that shape member states' co-operation in this field. The governance perspective emphasizes the role of formal and informal principles, norms, rules, and procedures in a system of co-operation and allows us to highlight the interplay between these structures and the contents of co-operation (Jachtenfuchs and Kohler-Koch 2004: 97; see also Wagner 2007). The institutional modes of policy-making have implications for the likelihood that common standards are adopted in the first place and also affect the contents of common rules. At a more informal level, the ideational or normative foundations of co-operation circumscribe the societal basis of mutual recognition and in particular the requirement of transnational trust in its realization. It will be argued that the predominance of transgovernmentalism in JHA co-operation limits the scope for legal approximation as a complement to mutual recognition, whereas the lack of mutual trust between member states' judicial organs circumscribes the application of the principle of mutual recognition.

Intensive transgovernmentalism, positive integration and mutual recognition
The mode of policy-making in JHA has been characterized as intensive transgovernmentalism (Wallace 2000; Lavenex and Wallace 2005).[3] In general terms, this mode underlines the prominent role of bureaucrats and state officials below the level of government representatives in establishing networks with their counterparts in other member states that develop a certain degree of autonomy in decision-making and implementation. Although important differences exist between those aspects of JHA that have moved to the first pillar and those that remain in the third, a common characteristic is the importance of such networks in both legislation and operational co-operation. This has implications for the scope and the consequences of applying mutual recognition in JHA and its 'management' in relation with other modes of positive integration such as harmonization and approximation of laws. On the one hand, transgovernmentalism gives the 'policemen of sovereignty' (van Outrive 1995: 395), the Ministers of Justice and the Interior, a particular weight in the legislative process, thereby limiting the scope for supranational legislation. On the other hand, transgovernmentalism emphasizes the role of operational co-operation that operates below the level of legislation. Again, this works against the idea of complementing mutual recognition through common supranational standards and enforcement institutions.

At the legislative level, intensive transgovernmentalism manifests itself in the limitation of supranational decision-making procedures. In the first pillar, the introduction of the exclusive right of initiative for the Commission, decision by qualified majority voting in the Council and co-decision by the European Parliament (EP) were only realized after a transition period of five (in practice seven) years. As a consequence, the so far most important directives establishing minimum standards were still adopted through the intergovernmental method and important reservations remain on the powers of the ECJ. Likewise, the third pillar still operates with unanimity which, with the EU's enlargement, has become increasingly difficult to achieve (Finnish Presidency 2006: 2). Another legacy of earlier modes of co-operation that prevails in both the first and third pillars is the working structure of the Council. This includes a fourth level of decision-making, the Strategic Committee on Immigration, Frontiers and Asylum (SCIFA), which gives a crucial role to member states' high-level law and order officials.

Intensive transgovernmentalism inhibits the scope for the adoption of supranational policies or 'positive integration' in two ways. First, by privileging governmental actors' respective interests over a comprehensive vision of a policy field, not all relevant aspects of a policy become subject to approximation, but only those where actors' interests converge. Second, if a legal text is finally adopted, it will usually reflect the lowest common denominator and reserve the member states a large degree of discretion in implementation. The lack of consistency in approximation is well reflected in the area of criminal law where most of the approximation has concerned substantive criminal law, and, in particular, the definitions of offences. By contrast, the areas of criminal sanctions and of criminal procedure, that are at the core of national sovereignty, have been largely neglected (Weyembergh 2005: 1585). Furthermore, the types of crime covered by this substantive approximation tend to reflect political conjunctures rather than objective criteria in terms of severity or the cross-border nature of crimes.[4] The second characteristic of positive integration measures in JHA is the weakness of obligations implied. Definitions are often formulated in a vague manner, so to rule out substantial adjustment of domestic legislation, the legal texts contain many exemption clauses and the member states retain a high margin of discretion in interpretation and application. This can be retraced both in third (Weyembergh 2005) and first pillar legislation (Lavenex 2006).

It seems that the Commission has noticed this lack of political will when it concedes in its report on the implementation of the Hague programme on JHA co-operation of June 2006 that results in legal approximation both in asylum and criminal law matters have remained behind expectations. A good example of the limits of positive integration in first pillar issues is the directive on minimum standards in asylum procedures adopted after multiple delays in December 2005. Fraught with exemption clauses, vague formulations and providing for minimum standards below those usual in national legislation, the directive has been criticized by the EP for constituting a threat to human rights and refugee law principles and for containing too many exceptions.[5] In the case of third pillar legislation, the Commission Report of 2006 notes that 'major delays ... sadly arose with the adoption of two flagship measures: political agreement on the Framework Decision on the evidence warrant was reached only in June 2006, and the one relating to certain procedural rights is still under discussion. Neither of them was adopted in 2005 as planned in the Hague programme' (COM(2006) 333 final §51). Whereas the evidence warrant extends the principle of mutual recognition to a new field, the Commission proposal for a Framework Decision on procedural rights applying in proceedings in criminal matters throughout the EU constitutes an attempt at legal approximation in procedural law. Already defensive in its wording, the Commission proposal has been criticized by the EP and the UK House of Lords for being too vague and non-committal (European Parliament 2005; House of Lords 2005: § 42). Indeed, its support among the member states can be questioned. Whereas some argue that the ECHR provides enough protection, others are concerned that such a measure would impose constraints on their domestic criminal justice systems and would thus infringe the subsidiarity principle (Morgan 2004). Stating the lack of progress in Council negotiations, a number of observers have voiced the concern that without a shift to qualified majority voting, it would become nearly impossible to agree on common provisions. An attempt by the European Commission and the Finnish Presidency to realize this shift through the application of the so-called *passerelle* of Art. 42 TEU, allowing for the introduction of supranational procedures, was however rejected in the informal JHA Council in September 2006.

Pending the introduction of supranational procedures, which is foreseen in the Constitutional Treaty, it seems that a majority of member states concentrate on operational co-operation which serves as one main avenue of integration next to legislative decision-making. Operational networks of law enforcement officials are created for exchanging information, for conducting joint investigations to enforce the law and for setting standards of co-operation in the form of memoranda of understanding. Originally developed 'bottom-up' between the relevant authorities of the member states, such operational networks have been complemented by more vertical structures created on the European level to spur their operations (den Boer 2005). The most prominent examples of vertical co-ordinating structures are Europol[6] and Eurojust.[7] These bodies fulfil the main purpose of exchanging information between the member states, and of co-ordinating the implementation of joint law enforcement activities. The clear distinction between operational and legislative integration in the Draft Constitutional Treaty suggests that the former is seen as an alternative to legal approximation. With regard to mutual recognition, network organizations such as Europol or Eurojust could fulfil the role of bundling and diffusing necessary information on laws, legal judgments, authorities or contact points. Whereas this would increase the transparency of legal systems, it would not reduce the problem of unbalanced effects of mutual recognition in the absence of legal approximation.

Trust and the normative foundations of mutual recognition
The horizontal transfer of sovereignty implied by applying mutual recognition is only possible if a high degree of trust exists among the participating countries (Majone 1994: 75; Scharpf 1997: 137f.). The requirement of trust is particularly important in the area of JHA, where mutual recognition not only means that member states accept that they will co-operate in the enforcement of each other's laws (see above), but where the judicial decisions at stake have immediate implications for human rights and fundamental freedoms (on trust and JHA, see also Anderson 2002; Walsh 2006). As pointed out by the ECJ in its first response to a preliminary reference on mutual recognition under third pillar legislation, 'there is a necessary implication that the Member States have mutual trust in their criminal justice systems and that each of them recognizes the criminal law in force in the other Member States even if the outcome would be different if its own national law were applied.'[8] In this case, the issue at stake was the mutual recognition of decisions to discontinue proceedings. Thus, whereas in one member state, a crime would lead to a court judgment, the former may be bound to recognize the solution in another member state, where a settlement is accepted for certain categories of crimes.

According to some observers, the realization of mutual recognition would imply 'a genuine paradigm shift in legal co-operation between member states' (Wouters and Naert 2004: 919). A look at relevant court decisions shows that the necessary level of trust in each other's judicial systems cannot be presupposed. A good example of this is the *Rachid Ramda* case of 2002 relating to an extradition warrant issued by France against Mr Ramda, an Algerian national, to stand trial for participation in terrorist bombings in France in 1995.[9] After stating the probability of ill-treatment in the gathering of evidence by the French police, a UK Division Court decided to quash the Secretary of State's decision to extradite Mr Ramda to France for want of proper consideration by the Home Secretary of the issue of the fairness of the evidence against him (Alegre and Leaf 2004: 200; Guild 2004: 227). Similar decisions can also be made by French judges in respect of Spanish extradition requests or by German courts in respect of French extradition requests, where the national courts have failed to be satisfied that the claim of the right to punish the individual made by another EU member state is justified (ibid.). The prevalence of mutual distrust is also visible in the second JHA area where the principle of mutual recognition has been codified: asylum law. As mentioned above, the implementation of the Dublin system of responsibility allocation for the examination of asylum claims presupposes the equivalence or at least acceptability of asylum determination standards among the member states. In reality, however, there is great variation between the level or procedural safeguards as well as differences in the interpretation of what constitutes a refugee, which will only partly be approximated once the recent directives on refugee status and asylum procedures are implemented. Meanwhile, a significant amount of jurisprudence shows the limits of the application of the Dublin system. In 1999, the British Court of Appeal quashed the Home Office's decision to transfer several applicants to France and Germany, noting that the applicants concerned could, in principle, have been entitled to refugee status in the United Kingdom, whereas this was not possible in Germany and France because of their more restrictive policies (Danish Refugee Council and European Commission 2001).[10] By 2006, the courts of nine member states had blocked transfers under the Dublin Regulation to Greece on protection grounds (ECRE 2006). Needless to say, enlargement to 27 + member states, with partly unconsolidated principles regarding the rule of law, will only exacerbate this problem. This is the reason why the JHA ministers, when debating about the introduction of the EAW, proposed limiting its use to the 'old' member states. This decision was later reversed by the Committee of Permanent Representatives on political grounds. The next section turns to the experience gathered with this instrument in practice.

THE PRACTICE OF MUTUAL RECOGNITION IN JHA

The first and also the most symbolic measure to officially apply the principle of mutual recognition in JHA is the Framework Decision of 13 June 2002 on the EAW and the surrender procedures between the member states. This will be followed by the European Evidence Warrant and framework decisions on freezing property or evidence, confiscation and financial penalties. What have been the experiences with the implementation of the EAW, and how far have its implementation and the further codification of mutual recognition been impeded by the lack of legal approximation and mutual trust? The relatively open wording of the EAW makes it a good indicator for assessing the desire on the part of the states to commit themselves on the route to the mutual recognition of judicial decisions in the law enforcement area. Since the Framework Decision only sketches the main guidelines, its realization is dependent on the behaviour of two main players: the national legislators who are responsible for the successful transposal of the European text and the competent judicial authorities for the application of the warrant.

The transposition into national law

On the surface, the implementation of the EAW has proceeded relatively smoothly. Whereas only half of the member states complied with the time limit laid down, by 22 April 2005 all member states had transposed the Framework Decision. Several member states had to revise their constitutions to do this. Nevertheless, in its first report on the implementation of the EAW, the Commission took a rather critical stance on domestic transpositions. In an annexe to its Report the Commission has set out a detailed, article by article, analysis of how the Decision has been implemented in the law of the member states (SEC(2006) 79). One manifestation of member states' reluctance to fully apply the EAW is the extension of grounds for non-execution of a surrender request by other member states. Whereas some countries have transformed the optional grounds for non-execution of Art. 4 EAW into mandatory grounds, others have included non-execution clauses that were not part of the Framework Decision. British law says that after the decision to surrender on the part of the judge, the minister may decide not to execute if the person acted 'in the interest of national security'. Italian legislation stipulates that the judge must not only check the conformity of the procedure with regard to the fundamental principles of Italian law but he must also check the grounds of the affair to ensure that there is sufficient evidence of proof. Furthermore, the grounds for non-execution provided for in the EAW such as the violation of fundamental rights (article 1) or discrimination (preambles 12 and 13) have been sometimes implemented in a manner exceeding the wording of the Framework Decision. Under the third pillar, the Commission has no competence of appeal in the case of default by states who have not transposed the Framework Decision correctly.

The practice of national courts

By September 2004, 2,603 warrants were already issued, 653 persons arrested and 104 persons surrendered (COM(2006) 8: 4). Beyond these general numbers, however, few data exist on the actual application of the EAW by national courts. Nevertheless, two sources point to the existence of several difficulties with this practice: Eurojust's Annual Report and national constitutional courts' rulings. Eurojust has no competence to gather data on the number of EAWs issued, but member states must report failures to meet EAW deadlines to this body. Yet, in 2005, only seven out of the 25 member states responded to the Eurojust question- naire, thus limiting the scope for interpretation (Eurojust 2005: 35). A more indirect way to monitor implementation has been the organization of strategic meetings arranged by Eurojust with practitioners of the member states. At these meetings, many grounds for refusal to execute the EAW were mentioned, among which were those typically invoked in cases of limited mutual confidence such as insufficient description of facts and lack of complementary information (Eurojust 2005: 41).

In several member states constitutional courts ruled the Framework Decision to be incompatible with the provisions of the constitution, in particular con- cerning the extradition of nationals. In April 2005 the Polish Constitutional Tribunal found that the EAW offended the Polish Constitution's ban on extraditing Polish nationals. The Supreme Court of Cyprus has found that the EAW falls foul of a clause in the Constitution of Cyprus prohibiting their citizens from being transferred abroad for prosecution. In July 2005 the German Constitutional Court annulled Germany's law transposing the Frame- work Decision because it did not adequately protect German citizens' funda- mental rights. The case concerned the surrender of a suspected terrorist of German/Syrian origin to Spain. As a result of the decision, German nationals could not be extradited until new legislation was adopted. Within a short time, the Spanish Parliament took retaliatory measures, banning the surrender of Spanish nationals to Germany and demonstrating that national sovereignty is still very much the point of departure for European co-operation in criminal matters. As noted in a report by the House of Lords:

> if one Member State refuses to execute an EAW on grounds which are not permitted under the Framework Decision then other Member States might well feel justified in doing likewise. Were such practice to become widespread then the whole regime could break down and its benefits would be lost. Mutual recognition and reciprocity would seem to go hand in hand.
>
> (House of Lords 2006: § 29)

Finally, the legality of the EAW has been called into question. On 13 July 2005, in response to an annulment action challenging the Belgian legislation imple- menting the EAW, the Belgian Constitutional Court referred a preliminary question to the ECJ. It asked whether removal of the double criminality require- ment for 32 types of offence was contrary to the principle of non-discrimination and equality, and whether this derogation would be contrary to the principle of legality in criminal matters.

The questions raised by the Belgian Constitutional Court and the verdict handed down by the German Constitutional Court point to the tension between adopting mutual recognition in the absence of complementary positive integration such as approximation of substantive criminal law and procedural safeguards, and the development of rules on criminal jurisdiction.

CONCLUSION: AN EVOLUTIONARY APPROACH TO MUTUAL RECOGNITION?

This article has sought to show the limits of the single market analogy implied in the imitation of the principle of mutual recognition as an instrument of integration in JHA. These limits were retraced at three levels: the semantics of the term; the institutional and normative preconditions of the instrument; and its operation in practice. The semantic analysis showed that whereas mutual recognition functions as an instrument of liberalization in single market integration, its realization would amount to an instance of governmentalization in JHA. Here, it is not the societal sphere and its cross-border transaction that are facilitated but governments' cross-border law enforcement activities. This has much deeper implications in terms of horizontal transfers of sovereignty than in economic regulation. Whereas existing, mainly legal analyses of mutual recognition in JHA denounce its uneven effects on the balance between state prerogatives and individual rights, the governance perspective emphasizes institutional and normative obstacles to its full realization. In institutional terms, the modes of governance prevailing in this area prevent the adoption of strong complementary legislation promoting necessary legal approximation or harmonization. In normative terms, the agents responsible for the implementation of mutual recognition, national courts and judicial authorities, often lack the necessary degree of trust and transnational socialization for its full application. Therefore, its effects in the long run should not be over-estimated. But does this mean that mutual recognition has been just wishful thinking in the ambitions to realize an 'area of AFSJ'?

The difficulties encountered with the implementation of the EAW, and the failure to agree on accompanying minimum standards, have indeed slowed down co-operation on mutual recognition (House of Lords 2006; Finnish Presidency 2006). A good example of the caution that member states now apply towards this principle are the difficult and protracted negotiations surrounding the second measure implementing it, the European Evidence Warrant.[11]

Yet, these difficulties should not suggest that governments have completely given up on their support for mutual recognition. On the contrary, most of them have continued to issue EAWs, and legal reforms are sought to remedy the negative rulings by Constitutional Courts. At the same time, the Commission has intensified its efforts to surmount the main institutional and normative obstacles to its realization. Among these count the (failed) attempt to introduce supranational decision-making procedures in the Council and various initiatives to spur mutual trust among the member states. These include, for instance, judicial training, the exchange of judges between the member states, as well as enhanced communication between Eurojust and the member states in the implementation of common instruments. Even though these measures may promote judicial authorities' knowledge of each other's laws and procedural standards, and thus improve the necessary level of trust, they only tackle the implementation aspect of mutual recognition. Without the political will to agree on common minimum standards on substantive or procedural criminal law, the application of mutual recognition will not only have uneven effects on the balance between suspects' rights and states' discretion, it will also remain limited to those aspects where an acceptable level of equivalence exists.

Taking these difficulties into account, and the lack of political will on the part of the member states to take on binding supranational commitments in these core areas of sovereignty, there might be a third perspective on prospects for mutual recognition in JHA. Against common interpretations that the principle's adoption might have been 'a step too far too soon' (Alegre and Leaf 2004), its premature endorsement might be a strategy in itself: a measure to change the rules of the game on the ground so as to increase the functional pressure for approximation or harmonization in the future. Seen from this perspective, the primary ambition of the supranational promoters of mutual recognition could be less its immediate effectiveness than the long-term promotion of judicial communication, mutual learning, and ultimately also approximation and trust. As it was hoped in the single market, legal approximation would thus be achieved by default, through a decentralized diffusion mechanism that circumvents the politicized debates in the Council of Ministers (see Benz 2005; Scharpf 1997). Here again, however, the single market analogy has its limits. The reason is that for such approximation to occur, participating actors need to see the benefits of changing their laws that outweigh the costs of adaptation. Such an evolutionary approach to mutual recognition relies on market dynamics in a competition for the 'better' kind of regulation (Benz 2005). Contrary to, for example, consumer protection standards, where one may expect a certain public pressure for upward approximation, however, no comparable incentives exist in areas such as refugee law or the rights of criminal suspects. In addition, it may be questioned how far a strategy that consciously counts on imperfections at the beginning in order to increase pressure for adaptation in the future is legitimate in the light of its direct repercussion on human rights and individual freedoms.

To conclude, it remains the task of national constitutions and eventually the European constitution to circumscribe the scope for the transnationalization of states' monopoly of force. For the reasons outlined above, mutual recognition may not carry far without the move towards truly supranational structures. Whether the member states are willing to go this step towards a political Union, in the current context of enlargement and constitutional perplexity, however, is doubtful.

Biographical note: Sandra Lavenex is Professor of International Politics at the University of Lucerne, Switzerland.

ACKNOWLEDGEMENTS

The author would like to thank the participants at the workshop on mutual recognition at the University of Bielefeld in June 2006 and in particular Susanne K. Schmidt, Kalypso Nicolaïdis, Miguel Poiares Maduro, Wolfgang Wagner and Nicole Wichmann for their helpful comments on earlier versions of the article. The usual disclaimer applies.

NOTES

1 This argument that European integration strengthens the governmental sphere resonates with liberal intergovernmentalism (Moravcsik 1994) and Klaus-Dieter Wolf's thesis of a new '*raison d'état*' (Wolf 1999). For a discussion in the context of JHA, see Lavenex (2006); Lavenex and Wagner (2005); Wagner (2007).

2 I owe this point to Miguel Maduro.

3 Nicole Wichmann (2006) analyses the consequences of the shift from looser forms of transgovernmental cooperation to mutual recognition for Schengen associates.

4 For example, the Joint Action of 24 February 1997 concerning action to combat trafficking in human beings and sexual exploitation of children adopted in the aftermath of the Belgian Dutroux case; the Framework Decision and Directive of 28 November 2002 concerning the facilitation of unauthorized entry, transit and residence, adopted after the death of 58 illegal immigrants in a container lorry at Dover; or the Framework Decision of 13 June 2002 on combating terrorism in the aftermath of 9/11; see Weyembergh (2005: 1585f.).

5 European Council on Refugees and Exiles (ECRE), ECRAN Weekly Update of 17 March 2005, online at http://www.ecre.org/Update/Index.shtml. Similar criticisms have also been raised with regard to the minimum standards directives adopted in the area of legal migration (on family reunification and long-term residents; see Brinkmann 2004).

6 Europol is the EU's criminal intelligence agency. Its aim is to improve the effectiveness and co-operation between the competent authorities of the member states primarily by sharing and pooling intelligence to prevent and combat serious international organized crime.

7 Eurojust is a body of senior prosecutors, judges and police officers from each member state, whose main role is to help national authorities work together on investigations and prosecutions of serious crimes.

8 Joint ECJ rulings C-187/01 and C-385/01 Gözütok and Brügge of 11.2.2003, ECR-1395 §33.

9 CO/4894/2001; [2002] EWCH 1278 (Admin.).

10 R v. SSHD, ex parte Adan, Subaskaran and Aitseguer, 1999 INLR 472.

11 For instance, for a transitional period of five years after the legislation comes into force, Germany will be allowed to check whether offences mentioned in a warrant are offences under German law, if they fall within six categories which Germany says are poorly defined. The Netherlands, afraid of being swamped with requests about the purchase of drugs, insisted on a clause saying that a country need not provide the requested evidence if the crime in question occurred wholly or partly on its own territory.

REFERENCES

Albrecht, P.-A. (2004) 'Europäischer Strafrechtsraum: Ein Albtraum?', *Zeitschrift für Rechtspolitik* 37(1): 1–32.

Alegre, S. and Leaf, M. (2004) 'Mutual recognition in European judicial cooperation: a step too far too soon? Case study – the European Arrest Warrant', *European Law Journal* 10(2): 200–17.

Anderson, M. (2002) 'Trust and police cooperation', in M. Anderson and J. Apap (eds), *Police and Justice Cooperation in the New European Borders*, The Hague: Kluver, pp. 35–46.

Benz, A. (2005) 'Governance in Mehrebenensystemen', in G.F. Schuppert (ed.), *Governance-Forschung. Vergewisserung über Stand und Entwicklungslinien*, Baden-Baden: Nomos, pp. 95–120.

Brinkman, Gisbert (2004) 'The Immigration and Asylum Agenda', European Law Journal 10(2): 182–199.

Danish Refugee Council and European Commission (2001) The Dublin Convention. Study on its Implementation in the 15 Member States of the European Union, Copenhagen. http://www.flygtning.dk/fileadmin/uploads/pdf/Materialer/dublin.pdf.

den Boer, M. (2005) 'Copweb Europe – venues, virtues and vexations of transnational policing', in W. Kaiser and P. Starie (eds), Transnational Europe – Towards a Common Political Space, London: Routledge.

Eurojust (2005) Annual Report, The Hague.

European Commission (2000) Communication on Mutual Recognition of Final Decisions in Criminal Matters, COM(2000) 495 final of 26 July 2000.

European Commission (2006a) Report on the Implementation of the Hague Programme, COM(2006) 333 final of 28 June 2006.

European Commission (2006b) Report on the European Arrest Warrant and the Surrender Procedures between Member States, COM(2006) 8 final of 24 January 2006.

European Commission (2006c) Commission Staff Working Document, Annex to COM(2006) 8 final, SEC(2006) 79 of 24 January 2006.

European Council on Refugees and Exiles (ECRE) (2006) Summary Report on the Application of the Dublin II Regulation in Europe, AD2/3/2006/EXT/MH.

European Parliament (2005) Report on the Proposal for a Council Framework Decision on Certain Procedural Rights in Criminal Proceedings Throughout the European Union, Rapporteur: Kathalijne Maria Buitenweg, A6–0064/2005 of 1 March 2005.

Finnish Presidency (2006) Informal JHA Ministerial Meeting Tampere, 20–22 September 2006. Follow-up to the mutual recognition programme: Difficulties in negotiating legislative instruments on the mutual recognition of judicial decisions in criminal matters, and possible solutions, 4 September 2006.

Guild, E. (2004) 'Crime and the EU's constitutional future in an area of freedom, security and justice', European Law Journal 10(2): 218–34.

House of Lords (2005) The Hague Programme: A Five-year Agenda for EU Justice and Home Affairs, London: Tenth Report of the House of Lord's Select Committee on the European Union, 23 March 2005, http://www.parliament.the-stationery-office.co.uk/pa/ld200405/ldselect/ldeucom/84/8402.htm.

House of Lords, Select Committee on European Union (2006) European Arrest Warrant – Recent Developments, Thirtieth Report, http://www.parliament.the-stationery-office.co.uk/pa/ld200506/ldselect/ldeucom/156/15604.htm

Jachtenfuchs, M. and Kohler-Koch, B. (2004) 'Governance and institutional development', in T. Diez and A. Wiener (eds), European Integration Theory, Oxford: Oxford University Press, pp. 97–115.

Jachtenfuchs, M., Friedrichs, J., Herschinger, E. and Kasack, C. (2006) 'Policing among nations. Internationalizing the monopoly of force'. Paper presented at the UACES Annual Convention, Limerick.

Kaunert, C. (2005) 'The area of freedom, security and justice: the construction of a "European public order"', European Security 14(4): 459–83.

Keohane, R.O. and Nye, J.S. (1974) 'Transgovernmental relations and international organizations', World Politics 27(1): 39–62.

Knelangen, W. (2001) Das Politikfeld innere Sicherheit im Integrationsprozess. Opladen: Leske + Budrich.

Lavenex, S. (2006) 'Towards the constitutionalization of aliens' rights in the European Union?', Journal of European Public Policy 13(8): 1284–1301.

Lavenex, S. and Wagner, W. (2005) 'Which European public order? Sources of imbalance in the European area of freedom, security and justice'. Paper presented at the International Studies Conference of the German Political Science Association, Mannheim, 6–7 October 2005.

Lavenex, S. and Wallace, W. (2005) 'Justice and home affairs. Towards a "European public order"?', in W. Wallace, H. Wallace and M. Pollack (eds), *Policy-Making in the European Union*, Oxford: Oxford University Press, pp. 457–80.

Lööf, R. (2006) 'Shooting from the hip: proposed minimum rights in criminal proceedings throughout the EU', *European Law Journal* 12(3): 421–30.

Majone, G. (1994) 'Mutual recognition in federal type systems', in A. Mullins and C. Saunders (eds), *Economic Union in Federal Systems*, Sydney: Federation Press, pp. 69–84.

Mitsilegas, V., Monar, J. and Rees, W. (2003) *The European Union and Internal Security. Guardian of the People?*, Basingstoke: Palgrave Macmillan.

Moravcsik, A. (1994) 'Why the European Community strengthens the state: domestic politics and international institutions', *Center for European Studies Working Paper Series* 52. Cambridge, MA: Center for European Studies.

Morgan, C. (2004) 'The European Arrest Warrant and defendants' rights: an overview', in R. Blekxtoon (ed.), *Handbook on the European Arrest Warrant*, Cambridge: Cambridge University Press, pp. 195–208.

Nicolaïdis, K. (1993) 'Mutual recognition among nations: the European Community and trade in Services', Ph.D. dissertation, Harvard, Cambridge, MA.

Nicolaïdis, K. (2007) 'Trusting the Poles? Constructing Europe through mutual recognition', *Journal of European Public Policy* 14(5): 682–98.

Outrive, L. van (1995) 'Commentary on the third pillar and the 1996 Intergovernmental Conference: what should be on the agenda?', in R. Bieber and J. Monar (eds), *Justice and Home Affairs in the European Union: The Development of the Third Pillar*, Brussels: Interuniversity Press, pp. 391–6.

Scharpf, F.W. (1997) *Games Real Actors Play. Actor-Centered Institutionalism in Policy Research*, Boulder, CO: Westview Press.

Scharpf, F.W. (1999) *Governing in Europe. Effective and Democratic?*, Oxford and New York: Oxford University Press.

Schmidt, S.K. (2005) 'Notwendigerweise unvollkommen: Strukturprobleme des Europäischen Binnenmarktes', *Zeitschrift für Staats- und Europawissenschaften (ZSE)/Journal of Comparative Government and European Policy* 3(2): 185–210.

Wagner, W. (2007) 'Europäisches Regieren im Politikfeld Innere Sicherheit?', in I. Tömmel (ed.), *Die Europäische Union: Governance und Policy-Making*, special issue of Politische Vierteljahresschrift PVS 2007(2) (forthcoming).

Wallace, H. (2000) 'The institutional setting: five variations on a theme', in H. Wallace and W. Wallace (eds), *Policy-Making in the European Union*, Oxford: Oxford University Press, pp. 3–36.

Walsh, J.I. (2006) 'Intelligence-sharing in the European Union: institutions are not enough', *Journal of Common Market Studies* 44(3): 625–43.

Weyembergh, A. (2005) 'Approximation of criminal laws, the Constitutional Treaty and the Hague Programme', *Common Market Law Review* 42(6): 1567–97.

Wichmann, N. (2006) 'The participation of the Schengen associates: inside or outside?', *European Foreign Affairs Review* 11(1): 87–107.

Wolf, K.-D. (1999) 'The new *raison d'état* as a problem for democracy in world society', *European Journal for International Relations* 5(3): 333–63.

Wouters, J. and Naert, F. (2004) 'Of arrest warrants, terrorist offences and extradition deals: an appraisal of the EU's main criminal law measures against terrorism after 11 September', *Common Market Law Review* 41(4): 909–35.

Embedding mutual recognition at the WTO

Joel P. Trachtman

1. INTRODUCTION

Mutual recognition is a useful tool for international liberalization in particular contexts. However, it has two types of limit, and to the extent that it may exceed these limits it poses two important types of risk.

The first limit of mutual recognition is set by the degree and importance of achievement of the relevant regulatory goal: the degree to which the foreign regulation achieves the goals of the domestic regulatory scheme, and the importance of meeting these goals. Thus, the first risk is that mutual recognition is implemented in a way that sacrifices important regulatory goals without adequate justification – without 'sufficient' achievement of the regulatory goal. States may at times accept compromises of their regulatory goals, but they should not do so unless they are compensated with enhanced welfare from free trade, or from other sources. The second limit of mutual recognition relates to the material capacities of developing countries. The risk is that mutual recognition is established by developed countries in a way that disadvantages exports of poor countries.

Mutual recognition as developed in the European Community (EC) has managed the first risk through a nuanced deliberative process that includes both legislative and adjudicative capacity, and has experienced only an attenuated form of the second risk, due in large part to the relative economic homogeneity of EC member states (at least up until the most recent enlargement).

This paper argues that mutual recognition at the World Trade Organization (WTO), as a type of liberalism, must be embedded in a process of governance that has two components. First, mutual recognition can only take place to the extent of satisfactory essential harmonization: to the extent that states can legitimately agree on an appropriate level of regulatory protection. This political process is necessary in order to establish an agreed minimum level of regulation.

Second, mutual recognition cannot be permitted to leave poor countries at a disadvantage in international trade. Therefore, essential harmonization must be established in a way that protects poor countries. This will require technical assistance, transfer of resources, and accommodation of difference. The liberalism of recognition must be embedded in a redistributive framework. In using this concept of 'embedded liberalism', I draw on the work of Karl Polanyi (1957) and John Ruggie (2002). They believe that states must regulate the distribution of gains from trade in order to avoid political discontent, and, ultimately, a 'backlash' that would destroy the liberal system. In Ruggie's interpretation, individual states must cushion the domestic 'losers' from the loss of wages, livelihoods, and investments that results from liberalization – Ruggie extends Polanyi's approach to relate free international trade to a domestic welfare state. The embedded liberalism 'bargain', in short, is one in which the state takes care of its own through regulatory intervention in order to maintain its political ability to liberalize. But, importantly, embedded liberalism calls for national regulatory intervention, not global regulatory intervention. Its call for redistribution is state-centered, and limited by domestic politics and budgetary capacity.

Further, while embedded liberalism has generally been thought to call for national regulatory intervention in order to support a national market, it is important to recognize that global liberalism embedded within a domestic welfare state is not quite analogous to the system described by Polanyi (Ruggie 2002). Polanyi saw the need for society-wide regulatory intervention to make adjustments in connection with a society-wide market. The true analog in connection with global markets is global regulatory intervention – a global welfare state. Thus, if the scope of the market is to some degree global, then it would seem appropriate that the scope of regulatory intervention in the market would need to be roughly commensurately global.[1]

So, liberalism in the form of mutual recognition is embedded, and indeed its scope is circumscribed, for two purposes: to achieve agreed minimum levels of regulation, and because the material conditions necessary to include poor countries in these minimum levels of regulation may not be met. It must be recognized that among states that are diverse in terms of their economic development and preferences, either implicit or explicit compensation payments to developing countries may be necessary in order to satisfy the second form of embedded liberalism without sacrificing the first form.

After defining critical terms below in this introduction, and providing a jurisdiction-based understanding of recognition, this paper examines the existing WTO legal doctrine. The WTO legal doctrine generally declines to adopt the broad judicially enforced doctrine of equivalence that has emerged in the European Union (EU), but the WTO does have limited capacity for case-by-case judicial evaluations of equivalence: judicial findings that the home or exporting country regulation satisfies the regulatory concerns of the host or importing country. Nor does the WTO include the internal legislative will or capacity to legislate rules of essential harmonization, as also has been common within the EU. While essential harmonization is, indeed, a necessary predicate for mutual recognition, the WTO does not have internal capacity for significant essential harmonization. On the other hand, the WTO has the capacity to refer to other organizations' normative efforts as sources of essential harmonization.

Looking beyond the WTO itself, at plurilateral or regional arrangements for mutual recognition, this paper evaluates the risk that these arrangements may violate the most-favoured nation (MFN) principle of WTO law. This is more than a technical issue, as plurilateral or regional arrangements for mutual recognition may adversely affect the competitive position of excluded states. This substantive issue raises special concerns to the extent that the excluded states are poor states. Even if poor states are not arbitrarily excluded, it is difficult and costly for poor states to participate meaningfully in efforts toward essential harmonization and mutual recognition. Thus, the MFN obligation may be understood as a potential source of protection for poor states against being disadvantaged by mutual recognition initiatives. The WTO does have limited capacity for case-by-case judicial evaluations of equivalence, which can support recognition in particular cases: judicial findings that the home or exporting country regulation satisfies the regulatory concerns of the host or importing country.

In order to develop a coherent analysis of mutual recognition at the WTO, it is useful to begin with careful delineation of the meaning of relevant terms. Once we define terms carefully, we see that mutual recognition itself is not a form of governance. I understand governance *in this context* as equivalent to regulation: as governmental intervention in the market by imposing requirements, costs or benefits, in order to achieve a governmental goal.

1.1   Recognition

Recognition, in simple legal terms, is a choice of law rule. Recognition is a selection by importing (or host) states of the rule of the home or exporting state, to the exclusion of the rule of the importing state. Pure recognition regimes diminish barriers to trade, by dismantling importing country regulatory barriers: because the importing country law is inapplicable, it cannot serve as a barrier. Finally, in this sense, recognition is by its nature purely deregulatory (presuming that the exporting country rules are less onerous than the importing country rules). Thus, recognition is not so much a rule of governance in the normal sense, but a rule of choice of governance. In light of the deregulatory bias of pure recognition mentioned above, it is a choice of reduced governance. Recognition, at its core, entails an agreement to compromise local regulatory autonomy, by accepting that the exporting state regulation is 'good enough'. So, we cannot lightly accept the compromise implicit in recognition arrangements.

The context of recognition arrangements – in terms of the possibility for externalization, the possibility for detrimental regulatory competition, and the possibility for discrimination against outsiders – is critical to an understanding of the utility of recognition arrangements. States may have regard to these concerns as they determine whether to engage in recognition arrangements. Institutional mechanisms may be established to reduce potential harmful effects of externalization. Essential harmonization is a critical component of these mechanisms. It should be clear that the value of engaging in mutual recognition will depend entirely on the context, both factual and institutional.

1.2   Mutual

When added to 'recognition', the word 'mutual' denotes narrow reciprocity in the sense described by Keohane (1986): a specific exchange of equivalent promises. You recognize my regulation, and I will recognize yours. In this sense, it is a trade concept – a concept of reciprocal liberalization – much more than it is a governance or regulatory concept. This type of narrow reciprocity exists in specialized bilateral agreements, but regional and multilateral integration agreements generally provide simply for recognition, without specifically conditioning Country A's recognition on Country B's compliance with its recognition obligations. Under this type of diffuse reciprocity (in the sense described by Keohane) the bargain is supported by a broad exchange, and narrow reciprocity– mutuality – is unnecessary. The question answered by mutuality is how does one state compensate the other for its recognition? This question is not interesting from the standpoint of an examination of the legal and public policy aspects of recognition. Therefore, I focus simply on recognition.

1.3   Essential harmonization

Essential harmonization is not necessary to recognition, but to the extent that the regulation at stake is meaningful, host or importing states would be expected before agreeing to recognition to (i) check the partner's regulation to ensure that it satisfies the host or importing state's regulatory goals, and (ii) to the extent that it does not, require modifications to the partner's regulation to ensure that it does. To the extent that a general minimum standard of harmonization can be agreed in a legislative context, this is understood as 'essential harmonization'.

In this context, essential harmonization plays two roles. First, it is a product of multilateral legislation. Exporting states, or at least their exporting firms, are required to comply with harmonized standards, or to forgo the benefits of exporting the relevant goods or services. Second, by serving as a predicate for recognition, it serves as an agreement on the scope or depth of regulatory competition. States are permitted to apply higher standards to their own suppliers, but regulatory competition might be expected to suppress the application of standards above the level of the essential harmonization. To the extent that this regulatory competition is expected, essential harmonization may be understood as simply 'harmonization'. The political process of essential harmonization provides an opportunity to decide collectively how far states will accept pressure on their standards from regulatory competition. By accepting recognition on the basis of essential harmonization, states accept competitive incentives to reduce the cost of the regulation that they apply to their own producers to the level required by the essentially harmonized rule.

According to the definitions provided in this subsection, recognition is not a means of governance, but is actually a means of reducing governance. As Margaret Thatcher recognized in the 1980s, it is a means of deregulation. On the other hand, essential harmonization, or a *requirement* of *actual* equivalence, may be understood as a means of governance. Essential harmonization may set the minimum standard at any level, including one that is higher than the average level existing prior to essential harmonization.

1.4   Equivalence

Although there is some ambiguity in the literature, 'equivalence' is not the same thing as 'recognition'. I follow Joseph Weiler's suggestion that the relevant judicial doctrine, announced by the European Court of Justice (ECJ) in *Cassis de Dijon*, is best termed 'functional equivalence', or, in this paper, simply 'equivalence' (Weiler 2005: 45). Equivalence, as compared to mutual recognition, is a more particular, case-based, finding that the home or exporting country regulation is equivalent – in the sense of satisfying the regulatory goal – to the host or importing country regulation. Mutual recognition, on the other hand, involves broad and automatic recognition of foreign regulation, without case-based evaluation.

Thus, under a doctrine of equivalence, an administrative agency or a court might find that the home state regulation is functionally equivalent to – for example, that it satisfies the regulatory concerns of – the host state regulation. One way of understanding the relationship between equivalence and recognition is in terms of the institution that makes the decision. Thus, equivalence is a case-by-case determination, based on a standard, and usually administered by a court. Recognition is a legislatively (or treaty) determined rule, usually established by a legislature or an administrative agency.[2]

2. THE JURISDICTIONAL ANALYSIS OF RECOGNITION

A rule of recognition is best understood as a rule of allocation of regulatory authority: of jurisdiction (Trachtman 2001a, 1995). That is, recognition simply means that the recognizing (host) state defers to the recognized (home) state in connection with the specified regulatory authority. So, for example, if the subject of the recognition is the prudential regulation of banking institutions, as in the EC's Second Banking Directive, then perhaps Germany, as host state, defers to the United Kingdom, as home state, in connection with the prudential regulation of United Kingdom banks doing business in Germany. Similarly, for goods, recognition requires, for example, that compliance with the pharmaceutical safety standards of the recognized state be a sufficient basis for marketing the relevant medicine in the recognizing state.

Recognition is the opposite of a jurisdictional rule of territoriality, assuming that the foreign producer is either engaging in conduct (territorial conduct) or is producing effects (territorial effects) in the recognizing state. Recognition involves deference by territoriality to nationality. Recognition commitments provide substantial clarity in allocation of prescriptive jurisdiction, as well as avoiding substantial overlaps. However, they do so at the risk of substantial possibilities of externalization: of imposing costs on the recognizing state. That is, the recognizing state transfers regulatory authority to the recognized state, despite the fact that whatever negative outcomes may occur will be experienced in the recognizing state.

What we might call 'rootless recognition' entails acceptance of foreign regulation as exclusively regulating foreign companies operating in a host jurisdiction, without any predicate where a predicate may be substantively appropriate – without 'essential harmonization'.

The expected benefit of recognition includes not just reduced costs of compliance for international companies, but also enhanced regulatory competition. '[C]ompetition facilitates the control and regulation of the exercise of political power' (Breton *et al* 1998: 43; Trachtman 2000). On the other hand, if we assume the beneficial character of regulation, competition diminishes the authority of regulators, jeopardizing their ability to maximize the public interest (Trachtman 2001a). The scope for regulatory innovation is equally great under rootless recognition and territoriality-based national treatment. However, proponents of regulatory competition would argue that the incentives for innovation are stronger under rootless recognition.

The greatest problem with rootless recognition is the risk of externalization: these risks must be compared with the benefits that are expected from greater competition. Moreover, it is worth asking whether there is a structure that would provide the benefits of competition with reduced risks of externalization. Of course, externalization reduces the benefits of competition, and what we are really seeking is a structure that has aggregate benefits greater than the other available structures. Thus again, territoriality-based national treatment, or managed recognition, would allow host states to forestall externalization by imposing their own regulation. More interestingly, managed recognition would provide an opportunity for states to reveal their anti-externalization preferences in negotiation over essential harmonization. This process requires states to revisit – and perhaps to modify – their preferences for regulation. As states use these processes to modify their regulation, democratic accountability for harmonization agreements becomes important.

A more refined approach to recognition could utilize one or more of the following instruments, all derived from EC practice, to reduce the risk of externalization:

- Judicial examination of equivalence. 'Equivalence' could be mandated by a court under a general constitutional or treaty-based free trade provision, based on an examination of the home country regulation to determine that they achieve the host country's purported regulatory goals. Such requirements may be applied pursuant to necessity or 'least trade restrictive alternative' requirements, of the Agreement on Technical Barriers to Trade (TBT Agreement) or the Agreement on Application of Sanitary and Phytosanitary Measures (SPS Agreement), or pursuant to other international mechanisms in other sectors. It is feasible that these disciplines could be extended to other fields. The result would be that recognition would only be required where the host state's regulatory goals are met by the home state regulation, ensuring against externalization.

- Legislative establishment of essential harmonization. International integration organizations such as the EC or the WTO, or international functional organizations, such as Codex Alimentarius or the International Accounting Standards Committee, may engage in efforts that amount to 'legislative' establishment of essential harmonization. Unlike in the EC (since the 1987 Single European Act) the international system does not generally provide for majority voting.[3] The EC often engages in essential harmonization, as a predicate to mutual recognition, to forge the single market. In negotiating harmonization directives, states understand that the increased regulatory competition that will result from the proposed mutual recognition will place pressure on their ability to maintain regulation that, by definition, is otherwise desirable from a purely local standpoint, having been legislated through presumptively legitimate processes. Before agreeing to mutual recognition, they agree on a minimum level of regulation that will insulate their home regulation from being reduced in unacceptable ways. Furthermore, they exact a quid pro quo, both in terms of essential harmonization and in terms of other market liberalization in other areas.

- Maintenance of 'safeguards' that would allow states to address threats to their public policy. EC harmonization and mutual recognition initiatives such as the Second Banking Directive contain provisions that allow host states to act in derogation from their ordinary recognition obligations in order to protect the 'general good'. These provisions provide a safeguard against externalization, at least in more egregious cases.

These devices could be used to determine, in specific cases relating to particular regulatory systems, and particular regulatory rules, whether competition or coordination is the superior alternative.

Roberta Romano, and Stephen Choi and Andrew Guzman, have argued for rootless recognition in the field of securities regulation: recognition of foreign regulation without evaluation or predicate (Romano 1998; Choi and Guzman 1998; but see Fox 1999; Trachtman 2001b). This approach fails to take into account the state preferences – the regulatory concerns – involved. Securities disclosure regulation is motivated by externality or asymmetric information problems, and rootless recognition fails to address those problems. This failure threatens any benefits of regulatory competition.

In the EC context, a process that Kalypso Nicolaïdis has termed 'managed mutual recognition' has been the rule in a number of areas, including securities regulation (Nicolaïdis and Shaffer 2005: 290). Indeed, in the international securities regulation context, the work of the International Accounting Standards Committee and the International Organization of Securities Commissions seems to suggest that managed recognition will be the rule. Rootless recognition does not seem to have substantial advantages over managed recognition, once one puts aside a generalized suspicion of government action (Trachtman 1997).

3. THE DOCTRINES OF RECOGNITION AND EQUIVALENCE AT THE WTO

In this section, I review existing WTO legal doctrine to achieve an understanding of the extent to which recognition and equivalence are part of the WTO legal system, and the extent to which they are embedded in structures for essential harmonization and redistribution.

The WTO has extended its reach from anti-discrimination to more extensive forms of negative integration, requiring necessity or least trade restrictive character, and rational bases for regulation, under the TBT Agreement and the SPS Agreement.

The WTO has itself effected little positive integration, either in the form of harmonization (other than in intellectual property rights) or in the form of requirements of mutual recognition. (While Article 4.1 of the SPS Agreement, for example, calls for a kind of conditional equivalence, predicated on proof of equivalent protection, it is unclear that this provision has had significant effect.) These two types of positive integration – harmonization and recognition – are complementary, or synergetic. (Here it should be made clear that recognition, and not equivalence, is a type of positive integration, as it is general and is provided by broader regulation. On the other hand, equivalence is case-based, and is determined by courts as part of a determination that a national regulatory measure is excessive because it fails to take into account the equivalence of foreign regulation.) States would not agree to recognition without some degree of harmonization, or some opportunity to check in advance the protective qualities of the home country regulation. The measure of harmonization necessary as a predicate for mutual recognition in the EC is known as 'essential harmonization', meaning that the essence or the core of the regulatory purpose is harmonized. Recall that essential harmonization in the EC did not become common until the advent of majority voting under the 1987 Single European Act.

3.1   GATT

The General Agreement on Tariffs and Trade (GATT) itself contains no explicit equivalence requirement or facility of recognition. However, it is possible that necessity requirements under the exceptions provided in Article XX (b) or (d) (exceptions for protection of life or compliance with law) could require recognition. These provisions, which provide a defense after a finding of violation, have been found to require that the national measure be the least trade restrictive alternative. Sometimes, the least trade restrictive alternative will be simple recognition of the effectiveness of home country regulation.

In addition, the Appellate Body in *US – Shrimp (Article 21.5)* seems to have identified an embryonic equivalence requirement in the *chapeau* of Article XX (exceptions). The Appellate Body held as follows:

> In our view, there is an important difference between conditioning market access on the adoption of essentially the same programme, and conditioning market access on the adoption of a programme *comparable in effectiveness.* Authorizing an importing Member to condition market access on exporting Members putting in place regulatory programmes *comparable in effectiveness* to that of the importing Member gives sufficient latitude to the exporting Member with respect to the programme it may adopt to achieve the level of effectiveness required.[4]

A measure requiring United States and foreign regulatory programmes to be 'comparable in effectiveness', as opposed to being 'essentially the same' would comply with the prohibition against arbitrary or unjustifiable restrictions on trade. This appears to function as a 'soft' equivalence discipline, which only arises after a violation of another provision of GATT.

3.2   SPS Agreement

Article 4.1 of the SPS Agreement requires that equivalence be accorded to other states' regulations. In 2001, the WTO's SPS Committee adopted a decision on the implementation of Article 4 on equivalence to 'make operational the provisions of Article 4 of the Agreement on the Application of Sanitary and Phytosanitary Measures'.[5] It sets up the possibility for other states to serve as 'regulatory laboratories' to come up with alternate means to achieve the same regulatory goals. It imposes an obligation on an importing Member, upon the request of the exporting Member, to explain the objective and rationale of the SPS measure, to identify clearly the risks that the relevant measure is intended to address, and to indicate the appropriate level of protection, which its SPS measure is designed to achieve.[6] In addition, the exporting Member must provide reasonable access, upon request, to the importing Member for inspection, testing and other relevant procedures for the determination of equivalence. Such requests should proceed rapidly, especially with traditional imports, and should not in themselves disrupt or suspend ongoing imports.

3.3   TBT Agreement

The requirement of the SPS Agreement is stronger than the more hortatory obligation of Article 2.7 of the TBT Agreement, which simply requires Members to give positive consideration to accepting foreign regulation as equivalent, if the foreign regulation fulfills the importing state's objectives. In the Second Triennial Review, the TBT Committee considered that 'Members may find it useful to further explore equivalency of standards as an interim measure to facilitate trade in the absence of relevant international standards.'[7]

Since Article XX requires that Members maintain an appropriate level of flexibility in the administration of their regulatory distinctions,[8] it is probable that Article 2.7 (or Article 2.2 in a manner parallel to Article XX) will be interpreted as requiring sufficient flexibility in normative determinations and good faith consideration of the alternative and equivalent standards suggested by the exporting country.

3.4   GATS

Article VI:4 of the General Agreement on Trade in Services (GATS) calls on the Council for Trade in Services (CTS) to develop any necessary disciplines to ensure that measures relating to qualification requirements and procedures, technical standards and licensing requirements do not constitute unnecessary barriers to trade in services. Prior to the agreement and entry into force of more specific rules under Article VI:4, disciplines on national measures are available under Article VI:5 in sectors in which the importing member has undertaken specific commitments. In order for these disciplines to apply, two sets of criteria must be satisfied:

1. The licensing or qualification requirements or technical standards must nullify or impair specific commitments in a manner that could not reasonably have been expected at the time the specific commitments were made; and
2. The measure must be (a) not based on objective and transparent criteria, or (b) more burdensome than necessary to ensure the quality of the service, or (c) in the case of licensing procedures, in itself a restriction on the supply of the service.

In 1998, the Committee on Trade in Services adopted the *Disciplines on Domestic Regulation in the Accountancy Sector* (the 'Accountancy Disciplines'),[9] developed by the GATS Working Party on Professional Services (now the Working Party on Domestic Regulation). These disciplines apply to all member states that have made specific commitments in accountancy (positive list) but do not apply to national measures listed as exceptions (negative list) under Articles XVI (market access) and XVII (national treatment). They generally articulate further and tighten the principle of necessity: that measures should be the least trade restrictive method to effect a legitimate objective. In fact, these provisions replicate requirements that have been imposed in the EC pursuant to the ECJ's single market jurisprudence. They also replicate the approach of the EC's General System Directives on professions, codifying principles of proportionality, or necessity. They have the following features relevant to equivalence and recognition:

> *Necessity.* Member states are required to ensure that measures relating to licensing requirements and procedures, technical standards and qualification requirements and procedures are not prepared, adopted or applied with a view to or with the effect of creating unnecessary barriers to trade in accountancy services. Such measures may not be more trade restrictive than necessary to fulfill a legitimate objective, including protection of consumers, the quality of the service, professional competence and the integrity of the profession. This necessity requirement is substantially stronger than that contained in Article VI:5 of GATS.
>
> *Qualification requirements.* Member states must take account of qualifications acquired in the territory of another member state, on the basis of equivalency of education, experience and/or examination requirements. Examinations or other qualification requirements must be limited to subjects relevant to the activities for which authorization is sought.
>
> *Technical standards.* Technical standards must be prepared, adopted and applied only to fulfill legitimate objectives. In determining conformity, member states must take account of internationally recognized standards (of international organizations) applied by that member.

Note that Article VII of GATS and paragraph 3 of the Annex on Financial Services do not require recognition, but merely authorize it. Although a strong GATS standard of necessity might eventually lead to judicially required equivalence, this is unlikely to be the case under current treaty language. But the necessity test might nevertheless mandate equivalence of some regulations and not others, whereby partial equivalence becomes the operational consequence of the principle of proportionality.

4.   THE WTO LEGALITY OF MUTUAL RECOGNITION

Sub-multilateral mutual recognition is a challenge to the MFN non-discriminatory structure of the multilateral trading system. Mutual recognition may be discriminatory in the MFN sense. Mutual recognition under the GATS requires that equivalent opportunities are offered to other states. It seems clear that mere mutuality is not a permissible basis for discrimination. There is even a question under WTO law regarding the degree to which regional trade agreements may limit mutual recognition arrangements to their members, as opposed to making recognition available to other WTO member states.

Does mutual recognition violate the MFN obligation under Article I:1 (MFN) of GATT?[10] This analysis requires review of the scope of MFN obligations (see generally Davey and Pauwelyn 2000). There are two issues. First, does the MFN obligation apply on a product-by-product basis? Second, does the MFN obligation apply to provide WTO member states that are not party to a mutual recognition agreement an opportunity to qualify for recognition?

Mutual recognition arrangements are an important mechanism, both within and without regional trade agreements,[11] to reduce regulatory barriers to trade (see Nicolaïdis 2000). The legal question for us is whether, and under what circumstances, a state may recognize foreign regulation without recognizing the similar regulation of all WTO members. Recall that in the *Canada-Autos* case, the Appellate Body confirmed that Article I:1 addresses de facto, as well as de jure, discrimination. The Appellate Body emphasized the unconditional and broad scope of Article I:1 in finding that mere differential treatment of products originating in different member states, regardless of the producer-based rationale, violates Article I:1. Although the Appellate Body did not emphasize this, its interpretation is based on the 'like products' reference of Article I:1 – automobiles are like products regardless of whether their manufacturers have or have not invested in Canada.[12] Given the focus on Article I:1's reference to the matters referenced in Article III:4 (national treatment), and to 'any advantage', it appears possible that 'like products' treated differently due to different recognition arrangements might result in a violation of MFN.[13] There would seem to be a conflict between mutual recognition and a strict understanding of the MFN obligation, to the effect that imported 'like' products cannot be treated differently from 'like' products from other member states. Mutual recognition focuses on the regulatory context in which products or services are produced, rather than the actual characteristics of the products or services. The question of the legality of mutual recognition arrangements may thus turn on the question of whether 'likeness' under Article I focuses on products themselves, or on production processes as well. The answer to this question is not clear in WTO law.

In the *Asbestos* case, the Appellate Body articulated a fairly broad definition of 'like products' for application under Article III:4 (Hudec 2000: 101). Although the definition of 'like products' in Article I:1 may be narrower, the Appellate Body's *response* to this broad definition may be useful to refer to in the Article I:1 context. The Appellate Body recognized that this interpretation of 'like products' would result in a relatively broad scope of application of Article III:4. In order to avoid a commensurately broad scope of invalidation of national law, the Appellate Body focused on the second element required under Article III: 4: 'A complaining Member must still establish that the measure accords to the group of "like" imported products "less favourable treatment" than it accords to the group of "like" domestic products. The term "less favourable treatment" expresses the general principle, in Article III:1, that internal regulations "should not be applied . . . so as to afford protection to domestic production.".'[14]

Thus, two dimensions of discriminating treatment are required: first, like products must be treated differently; second, foreign like products as a class must be treated differently from, and less favourably than, domestic like products. It is not enough to find a single foreign like product that is treated differently from a single domestic like product. Rather, the class of foreign like products must be treated less favorably than the class of domestic like products. In order for this to occur, it would seem necessary that the differential regulatory treatment be predicated, either intentionally or unintentionally, on the national origin of the product. However, in *Korea–Various Measures on Beef*, the Appellate Body made clear that differential treatment based on nationality, alone, would not necessarily amount to 'less favourable' treatment.[15] Differential treatment based on nationality could have a rationale and/or a benign effect on trade that would leave it consistent with the national treatment obligation. The area left for panel or Appellate Body discretion is in determining, in cases of de facto and unintentional disparate regulatory treatment, whether there is a violation of the national treatment requirement. It is possible that this 'less favourable treatment' test (even though this language is not directly replicated in Article I:1) would apply, *mutatis mutandis*, to protect *bona fide* mutual recognition from criticism under Article I MFN, especially where it is administered on a non-preferential basis: where any WTO member state may satisfy the requirements for mutual recognition.

In this light, I might note that the TBT Agreement and the SPS Agreement contain provisions encouraging recognition regimes. This encouragement, in order to have *effet utile*, might be interpreted as providing some form of protection against Article I:1 challenge. However, a more textualist approach, which might be more likely to be applied by the Appellate Body, would not permit an exception based on these TBT Agreement and SPS Agreement provisions. Furthermore, the language of these agreements would not appear to condone artificial, regional trade agreement-based, limitations on the right to 'qualify' for recognition.[16] Such agreements would be required to be justified under Article XXIV (regional integration) of GATT, as discussed below.

Furthermore, any arguable exception under Article XX of GATT (or *compliance* with the necessity requirements of the TBT Agreement and SPS Agreement) would require that the recognition regime not discriminate in an arbitrary manner, and may require that the recognition regime be necessary. These requirements would seem to argue that recognition regimes could not be exclusive to members of a regional trade agreement, but would be required to be offered on an open basis.

Interestingly, this logic would have results similar to those explicitly stated in Article VII of GATS. Indeed, the language of Article 4 of the SPS Agreement requires recognition on an open and objective basis. Under this provision, the fact of intra-regional trade agreement recognition arrangements would make it more difficult to resist extra-regional trade agreement recognition. Article 2.7 of the SPS Agreement does not provide as strong a requirement, calling on members to 'give positive consideration' to accepting foreign technical regulations as 'equivalent'. Furthermore, the application of the necessity requirements in Article 2.2 of the SPS Agreement and Article 2.2 of the TBT Agreement might be affected by regional trade agreement recognition arrangements in the following way. Once a state enters into a recognition arrangement, and accepts that some products need not comply with its own regulation, it becomes more difficult to argue that its own regulation is necessary when applied to other imports, if those other imports are regulated similarly to the imports that benefit from the recognition arrangements. In other words, the recognition arrangement may set a lower standard of necessity.

Thus, while it appears that there is a possible argument that recognition arrangements may be legal under WTO law, there seems to be little support for 'closed' recognition as it might appear within a regional trade agreement, such as the EC. It might be argued that Article XXIV of GATT provides an exception that would allow such 'closed' intra-regional trade agreement recognition. It is critical to point out, though, that Article XXIV by its terms only provides an exception from requirements contained in GATT itself, and not from the requirements of the TBT Agreement or SPS Agreement. The MFN obligations of the TBT Agreement and the SPS Agreement would appear to apply independently of the MFN obligations of GATT, but would not be eligible for exception under Article XXIV of GATT.

Even considering GATT alone, the requirements of Article XXIV of GATT with respect to regional trade agreement recognition measures are somewhat unclear (see Trachtman 2003), in large measure due to the imprecision of the definitions of 'other restrictive regulations of commerce' in Article XXIV:8, and 'other regulations of commerce' in Article XXIV:5 and 8. In the Turkey–Restrictions on Imports of Textile and Clothing Products decision,[17] the Appellate Body examined the relationship between Article XXIV and other provisions of GATT. Under the Appellate Body's decision, it is at least arguable that the exception of Article XXIV is only available with respect to measures that are *necessary* in order to form a free trade area or customs union as defined in Article XXIV. As Article XXIV:8 does not appear to *require* harmonization or mutual recognition arrangements, mutual recognition arrangements may not be protected.

Therefore, it appears that to the extent that regional trade agreements engage in mutual recognition, their mutual recognition arrangements must conform to all the requirements of WTO law, including the MFN requirements of GATT, the TBT Agreement, and the SPS Agreement.

5.   EMBEDDED LIBERALISM I: MUTUAL RECOGNITION AND ESSENTIAL HARMONIZATION AT THE WTO

The WTO should not be seen as calling for mutual recognition *without* a process of essential harmonization: mutual recognition, as a fundamentally liberalizing rule, should be embedded in appropriate prudential regulation. This prudential regulation will prevent externalization and inappropriate regulatory competition. Essential harmonization is the occasion for a political process that sets the limits for externalization and regulatory competition.

In light of this need for essential harmonization, the WTO is not today institutionally capable of delivering significant mutual recognition arrangements on its own. There may be exceptions, such as the Agreement on Trade Related Aspects of Intellectual Property Rights (TRIPS), effected through new treaty arrangements. Nor will the WTO emerge soon as a locus for essential harmonization. Rather, mutual recognition arrangements will develop based on functionally specialized efforts toward essential harmonization, such as the development of international standards for products or services. These efforts will generally take place in functionally specialized agencies, such as the International Organization for Standardization (ISO) or Codex Alimentarius. In limited areas, these essential harmonization arrangements will be incorporated within the WTO system as the basis for recognition arrangements. That is, compliance with these international standards will serve as essential harmonization for the purposes of mutual recognition.

Compliance with these international standards will thus serve as a basis for acceptance of foreign goods and services without cumulative application of host country law: for recognition of the home country regulation or simply of the international regulation. It is in this sense that international standardization and mutual recognition are complementary in the multilateral system.

Even if the essential harmonization occurs outside the WTO, recognition arrangements may be required to be validated within the WTO legal system, in order to avoid running afoul of the MFN requirements, at least for goods. For services, Article VII of GATS may validate open recognition arrangements, but may call for disapproval of closed recognition arrangements.

6.   EMBEDDED LIBERALISM II: MUTUAL RECOGNITION AND DEVELOPING COUNTRIES

For developing countries, plurilateral or multilateral mutual recognition represents a danger of market foreclosure. Developing countries may lack the material capacity to participate, the power to control the agenda, and the resources to comply with harmonized standards established through multilateral processes. They therefore are in danger of failing to benefit from mutual recognition, and finding that harmonized standards and mutual recognition put their, non-participating, products at a disadvantage compared to products of states that are able to participate in mutual recognition processes. In the 1980s the US and Japan feared a 'Fortress Europe'. Today, it is not out of the question for poor countries to fear that mutual recognition will help build the walls of a 'Fortress North'. A nuanced, inclusive, and redistributive political process is needed: embedded mutual recognition.

Within the trade and regulation context, poor countries will achieve the greatest possible benefit from MFN-based liberalization in connection with goods that are of export interest to them (Hoekman *et al.* 2004). So, reduction of tariffs charged by developed countries on goods produced by poor countries is helpful. To the extent that these tariffs are replaced by non-tariff barriers, this benefit is reduced.

Mutual recognition arrangements among developed countries, failing to include poor countries, are highly likely to place the products of poor countries at a disadvantage relative to the products of countries participating in the mutual recognition arrangements. So, mutual recognition arrangements within north–north free trade agreements or customs unions pose the risk of erecting even greater trade diversion than that which would be indicated by the internal zero tariff treatment that characterizes these regional integration arrangements. As noted above, this type of closed recognition may violate WTO MFN obligations.

It may well be that a regime of 'open recognition' – allowing all states to submit their regulatory regimes for review and possible acceptance for recognition – would satisfy the requirements of MFN. However, this approach may not provide sufficient market access for poor countries if individual developed countries, or groups of developed countries, establish high standards that are excessively difficult or costly for poor countries to meet. In fact, just as domestic standards may be set to provide protection against imports, it may be that the standards applied in recognition regimes are set by the parties to provide *de facto* protection. To the extent that recognition regimes are established without transparency and input to allow poor countries to influence their development, this is a risk.

Moreover, it may be excessively costly for poor countries to qualify for recognition, either in connection with their regulatory standards or in connection with their certification arrangements. In connection with the Doha Round, there have been discussions of technical assistance to enable poor countries to participate in, and qualify for, harmonization and recognition processes. Arrangements should be made to ensure that even open recognition arrangements do not place poor countries at a competitive disadvantage, or require poor countries to expend excessive amounts of their own resources in order to comply.

7.   CONCLUSION: MUTUAL RECOGNITION AND GOVERNANCE

As noted at the beginning of this article, mutual recognition is a technique of trade facilitation that involves regulatory deference by importing or host countries. In this sense it is not a technique of governance. Rather, governance is provided either by harmonization or by agreements for equivalence predicated upon regulatory sufficiency. Harmonization requires each state to impose at least a minimum standard of regulation, which is then set as a predicate for mutual recognition. Equivalence does not require each state to legislate at a particular harmonized level, but allows the importing or host state to evaluate the regulatory structure of the exporting or home state in order to determine whether the regulatory goals are sufficiently met.

It is perfectly rational for states to decide to compromise some of their regulatory goals as they engage in international commerce. They may do so through recognition without predicate ('rootless recognition') where the value of their regulation is small relative to the value of expanded commerce. Alternatively, they may engage in managed recognition to maximize the combined value of regulation and expanded commerce. Managed recognition would include either harmonization or equivalence regimes.

However, the WTO has little capacity to produce harmonized rules, but may increasingly select harmonized rules from other regimes, such as Codex Alimentarius, as predicates for recognition. On the other hand, particularly within the SPS Agreement, the WTO has some capacity for adjudicated equivalence disciplines: requirements that importing states faithfully evaluate the equivalence of the regulatory structure of the exporting state.

Mutual recognition may also pose dangers to poor country market access. Mutual recognition regimes should be structured so as not to reduce poor country market access, and so as not to require poor country expenditures of excessive amounts of resources. Arrangements for technical assistance may be made to address the latter concern.

Thus, mutual recognition, like any form of liberalism, must be embedded in two ways. First, it should not jeopardize a satisfactory level of prudential regulation. Thus, capacity for harmonization and/or equivalence evaluation will set the limit on the scope of mutual recognition. Second, mutual recognition should not disadvantage poor states, either *de jure* through closed recognition among developed states or *de facto* through harmonization or equivalence conditions that are excessive, or excessively costly, for poor states.

Biographical note: Joel P. Trachtman is Professor of International Law at the Fletcher School of Law and Diplomacy, Tufts University, Medford, Massachusetts, USA.

ACKNOWLEDGEMENTS

I am grateful for comments and suggestions to Miguel Maduro, Jacques Pelkmans, Susanne Schmidt, and Greg Shaffer, and for research assistance to Nirmalaguhan Wigneswaran. Errors are mine.

NOTES

1 It is a question of subsidiarity. For a brief statement of this issue, see Trubek (2002).
2 For an introduction to the rules versus standards discussion in law and economics, see Kaplow (1998, 1992). See also Sunstein (1995). For an application of this literature in the international law context, see Trachtman (1999).

3 In the EC – Sardines case, the WTO Appellate Body accepted that certain standards adopted by majority voting in Codex Alimentarius could qualify as relevant international standards for the purposes of Article 2.4 of the TBT Agreement. Appellate Body Report, EC – Trade Description of Sardines, WT/DS231/AB/R, adopted 23 October 2002.
4 Appellate Body Report, US – Shrimp (Article 21.5), WT/DS58/AB/R, at para. 144 (emphasis in original).
5 See document G/SPS/19. This document was clarified in 2004, in G/SPS/19/Rev.2.
6 It adds that, in doing so, Members should take into account the *Guidelines to Further the Practical Implementation of Article 5.5* adopted by the Committee on Sanitary and Phytosanitary Measures at its meeting of 21–22 June 2000 (document G/SPS/15, dated 18 July 2000).
7 *TBT Triennial Review*, para. 23, G/TBT/9.
8 Appellate Body Report, *US–Shrimp*, WT/DS58/AB/R, at para. 165; and Appellate Body Report, *US – Shrimp (Article 21.5)*, WT/DS58/AB/RW, at paras 135–152.
9 WTO (1998), Disciplines on Domestic Regulation in the Accountancy Sector, S/L/64, 17 December 1998, reprinted in *WTO Focus*, December 1998, 10–11.
10 See Bartels (2005).
11 The EC has entered into a number of mutual recognition arrangements with third states. See, for example Agreement on Mutual Recognition Between the European Community and the United States of America, OJEC No. L31, 4 February 1999.
12 Appellate Body Report Canada – Certain Measures Affecting the Automotive Industry, WT/DS139/AB/R, WT/DS142/AB/R, adopted 19 June 2000, para. 85.
13 For an example of a circumstance in which the fact of government certification did not provide sufficient distinction to support a finding that products were not 'like', see Panel Report, European Economic Community–Imports of Beef from Canada, adopted 10 March 1981, 28 B.I.S.D. 92. For an example of differential import licensing procedures violating Article I:1, see Panel Report, EC–Regime for the Importation, Sale and Distribution of Bananas, adopted 25 September 1997, WT/DS27/R, paras. 7.188–7.193; 7.251–7.256; 7.235–7.241.
14 WTO Appellate Body Report: European Communities – Measures Affecting Asbestos-Containing Products, WT/DS135/AB/R, para. 100, adopted 5 April 2001.
15 Appellate Body Report, Korea – Various Measures on Beef, WT/DS161/AB/R and WT/DS169/AB/R, at para. 134.
16 See Davey and Pauwelyn (2000: 23–4), evaluating mutual recognition agreements under the MFN principle.
17 WT/DS34/AB/R, adopted 19 November 1999.

REFERENCES

Bartels, L. (2005) 'The legality of the EC mutual recognition clause under WTO law', *Journal of International Economic Law* 8(3): 691–720.
Breton, A., Cassone, A. and Fraschini', A. (1998) 'Decentralization and subsidiarity: toward a theoretical reconciliation', *University of Pennsylvania Journal of International Economic Law* 19(1): 21–51.
Choi, S. and Guzman, A. (1998) 'Portable reciprocity: rethinking the international reach of securities regulation', *Southern California Law Review* 71: 903–52.
Davey, W. and Pauwelyn, J. (2000) 'MFN unconditionality: a legal analysis of the concept in view of its evolution in the GATT/WTO jurisprudence with particular reference to the issue of "Like Product"', in T. Cottier, P.C. Mavroidis and P. Blatter

(eds), *Regulatory Barriers and the Principle of Non–Discrimination in World Trade Law*, Ann Arbor: Michigan University Press, pp. 13–50.

Fox, M. (1999) 'Retaining mandatory disclosure: why issuer choice is not investor empowerment', *Virginia Law Review* 85(7): 1335–420.

Hoekman, B., Michalopolous, C. and Winters, L. (2004) 'Special and differential treatment in the WTO: moving forward after Cancún', *The World Economy* 27(4): 481–506.

Hudec, R. (2000) '"Like product": the differences in meaning in GATT Articles I and III', in T. Cottier, P.C. Mavroidis and P. Blatter (eds), *Regulatory Barriers and the Principle of Non–Discrimination in World Trade Law*, Ann Arbor: Michigan University Press, pp. 101–24.

Kaplow, L. (1992) 'Rules versus standards: an economic analysis', *Duke Law Journal* 42(3): 557–629.

Kaplow, L. (1998) 'General characteristics of rules', in B. Bouckaert and G. De Geest (eds), *Encyclopedia of Law and Economics*, Cheltenham: Edward Elgar, pp. 502–28. <http://users.ugent.be/ ~ gdegeest/9000book.pdf>.

Keohane, R. (1986) 'Reciprocity in international relations', *International Organization* 40(1): 1–27.

Nicolaïdis, K. (2000) 'Non-discriminatory mutual recognition: an oxymoron in the new WTO lexicon', in T. Cottier, P.C. Mavroidis and P. Blatter (eds), *Regulatory Barriers and the Principle of Non–Discrimination in World Trade Law*, Ann Arbor: Michigan University Press, pp. 267–302.

Nicolaïdis, K. and Shaffer, G. (2005) 'Transnational mutual recognition regimes: governance without global government', *Law and Contemporary Problems* 68(3–4): 263–318.

Polanyi, K. (1957) (1944) *The Great Transformation: The Political and Economic Origins of Our Time*, Boston: Beacon Press.

Romano, R. (1998) 'Empowering investors: a market approach to securities regulation', *Yale Law Journal* 107: 2359–430.

Ruggie, J. (2002) *Taking Embedded Liberalism Global: The Corporate Connection*, Miliband Public Lecture on Global Economic Governance. The London School of Economics and Political Science. 6 June 2002 <www.globaldimensions.net/articles/ruggie/globalliberalism.html>.

Sunstein, C. (1995) 'Problems with rules', *California Law Review* 83(4): 953–1026.

Trachtman, J.P. (1995) 'Trade in financial services under GATS, NAFTA and the EC: a regulatory jurisdiction analysis', *Columbia Journal of Transnational Law* 34: 37–122.

Trachtman, J.P. (1997) 'Accounting standards and trade disciplines: irreconcilable differences?', *Journal of World Trade* 31: 63–98.

Trachtman, J.P. (1999) 'The domain of WTO dispute resolution', *Harvard International Law Journal* 40: 333–77.

Trachtman, J.P. (2000) 'Regulatory competition and regulatory jurisdiction', *Journal of International Economic Law* 3: 331–48.

Trachtman, J.P. (2001a) 'Economic analysis of prescriptive jurisdiction and choice of law', *Virginia Journal of International Law* 42: 1–79.

Trachtman, J.P. (2001b) 'Regulatory competition and regulatory jurisdiction in securities regulation', in D. Esty and D. Gerardin, (eds), *Regulatory Competition and Economic Integration: Comparative Perspectives*, Oxford: Oxford University Press, pp. 289–310.

Trachtman, J.P. (2003) 'Toward open recognition: standardization and regional integration under article XXIV of GATT', *Journal of International Economic Law* 6: 459–92.

Trubek, D. (2002) 'Book review: Governance in a globalizing world', *American Journal of International Law* 96: 748–52.

Weiler, J. (2005) 'Mutual recognition, functional equivalence and harmonization in the evolution of the European common market and the WTO', in F. Kostoris Padoa Schioppa (ed.), *The Principle of Mutual Recognition in the European Integration Process*, Basingstoke: Palgrave Macmillan, pp. 25–84.

Mutual recognition: comparing policy areas

Adrienne Héritier

1. INTRODUCTION

Why and how did mutual recognition emerge in European policy areas as different as the free trade of goods and justice and home affairs? The contributions of this volume expose in a very insightful and differentiated way how mutual recognition as a mode of governance has been more or less successfully established in different policy areas and, once established, more or less successfully implemented. The differences between the policy areas of free movement of goods, services, taxation, and justice and home affairs are striking. How can we account for the divergent outcomes? Why does mutual recognition in a pure form not exist in any of these areas, but only as a form of 'managed' mutual recognition? And why has 'managed' mutual recognition been successfully established in the free movement of goods (Pelkmans 2007), and why has the free movement of temporary services been rejected (Nicolaïdis and Schmidt 2007)? Why is it that in the area of value added taxes (VAT) mutual recognition has not been seriously tackled, but national treatment linked to a fragmented regime of border tax adjustment has persisted (Genschel 2007)? And how can it be explained that mutual recognition in justice and home affairs has been declared as a loose principle of action which has remained void in practice (Lavenex 2007)? Based on the analysis of the different policy areas discussed in this volume, I will propose a strategic choice argument to account for the differential outcomes in the establishing of mutual recognition and, if instituted, for the divergent outcomes of its implementation in the different policy areas.

2. MUTUAL RECOGNITION AS AN INSTITUTIONAL RULE CREATING RELIABLE BEHAVIOURAL EXPECTATIONS

Mutual recognition constitutes an institutional rule or rule of behaviour prescribing a particular behaviour among member states in the European Community/European Union. Institutional rules defined as rules of behaviour are created by actors and, in turn, shape actors' behaviour (North 1990). They may be regarded as condensed information about the likely behaviour of actors engaged in interaction. Assuming that actors will seek to maximize their utility and will abide by the prevalent institutional rules, knowledge of the valid institutional rules allows actors to devise their strategies in order to reach their preferred outcomes in the light of other actors' objectives and expected behaviour. In a rational choice framework, as Knight formulated it:

> social institutions affect the calculus used by rational actors to assess their potential strategies and to select their rational choice of action. These effects alter the chosen strategies and affect the outcomes of conflict. They change these outcomes by altering what is rational for social actors to do. Institutional rules do this by providing two types of information: (1) the nature of sanctions for non-compliance and (2) the probable future actions of others. A key to their effectiveness is that they are socially shared: the knowledge of their existence and applicability is shared by the members of the relevant group or community. The fact that the rules are known to be generally applicable guides not only our own future actions, but also our expectations about the future actions of others with whom we interact.
>
> (Knight 1992: 17)

Mutual recognition as an institutional rule governing market integration allows for the free movement of goods, services and persons, based on home-country rule and the recognition of the legitimacy of different, but equivalent, regulation in the other member states (Nicolaïdis 1997). As such, it is different from the institutional rules of harmonization and national treatment, and represents an institutional rule of eminent importance in dealing with the diversity of member states. 'Managed' mutual recognition, as a combination of country of origin principle and equivalence rules (Pelkmans 2007), since it operates through market processes and case law linked to judicial principles such as legislation cannot be easily observed. In particular, judicial mutual recognition 'seems to be "invisible" as it were' (Pelkmans 2007: 703). This is one reason why – although a very powerful institutional rule in some policy areas – it has been a neglected subject in political science research, a neglect which this volume seeks to remedy.

3.   THE DIFFERENTIAL OUTPUTS AND OUTCOMES OF MUTUAL RECOGNITION: A STRATEGIC CHOICE EXPLANATION

I argue that a rational strategic choice argument may help to account for the differences in output, outcome and impact of mutual recognition across policy areas. The approach analytically distinguishes between two elements of strategic interaction: actors and their environments. Actors and their environments are further disaggregated into two attributes. Strategic *environments* are composed, first, of the actions which are available to the actors. They summarize what could be the outcome of the interactions of actors, or the outcome of how decisions and events can unfold (Lake and Powell 1999: 8, 9). Second, the environment is composed of an information structure that defines what the actors can know for sure and what they have to infer from the behaviour of others. Institutional rules play an eminent role here. Keohane (1984) argued that one way in which institutions facilitate co-operation among states is by providing more information to state actors, especially by providing better possibilities of monitoring each other's behaviour (Lake and Powell 1999: 9).

On the *actor side*, strategic choice analysis distinguishes between two attributes. First, actors are assumed to have preferences, defined simply as how they rank the possible outcomes defined by the environment (Lake and Powell 1999: 9). Actors' *basic* preferences are desires that remain the same across a wide variety of situations. Actors' *situational* preferences (Frieden 1999) consist of the ranking of preferred outcomes in more specific situations and depend upon the particular problem constellation. The second attribute of an actor are her or his prior beliefs about the preferences of others. In particular, when actors are uncertain, these beliefs are crucial for the decision about which strategy to choose, and, in consequence, for the outcome of interaction (Lake and Powell 1999: 11).

The analytic distinction of actors' attributes and the attributes of the environment implies the possibility of two broad kinds of 'conceptual experiments' (Lake and Powell 1999). The first conceptual experiment varies the properties of the actors, i.e. their preferences and beliefs, while holding the environment in which they interact constant, and derives conclusions, i.e. hypotheses, about the likely outcome. The second conceptual experiment varies attributes of the environment while the actors' attributes are held constant, and derives conclusions or hypotheses about the likely outcome of the interaction. The argument I want to make here is that – holding constant the preferences of the involved actors – the differential outcomes regarding mutual recognition in the different policy areas may be understood as a function of the variation of environmental/institutional factors relevant for the individual policy area. An important variation on the environment side would be a variation of the existing macro-institutional domestic or European rules. Do the changes in the valid European institutional rules affect the information or actions available to the actors when they have to act, and do these changes affect the outcomes of the interaction (Lake and Powell 1999: 11, 12)? In a second step I will also vary preferences in order to see how this affects outcomes.

In the following text I will put two questions asking (1) why mutual recognition has been more or less successfully established in different areas of European policy-making, as a policy-output, and, if once established, (2) why the implementation of mutual recognition produced particular policy effects and structural impacts in one area, but not in others.

4.   POLICY OUTPUT: WHY AND HOW HAS MUTUAL RECOGNITION BEEN INTRODUCED?

Turning to the *first question* and trying to explain the different policy outputs in the different policy areas analysed in this volume, I will (a) engage in the conceptual experiment varying *environmental factors* as a prime independent variable, i.e. institutional conditions[1] (while holding actors' preferences constant), in order to see how this affects the observed outcomes. Of the relevant political/institutional conditions, i.e. Commission initiatives, Council decisions and initiatives of the European Parliament, it is in particular Court activism which makes a difference. More specifically, I will first argue (hypothesis 1) that the systematic variation of the information/institutional aspect of the environment, i.e. the existence or absence of the activism of the European Court of Justice (ECJ), may explain whether mutual recognition was established and which type of mutual recognition was established, i.e. whether it was 'pure' mutual recognition or 'managed' mutual recognition.

In a second conceptual experiment (b) preferences are varied in order to observe the impact upon policy output while holding the environmental factors constant. It is argued that, given certain institutional conditions, the intensity of pro- and anti-market integration preferences may account for the policy output.

The assumed actors' preferences are that *member states* in general (basic preferences) seek to increase their economic welfare (i.e. share in trade of exported goods and services) while preserving their domestic levels of product[2] and process regulation. More specifically, it is assumed that *high-regulating member states'* preferred outcome would be mutual recognition under conditions of strong equivalence rules, the second preferred outcome harmonization and the least preferred outcome would be national treatment because it would not allow an increase in the export of goods. *Low-regulating countries*, however, are assumed to prefer mutual recognition without strict rules of equivalence over framework harmonization with a good deal of latitude. The least preferred outcome is assumed to be national treatment. The *Commission's* first preference is assumed to be harmonization, the second preferred outcome mutual recognition within rules of reason, and the third preferred outcome mutual recognition 'pure'. The *Parliament* is assumed to prefer strict harmonization over mutual recognition with strict rules of reason over mutual recognition 'pure' over national treatment.

The environmental (independent) variable which is varied under the first conceptual experiment is the existing institutional rule. The most important existing institutional rule, I argue, is the *existence or absence of judicial activism*, i.e. strict Court rulings to promote free movement. The existence of a clear Court ruling in favour of mutual recognition constitutes an institutional rule clearly indicating to all concerned actors what should guide their actions and which sanctions can be expected in case of non-compliance. The knowledge of this rule and its applicability is shared by all actors and is therefore expected to influence actions. The different values of the dependent variable, i.e. the policy output, are 'pure' mutual recognition, 'managed' mutual recognition, framework harmonization, strict harmonization, operative co-operation, or national treatment. The assumptions about preferences together with the first variation of the institutional rule (existence or absence of Court activism) leads to the general claim:

Hypothesis 1 'In the presence of a clear Court ruling in favour of mutual recognition, member states – in spite of divergent preferences – will accept mutual recognition albeit with strong rules of reason.'

Or conversely:

Hypothesis 1.1 'In the absence of a clear Court ruling in favour of mutual recognition, given divergent preferences among member states, mutual recognition will be weak or missing; loose framework legislation, national treatment or operative co-operation are more likely to prevail.'

In order to empirically assess this first hypothesis the case of *free movement of goods* (Pelkmans 2007), on the one hand, will be compared with the cases of *free movement of services* (Nicolaïdis and Schmidt 2007), (*VAT*) *taxes* (Genschel 2007), and *justice and home affairs* (Lavenex 2007), on the other hand.

In the area of *free movement of goods*, regulatory diversity initially impeded market integration in trade. In the 1960s, the Commission, which had first aimed at harmonization, but found that a large part of this harmonization programme had stalled, started to consider mutual recognition (Genschel 2007). In these endeavours it was greatly supported by the ECJ rulings of *Dassonville* and *Cassis de Dijon*. As Pelkmans argues, once the ECJ understood that guaranteeing market access would only function if free movement of goods was secured and a member state was only to deviate from this by explicit derogations, it went for 'an "economic" interpretation' (Pelkmans 2007: 700). In *Dassonville* it ruled that regulatory barriers 'capable of hindering, directly or indirectly, actually or potentially, intra-Community trade' are prohibited, but should be balanced by derogations (Pelkmans 2007: 700–1; Majone 1996). Thus, the ECJ with this change of paradigm in adjudication prepared the ground for the political victory of mutual recognition '[b]y reading the logic of mutual recognition into the text of the Treaty' (Genschel 2007: 748). This was followed by the ruling of *Cassis de Dijon* in which the

ECJ for the first time defines the 'origin principle'. Member states are held to follow the origin principle unless there are justified reasons for not doing so.

The outcome (dependent variable) was that the *free movement of goods* under mutual recognition restricted by strong rules of reason, i.e. 'managed' mutual recognition, was established as applying in a manner that buffers competition (Nicolaïdis 1997). The preconditions of the application of mutual recognition are spelled out ex-ante and ex-post, limiting the scope of activities covered by mutual recognition (Nicolaïdis 2007). This type of 'managed' mutual recognition does not constitute an alternative to harmonization or national treatment but combines both of them (Nicolaïdis 2007: 685) since it is never applied by itself, but is linked with other integration principles, i.e. with minimum harmonization/standardization thus creating a common baseline (Schmidt 2007).

Comparing the case of *free movement of goods* with the case of *free movement of services* (Nicolaïdis and Schmidt 2007), it becomes evident that, in the area of services, there has been no comparable judicial activism. Quite the opposite; the ECJ has interpreted the freedom to provide services more *restrictively* than the free trade with goods, as for instance in the case of the posted workers directive where the Court has emphasized the right of a strong host-country control (Nicolaïdis and Schmidt 2007). The outcome (dependent variable) is, as the analysis of Nicolaïdis and Schmidt shows, the abolishing of mutual recognition in the draft legislation on the services directive. Given the deep division between supporters and opponents of the directive, and its strong ideological underpinnings, the absence of Court pressure made it easier for the opponents of the free movement of services to insist on host-country control.

In the area of *(VAT) taxes*, Court pressure is absent as well. Genschel shows that, as opposed to the *free movement of goods*, Art. 90 (former Art. 95) of the Treaty cannot be used to force governments to accept origin-based taxation. 'However, the ECJ cannot ... prepare the legal ground for the mutual recognition of VAT because Article 90 explicitly allows the (non-discriminatory) taxation of imports' (Genschel 2007: 749). The political avenue of tax harmonization, for fear of tax competition and high implementation costs for governments, as Genschel convincingly argues, is not a viable political alternative. Here again, the absence of Court rulings allowing for a rule of reason protecting national tax revenue as a public policy justifying restrictive state measures plays an important role. This means that the transaction costs of tax arbitrage are lower and member states would have to fully mutually recognize their VATs. Consequently, companies would have an incentive to move to countries with low VAT rates, triggering off a race to the bottom among member states out-performing each other in the cutting of VAT rates. As Genschel emphasizes, the experience in the area of direct taxation underlines this expectation. Corporate taxes, levied by the member state of origin where its headquarters are, have induced companies to concentrate taxable profits in member states with low corporate taxes. '[T]he ECJ has done little so far to protect member states from arbitrage pressures and revenue losses' (Genschel 2007: 752).

The policy output (dependent variable) is the persistence of national treatment linked with a complicated system of border tax adjustments.

In *justice and home affairs or the area of freedom, security and justice* the shadow of the Court has also been weak. There has been no Court activism comparable to the rulings of *Dassonville* and *Cassis de Dijon* on the free movement of goods. Rather, important reservations regarding the powers of the ECJ prevail on the part of member states. Thus the ECJ cannot be invoked if there is a lack of implementation of framework directives in justice and home affairs.

The *policy output* (dependent variable) therefore was that – when the heads of state and governments adopted the principle of mutual recognition at the Tampere European Council (1999) – it was simultaneously linked to multiple derogations (Nilsson 2006; Lavenex 2007). And very similarly, the previously established principle of mutual recognition in asylum matters contains multiple grounds for non-application. *If* a harmonizing legal text is adopted, it will usually reflect the lowest common denominator and allow member states a large degree of discretion in implementation; it would contain weak obligations and many exemption clauses (Lavenex 2007). Only a few effective instruments to implement the political decisions have been introduced, i.e. the European arrest warrant and the freezing of accounts (Lavenex 2007; Nilsson 2006). As a result of the slowness of the formal political decision-making process, modes of co-operation in justice and home affairs have emerged which are informal, pragmatic and operational.

In conclusion, the comparative analysis of the cases lends some empirical plausibility to the first 'court activism' hypothesis.

In the second conceptual experiment institutional conditions are held constant and the preferences of the member state actors over policy outcomes are varied across policy areas. Under this 'intensity of preferences' hypothesis it is argued that actors' preferences diverge considerably with respect to different types of freedoms. They are relatively favourable as to the integration of the free movement of goods, less so in the case of the free movement of services, and even less so in the case of justice and home affairs, with respect to the free mobility of persons and the recognition of the adjudication of other member states. The divergence of preferences in these policy areas results in part from their closeness or distance to core aspects of national sovereignty. Taxes and justice and home affairs are very close to the core of national sovereignty. The divergence has also been deepened by the changing environmental context of economic internationalization and eastern enlargement.

Varying preferences while holding constant institutional conditions it is therefore claimed that:

Hypothesis 2 'The stronger actors' rejection of market integration and the closer an issue to national sovereignty, the less likely the introduction of mutual recognition, the less likely strict harmonization, the more likely only a loose co-operation.'

And conversely,

Hypothesis 2.1 'The stronger the support for market integration in an issue area, the greater the distance from national core sovereignty questions, the more likely mutual recognition.'

In order to empirically assess the plausibility of this hypothesis the cases of *free movement of goods*, on the one hand, and *taxes, service integration*, and *justice and home affairs*, on the other hand, will be compared.[3]

In the area of *free movement of goods* the pro-integration preferences are pronounced. The regulation of the production of goods is not close to the core sovereignty values of a member state; nor does it imply a direct redistribution (such as in the case of taxes). It aims at the correction of negative external effects of market and production processes on which member states reasonably agree, such as on a high level of health and environmental protection. Moreover, the costs of implementation lie with industry, not with governments (Genschel 2007). Hence it is comparatively easy to obtain acceptance of the regulation of goods of other member states as long as regulatory objectives are safeguarded, and the outcome is to be 'managed' mutual recognition.

The preferences for the co-ordination of *taxes* are much weaker than for the free movement of goods. For one thing, as Genschel argues, tax diversity is less harmful to trade in goods than diversity in the regulation of goods. Different rates of VAT do not affect the structure of production. Moreover, VAT is a completely transparent tax. The *outcome* (dependent variable), therefore, i.e. the persistence of national treatment linked with a complicated system of border tax adjustments, is not surprising.

As regards the *free movement of services*, the anti-integration preferences of member states may also be pronounced. Services differ from goods, as Nicolaïdis and Schmidt (2007: 719) point out, in that services come with people. They are frequently based on the 'uno-actu' principle, i.e. the service requires the movement of the provider to the point of consumption. The individuals arriving with the services deepen the existing fears of unemployment at a time when labour costs in highly developed economies have come under pressure. With eastern enlargement, the political and economic context has changed, the differences in economic development between member states have increased, and with them the fear of regulatory competition. Thus, the interests of the old and new member states in the political debate about the services directive were directly pitched against each other. As we have seen, the *outcome* (dependent variable) has been that mutual recognition was eliminated from the draft directive.

In *justice and home affairs* anti-free movement preferences are also very pronounced . What is at stake is safety and civil liberty, values which are much more polarizing than the values at stake under the free movement of goods, such as the standardization of the content of a beverage or the technical norms of an elevator. Also, issues of justice and home affairs are close to the essence of national sovereignty. When it comes to arresting people and accepting the judicial verdicts of other member states, member states are hesitant to agree to a horizontal shift of sovereignty and to pool sovereignty at the European level. Thus in asylum and immigration matters the powers of supranational actors were restricted until 2005. Although the Commission now has the right of initiative, and the Council decides on the basis of qualified majority voting and under codecision, the most important directives were still adopted through intergovernmental method and unanimity and there is a notorious lack of political will to co-ordinate (Lavenex 2007). Not surprisingly, therefore, the *policy output* (dependent variable) is a principle of mutual recognition with multiple grounds of derogations (Nilsson 2006; Lavenex 2007).

In conclusion, the variance of the intensity of pro- and anti-market integration preferences does throw some explanatory light on the differential outcome in the different policy areas, as claimed under the second 'intensity of preferences' hypothesis.

5.   THE IMPLEMENTATION OF MUTUAL RECOGNITION: POLICY EFFECTS AND STRUCTURAL IMPACTS

The second question tackled in the contributions of this volume (Pelkmans, Lavenex, Genschel and Nicolaïdis) concerns the *implementation* of mutual recognition, its policy effects and structural impacts. When discussing this question, the preferences of additional actors, i.e. firms and associations, have been taken into account. The assumed preferences of member states, the Commission and the Parliament are the same as under the first policy output question. Additionally, it is assumed that high-regulating member states seek to realize a strict implementation of mutual recognition with equivalence rules, while low-regulating member states are less keen to do so. The Commission and the Parliament, are both assumed to prefer strict implementation over lax implementation. Private actors, i.e. firms and trade associations, play an important role in the implementation of the rules in the four policy areas. They are keen to facilitate market transactions of goods (and services), i.e. to cut transaction costs for information, negotiation and the monitoring of implementation by abolishing the existing specific regulations for goods, services and professions in national markets (Pelkmans 2007). However, it seems plausible that firms and their associations in high-regulating member states prefer the strict implementation of mutual recognition and equivalence rules, while firms and their associations in low-regulating member states favour mutual recognition without a strict implementation of the rules of reason. Trade unions, on the other hand, prefer the strict application of the rules of reason over the strict application of 'pure' mutual recognition.

Holding constant these preferences, the *independent* variable is the institutional rules governing the implementation process, i.e. the existence or absence of a well-developed and strict instrument and an organizational infrastructure for the application of mutual recognition and functional equivalence; the existence or absence of case law regulating the application of mutual recognition, and the existence or absence of laws of approximation guiding the application of mutual recognition.

On the side of the *dependent* variable, the focus of investigation is *policy effects* as assessed by a strong degree or a low degree of market integration. As to the *structural impact*, we might find a strong or a weak horizontal and vertical transfer of state sovereignty to other member states and/or the European level. In the 'implementation hypothesis' it is therefore submitted that:

Hypothesis 3 'If mutual recognition is based on well-developed, viable instruments and an organizational infrastructure, implementation will lead to more extensive market integration and to a concomitant horizontal shift of state sovereignty.'

And correspondingly:

Hypothesis 3.1 'If the implementation of mutual recognition is not based on well-developed instruments and an organizational infrastructure, market integration will be less extensive, and a horizontal transfer of sovereignty will not occur.'

The comparison focuses on the two cases where mutual recognition has been instituted, i.e. the *free movement of goods* and *justice and home affairs*.

The case of *free movement of goods* is a very interesting case in which there are two different implementation regimes which differ strongly as to their policy effect and structural impact. The ECJ case law requires member states to accept equivalent products of other member states. However, in their assessment of equivalence, actors have much latitude which allows member states to claim exceptions from free trade (under Art. 30 and the existing ECJ case law), with the ECJ being the final arbiter under *judicial mutual recognition*. Establishing the equivalence of regulations to which products have been subject, however, is a demanding exercise which frequently needs to be backed up by scientific expertise. If the expertise shows that the country of origin pursues the same regulatory objective and this objective is considered as equivalent, the host country cannot invoke a derogation (Pelkmans 2007: 713–4).

If the equivalence of regulatory measures is not considered to be given, derogations apply. The only way to achieve free movement is through 'approximation'. Under the so-called New Approach, termed *regulatory mutual recognition*, regulatory safety, health, environmental and consumer protection objectives are defined and specified by means of standards. Once established, a lack of equivalence can no longer prevent imports of goods (Pelkmans 2007). Here the instruments of implementation are carefully developed. Voluntary European technical standards are elaborated on the basis of 'mandates' issued by the European Commission, 'in turn derived from the SHEC [safety, health, environment, consumer protection] objectives in the relevant directive(s). Market participants, and not Eurocrats or national civil servants, develop standards for the EU. The Commission recognizes these standards and, after official publication, business can rely on them for intra-EU free movement' (Pelkmans 2007: 703). Regulatory mutual recognition is much appreciated by companies because of the greater certainty about objectives and standards and the procedural obligations of member states. What is more, national legislation has to be notified in Brussels and must include clear references to mutual recognition, by for instance, referring to the standards of the European Committee for Standardization (CEN) and the European Committee for Electrotechnical Standardization (CENELEC) (Pelkmans 2007).

Because of these instruments the implementation of *regulatory* mutual recognition allows for policy effectiveness (dependent variable). It deepens and improves the quality of the internal market (Pelkmans 2007) and helps to contain over-regulation by member states since their rules cannot stop imports from other member states if they meet the equivalency standard (Pelkmans 2007).

By contrast, under *judicial* mutual recognition, as Pelkmans (2007) emphasizes, the information costs for business to find out whether mutual recognition applies to them are prohibitive. Also, the loss of reputation which may result in the case of the refusal of a product by the importing country and the waiting costs until the possible admission ('time to market') of the product are considerable. The prospect of going to court is not encouraging: the process is slow and costly too (Pelkmans 2007). Small and medium-sized enterprises in particular are not familiar with ECJ case law, only their national laws. They therefore tend not to consider mutual recognition as a viable mode of achieving their trade objectives and refrain from exporting to other countries or, alternatively, make adaptations before exporting, thus reducing their competitiveness (Pelkmans 2007). And, as Genschel points out, since companies cannot wait for a court to vindicate a claim of mutual recognition, they often comply with the rules of the importing country even when they could insist on the functional equivalence of their home-country regulation (Genschel 2007).

National authorities of the host country which – given the lack of a rule book for mutual recognition – are confronted with high information costs themselves tend to abide by *national* rules and not European case law. For these reasons, as Pelkmans argues, the implementation of *judicial* mutual recognition in view of existing differences in technical specifications between member states is 'weak, haphazard, unreliable and slow' (Pelkmans 2007: 711). The very companies relying on mutual recognition 'are hardly "protected" by its regime' (Pelkmans 2007: 711).[4]

Another important policy effect of mutual recognition which has been much discussed is a possible regulatory race to the bottom. However, according to existing empirical accounts 'managed' mutual recognition ensures that competitive pressures are being mediated and, arguably, instances of a regulatory race to the bottom are rare (Schmidt 2007: 676). As Pelkmans emphasizes, under judicial mutual recognition equivalence of regulatory measures must be observed and under regulatory mutual recognition objectives are commonly defined (Pelkmans 2007: 708). Moreover, the treaty prescribes a high level of protection in safety, health, environmental and consumer affairs. As a result, a regulatory race to the bottom is not likely to ensue (Pelkmans 2007: 708). Furthermore, since technical specification standards under regulatory mutual recognition are performance-oriented, there is a safeguard against a regulatory race to the bottom (Pelkmans 2007: 708).

As to the *structural impact* (dependent variable) mutual recognition avoids the centralization of political competences, which however, may imply a horizontal transfer of competences to other member states. Yet, this transfer is less far-reaching owing to the application of strict rules of equivalence, i.e. 'managed' mutual recognition. It is true, though, that the notification system in prospective barrier control has the structural impact of a 'semi-automatic suspension of the national legislative process' (Pelkmans 2007: 706). Additionally, as regards a structural impact beyond Europe, given that national legislation must include clear references to mutual recognition and equivalence rules, for example, by referring to standards of the CEN and CENELEC, and the latter, in turn, by refering to the norms of the International Standards Organization (ISO) and the International Electrical Commission (IEC), third countries are included in mutual recognition as well (see Trachtman 2007).

In the comparative case of *justice and home affairs* the instruments of *implementation* of the principle of mutual recognition have been notoriously weak. Under the only loose principle of mutual recognition, for instance in asylum matters, there are multiple grounds for the refusal of asylum seekers. As Lavenex (2007) emphasizes in her article, the framework decision is weak and its transposition has been very slow. Only two instruments are available: the European arrest warrant and the freezing of bank accounts. Member states cannot be brought to the ECJ for lack of implementation. In addition, implementation appears to be extremely difficult because of different constitutional traditions. To give an example, while child abduction by a parent may constitute a criminal act in one country, this may not be the case in another country, leading to uncertainty as to the application of the European arrest warrant (Nilsson 2006). What is more, justice ministers of member states sometimes refuse the implementation of court rulings of other member states (Nilsson 2006). Attempts at unified procedures, such as the agreement on a convention on mutual legal assistance, are rather weak instruments, and the right of preliminary rulings under Schengen has been accepted by only 15 of 25 member states. The new instrument of mutual evaluation to assess performance is not likely to produce quick changes either. The operational powers of Eurojust are weak; if they were not, a chamber of criminal justice which does not exist in the ECJ would have to be created (Nilsson 2006).

Therefore it does not come as a surprise that on the side of *policy effectiveness* (dependent variable) the results of mutual recognition in justice and home affairs are modest at best. Moreover, as Lavenex points out, there is an imbalance between security concerns and individual rights in favour of the former. The security element of the area of freedom, security and justice, i.e. competences for facilitating law enforcement measures, is stronger than the protection of civil rights, especially human and procedural rights in criminal proceedings

(Lavenex 2007). External events frequently drive change and create pressure for the development of security instruments which are more easily agreed on under unanimity than matters of civil rights.

As to the structural impacts of a de facto horizontal transfer of formal competences among member states, it has remained modest owing to the lack of implementation of the principle of mutual recognition in justice and home affairs. Nevertheless, it has given rise to a large number of operative co-operation measures at the administrative level (Lavenex 2007).

6.   CONCLUSION

As the comparative analysis of the accounts of mutual recognition offered in the contributions to this volume shows, the establishment of mutual recognition linked with serious instruments of implementation and rules of regulatory equivalence only came about if pressed by an active ECJ, and policy effectiveness is only secured if there are strict instruments of implementation. In addition, the diverging preferences for market integration and mutual recognition in areas as different as the free movement of goods, services, taxes, and justice and home affairs contribute to the establishing of a strict mutual recognition. However, since the cases discussed in this volume do not allow for a comparison of cases with different preferences holding constant institutional rules, it is not possible to discriminate between the independent influences of divergent preferences.

Mutual recognition is an important institutional rule or mode of governance guiding the behaviour of actors in the free trade of goods, but only linked with complementary institutional rules guaranteeing the scrutiny of the equivalence of national regulations, and if this is not considered to be given, of regulatory rules of approximation which have to be taken if free movement is to be accepted.

Biographical note: Adrienne Héritier is Professor of Public Policy; she holds a joint Chair between the Department of Political and Social Sciences and the Robert Schuman Centre for Advanced Studies at the European University Institute of Florence, Italy.

ACKNOWLEDGEMENTS

I would like to thank Susanne Schmidt for her helpful comments on earlier drafts of this article.

NOTES

1 Other variables of the environment may be features in strategic choice theories, 'but they take on significance only through their effects on one or more of the primary independent variables ... A full specification of the causal chain ...

would reveal that these factors matter because they affect either the preferences of actors over different types of policy outcomes or the possibilities of action' (Lake and Powell 1999: 9).

2 Scharpf has argued that product regulation, if it manifestly increases the quality of a product in the view of consumers, such as providing more safety in financial products, creates a 'certificate effect' and therefore is more competitive in an integrated market (Scharpf 1999: 96).

3 This comparison has a disadvantage in that the institutional aspect is not held constant.

4 He proposes the introduction of detailed product lists to reduce information costs (Pelkmans 2007).

REFERENCES

Frieden, J.A. (1999) 'Actors and preferences in international relations', in D.A. Lake and R. Powell (eds), *Strategic Choice and International Relations*, Princeton: Princeton University Press, pp. 39–76.

Genschel, Philipp (2007) 'Why no mutual recognition of VAT? Regulation, taxation and the integration of the EU's internal market for goods', *Journal of European Public Policy* 14(5): 743–61.

Keohane, R. (1984) *After Hegemony: Cooperation and Discord in the World Political Economy*, Princeton: Princeton University Press.

Knight, J. (1992) *Institutions and Social Conflict*, Cambridge: Cambridge University Press.

Lake, D.A. and Powell, R. (1999) 'International relations: a strategic choice approach', in D.A. Lake and R. Powell, *Strategic Choice and International Relations*, Princeton: Princeton University Press, pp. 3–38.

Lavenex, S. (2007) 'Mutual recognition and the monopoly of force: limits of the single market analogy', *Journal of European Public Policy* 14(5): 762–79.

Majone, G. (1996) *Regulating Europe*, London: Routledge.

Nicolaïdis, K. (1997) *Mutual Recognition of Regulatory Regimes: Some Lessons and Prospects*, Jean Monnet Working Paper No. 7/97, Harvard ⟨http://www.jeanmonnet-program.org/papers/97/97-07.html⟩.

Nicolaïdis, K. (2007) 'Trusting the Poles? Constructing Europe through mutual recognition', *Journal of European Public Policy* 14(5): 682–98.

Nicolaïdis, K. and Schmidt, S.K. (2007) 'Mutual recognition "on trial": the long road to services liberalization', *Journal of European Public Policy* 14(5): 717–34.

Nilsson, H. (2006) 'Council of the European Union. Presentation', Workshop on *New Modes of Governance in Europe*, organized by U. Diedrichs and W. Wessels. New Goverment Integrated Project, FP 6, Brussels, 3 November 2006.

North, D.C. (1990) *Institutions, Institutional Change and Economic Performance*, Cambridge: Cambridge University Press.

Pelkmans, J. (2007) 'Mutual recognition in goods. On promises and disillusions'. *Journal of European Public Policy* 14(5): 699–716.

Scharpf, F.W. (1999) *Governing in Europe. Effective and Democratic?*, Oxford: Oxford University Press.

Schmidt, S.K. (2007) 'Mutual recognition as a new mode of governance', *Journal of European Public Policy* 14(5): 667–81.

Trachtman, J.P. (2007) 'Embedding mutual recognition at the WTO', *Journal of European Public Policy* 14(5): 780–99.

So close and yet so far: the paradoxes of mutual recognition

Miguel Poiares Maduro

INTRODUCTION

An immediate conclusion that emerges from this set of contributions is the diversity of mutual recognition. The contributions cover a variety of different policy areas (from taxation to goods, from services to justice and home affairs) and even different multi-level systems or integration regimes. Such a panoramic view provides us with a perception of how different the potential for mutual recognition and its possible consequences may be depending on the policy and actors' dynamics and variables on those different areas. They also present us with different models of mutual recognition. Pelkmans (2007) talks of regulatory and judicial mutual recognition. Trachtman (2007) distinguishes between equivalence and strict mutual recognition and Nicolaïdis and Schmidt (2007) between pure mutual recognition and managed mutual recognition. Sandra Lavenex (2007) points to the risks of transferring the logic of mutual recognition developed in the area of the internal market into the area of justice and security where the same institutional conditions that supported the former are not met and where the degree of mutual trust is even weaker. In a similar vein, Philipp Genschel (2007), for example, explains how mutual recognition is the preferred instrument to eliminate regulatory barriers but not tax barriers. Adrienne Héritier's conclusion draws on this richness to develop some hypotheses on what environmental/institutional factors explain preferences for mutual recognition and the outputs of mutual recognition policies (Héritier 2007). To some extent, the present conclusion complements her analysis by adopting a more normative approach.

RULES RECOGNITION AND GOVERNANCE

A first issue arising from the diversity of forms taken by mutual recognition is whether it is indeed a form of governance and what consequences ought to follow from such a characterization. Though most contributions appear to argue that mutual recognition is a form of governance, Joel Trachtman (2007) argues in the opposite sense. For Trachtman mutual recognition determines which governance rule is to prevail and therefore cannot be a form of governance in itself. His view is perfectly understandable if one takes mutual recognition, at its face value, simply as a rule allocating regulatory competences among states. In such a light, it is a conflict rule: it determines which set of rules is to prevail in the regulation of a certain good or service, for example. However, mutual recognition is indeed a mode of governance if one looks at the processes which are generated by this rule and the social outcomes they produce. In fact, mutual recognition does not determine the final regulatory outcome but sets in motion a process of regulatory competition that is governed by a particular form of market (composed of both economic and political transactions). It is to this market that mutual recognition entrusts regulatory competition and it is this market that is a mode of governance, in the sense in which Susanne Schmidt (2007: 668) refers to governance: 'forms of social co-ordination'.

It is the particular mechanisms of decision-making inherent in mutual recognition that explain why it generates different assessments for different actors and in different policy areas. Mutual recognition changes the balance among different interests in the representation and participation that shape certain policies. As a consequence, it can be more or less 'democratic' than other forms of governance and will lead to different outcomes. When Schmidt (2007) compares national treatment (host-country control) with harmonization and mutual recognition, she rightly points out that the relationship between politics and trade is reversed from the first to the latter. What that reflects, however, is the different contexts and mechanisms of participation existent in the three modes of governance. Under national treatment, the primate of politics is, in effect, the primate of national politics. Policies will be the product of the participation of the different interests represented in the national political process and of the balance of power between them. Under harmonization, policies will be the product of participation by different national interests at supranational political process levels and of their respective voting and lobbying power at that level. Under mutual recognition, it is participation in the 'market for regulations' that determines the final policies. Such a market, responsible for policy choices under the regulatory competition generated by mutual recognition, is, however, different from the traditional market. It involves, first of all, the preferences that consumers express for certain goods or services (which favour the regulations according to which those goods and services are produced). It also involves the preferences that capital, companies, labour, taxpayers and other categories express for certain policies by moving to the states that adopt them and relying on the home-country control principle. But it is also a product of other forms of 'voting with one's feet' and the political votes and lobbying of those who remain in the host country and resist changing their domestic policies. The policy outcome of the regulatory competition inherent in mutual recognition is a product of these different variables and instances of participation. The final result of mutual recognition will be a product of how this market of economic and political transactions decides among the mutually recognized norms and policies. It is for this reason that the outcome of regulatory competition depends on the rules of competition and that it varies greatly depending on the issues and the forms of competition. It is also for this reason that Reich (1992: 867–8) has stated that 'competition between legal orders is as such neither efficient nor harmful. It is much more necessary to know the objectives, contents and form of the legal orders among which competition in a (quasi-)federal jurisdiction will take place.'

The different variables of participation and representation in mutual recognition explain the variety of forms of mutual recognition highlighted in the different contributions and its higher or lower success in different policy areas. One example which is addressed in some of the contributions is the different treatment accorded to process rules (which govern the conditions under which a product is produced or a service is prepared and do not accompany it to the importing state: labour rules, environmental rules regulating production, taxes, etc.) with regard to product rules (which govern the characteristics of the good or service and do accompany it: components, packaging, labelling or the nature of the activity involved in the service provided, for example). Process rules are, in general, mutually recognized. In spite of some recent challenges to this distinction in the World Trade Organization (WTO) context, the general rule is that a state cannot impose on the products or services from other states its own process rules. In principle, no state can legally prohibit the importation of a certain good because it is manufactured under different conditions from its domestic products, such as regarding the wages paid or taxes levied on the producing companies. The reason why mutual recognition regarding process rules is generally more accepted than mutual recognition regarding product rules may have to do with the way the market, as defined above, governs the process of mutual recognition regarding those two different types of rules. Product rules have externality effects in terms of costs that process rules do not necessarily have, and this hinders the capacity of the market to internalize in the decision-making process of the home-country state a large part of the costs generated by its policies.

I would also argue that it is the different participation mechanisms inherent in the forms of governance related to national treatment, harmonization and mutual recognition that often explain the different assessments made by different actors on the virtues and problems of mutual recognition. Again, the current set of contributions present us with a very clear view of these different assessments. Some point to actual instances of the race to the bottom or present its thesis in the abstract (as exemplified by Trachtman's (2007: 784) assertion that the least demanding rule always leads, in principle, to deregulation). Others make a rather positive assessment and either point to opposite examples of a race to the top or challenge the race to the bottom thesis. That is so either because they trust that the competitive process will, more often than not, promote more optimal regulation (Pelkmans 2007) or because they believe that mutual recognition creates, by itself, pressures towards some forms of harmonization (Nicolaïdis and Schmidt 2007). What I believe it is important to stress is that whether mutual recognition will actually lead to more or less regulation and to higher or lower regulatory standards (the two are not necessarily the same) depends on the dynamics of participation generated by the process of market decision-making inherent in mutual recognition and that this should be compared with those of the available alternatives.

The different assessments and applications of mutual recognition are a natural consequence of the participatory variables that determine the results of mutual recognition as a form of governance. Whether and how mutual recognition will operate depends on the interaction between the forms of participation and representation inherent in the decision-making process of regulatory competition and the contexts in which its application is suggested. This will also determine how mutual recognition is to be structured and in the context of which institutional alternatives this occurs. Such variables will determine how different interests will have a voice in the mechanisms associated with mutual recognition and this will, in turn, determine its likely social outcome.

One of the main values of this set of contributions lies precisely in the link they establish between these two issues: the regulatory consequences of mutual recognition and its conception as a form of governance. In my view, only a clear assumption of mutual recognition as a form of governance can highlight the institutional dimension associated with it, in terms of the mechanisms of participation and representation that it embodies and their importance in both explaining and modelling its regulatory impact.

This assumption is also the way to move on from the ideological debate that has been intimately linked to mutual recognition (Schmidt 2007) and reconstruct it under a more productive framework. A genuine and correct assessment of mutual recognition can only be made by addressing it as a form of governance whose forms of participation and representation operate differently in different sets of circumstances.

This discussion highlights three points:

- First, mutual recognition is an instrument of governance: it is a form of decision-making (based in a particular institutional form of the market) that produces social decisions. In this light, it favours certain mechanisms of participation over others with consequences for the way in which different interests are represented.
- Second, in the light of the governance qualities of mutual recognition and the differentiated representation it promotes, its legitimacy is reinforced the more it takes place in the context of alternative modes of decision-making. In other words, mutual recognition, to be fully legitimate, should be an institutional choice among a set of institutional alternatives. That institutional choice should be a function of the variables of participation and representation in all the alternative modes of social decision-making. The existence of these alternatives would guarantee that the risks inherent in the mechanisms of decision-making linked to mutual recognition can be corrected and controlled. These institutional alternatives can be national (to guarantee, for example, a fair domestic redistribution of the trade gains) or supranational (to reinstate at the supranational level the primacy of politics).
- Third, where mutual recognition imposes on states a broadening of the interests that they are to take into account in the definition and pursuit of their goals, it interferes with the redistribution of costs and benefits in those states. In these instances, there is a strong case for mutual recognition also to be supported by instances of redistribution at the supranational level (see also Trachtman 2007: 787). But this raises an additional question: what kind of political link is necessary between states, beyond their co-operative self-interest, when mutual recognition entails redistribution and requires solidarity? This question, which is mainly normative, can be linked with the conditions for mutual trust between states which are necessary to mutual recognition and which will be discussed in more detail below.

MUTUAL RECOGNITION AND DIVERSITY

As Schmidt (2007: 672) notes, harmonization requires a high degree of vertical transfer of sovereignty. It is no surprise, therefore, that a preference for mutual recognition is often expressed in terms of it being the instrument of political and economic integration which is more respectful of diversity and a state's autonomy (Nicolaïdis 2007). To a considerable extent this is true but the link between mutual recognition and the preservation of diversity should also not be exaggerated. Is the impact on sovereignty generated by the process of harmonization so much different from the impact of mutual recognition? Mutual recognition often leads to ex-post harmonization and what changes is not so much the degree of sovereignty transferred but more how it is transferred. What happens is that this ex-post harmonization is promoted in a decentralized manner by regulatory competition and the process of decision-making which I have previously described. It is a product of this decentralized process of decision-making that involves different national authorities and actors at a horizontal level. This is also a form of diversity but it could perhaps be better identified as a form of horizontal deliberation. Susanne Schmidt (2007: 672) talks appropriately, in this context, of a horizontal transfer of sovereignty. A state that has to recognize and give effect, in its jurisdiction, to the rules of another state can be said to transfer, in part, some of the exercise of its sovereign powers to that other state. However, the nature of the changes in a state's sovereignty in the context of mutual recognition is perhaps even more complex and varied than what can simply be deduced from the idea of horizontal transfer of sovereignty.

In this respect, a reconstruction of the nature of the impact of mutual recognition on a state's sovereignty must take into account two dimensions. The first is the extent to which mutual recognition impacts on the policy autonomy of states (the autonomy of a political community to determine its own policy preferences or self-government). The second is the extent to which it affects the autonomy of a political community in defining the participation and representation of different groups and citizens in its policies. Both of these instances can also be linked to different processes through which mutual recognition de facto leads to forms of implicit harmonization.

First, though the obvious point is to highlight the horizontal transfer of sovereignty inherent in the process of regulatory competition created by mutual recognition, the latter can also promote a vertical transfer of sovereignty. As several of the authors point out, mutual recognition is often linked to some sort of essential harmonization. At other times it is also implemented with reference to international standards that assume a more or less soft or hard law character. These standards are the product of technocratic bodies and committees that have an inherent rationality dominated by a particular set of normative values and are often not subject to a state's sovereign control.

The acknowledgement of the mixed character of mutual recognition also helps to highlight how mutual recognition changes the exercise of sovereignty within a state. I have already pointed to the circumstance that mutual recognition could, to a large extent, be defined as an alternative model of social decision-making, of a largely decentralized nature and, consequently, with a different representation of interests. There are, however, further dimensions to what it entails in terms of impact on the balance of power in the decision-making powers of a state. Lavenex (2007: 774–5) demonstrates this by claiming that mutual recognition in the area of justice and security is actually an instrument to reinforce the power of national governments over other branches of power within the states. Some resistance to mutual recognition, which either favours national treatment (primacy of national political control) or harmonization (primacy of European political control), has its origins precisely in this distrust of mutual recognition as affecting the balance of power within the states and not so much between states.

One perspective which aims at presenting mutual recognition as fully respecting policy diversity and national autonomy highlights its role as a kind of destroyer of policy prejudices or a 'substantive translator' of regulations. Pelkmans (2007: 702) presents this vision when he refers to the application of mutual recognition by the Court of Justice in the realm of safety, health, environment and consumer protection (SHEC). In his own words: 'SHEC regulation is in essence "risk regulation". If the risk reduction aimed for is similar, the regulatory objective is essentially the same, and a good can be freely imported.' In other words, since the goal is attained in an equal measure by the different policies of the exporting and the importing state, there is no reason why they should not be mutually recognized. Not to do so will be, as Pelkmans says, a regulatory failure, the consequence of a lack of mutual trust between member states where, at least in these cases, the identity of regulatory objectives will prove to be false. This is certainly true and a welcome outcome of mutual recognition but, again, it involves a shift in the balance of power within a state. Often, that lack of 'mutual trust' and 'equivalence' is the product of a captured or frozen domestic political process. In some instances, the process of deliberation on mutual recognition either empowers sub-represented groups in the national political process or allows dormant majorities (often consumers) to regain control over the political process in areas previously dominated by certain concentrated interests. In other instances, mutual recognition challenges existing legislative path dependencies at the state level. National legislation which may have been largely justified when adopted sometimes becomes outdated and unjustified but, nevertheless, remains in place since it has, in the meantime, created a community of vested interests and a set of social practices resistant to change. When a state is forced by the processes of mutual recognition to justify its own legislation in light of different but 'equivalent' legislations from other states, it is forced to question anew the wisdom of that legislation and a new deliberative moment tends to occur. Mutual recognition might lead again to implicit harmonization (in the form of equivalence or identical legislations) as a consequence of the change in the domestic politics of a state.

The form of mutual recognition to which Pelkmans (2007: 702) refers equates, as stated, mutual recognition with equivalence. This can certainly be conceived as one of the forms of mutual recognition and, as Trachtman (2007: 786) suggests in his contribution, appears to be the prevalent method in the WTO context. In the European Union context, however, it is doubtful if mutual recognition is only applicable where there is equivalence between the different national policies. One example is the largely consensual case law of the Court of Justice which in a series of matters, mainly regarding consumer protection, has struck down national law imposing certain product requirements (such as those regulating the mandatory composition of beer, vinegar, pasta, etc.) as unjustified in light of an alternative labelling policy. The Court considered that, in many instances, labelling information would be sufficient. However, what was at stake in these cases was not pure equivalence since a policy imposing mandatory product requirements is rather different from a policy based on consumer information. What takes place, in this instance, is that the judgment of the Court of Justice must take into account the interests of market integration that the national legislation simply ignored. In other words, judicially imposed mutual recognition is, often, an instrument for the Court of Justice to introduce EU interests of market integration in the national decision-making process and not simply a mechanism through which the Court assesses whether the different national legislations are identical. Again, the spectrum of interests to be taken into account changes in such decisions.

One relevant question concerns what is required for mutual recognition to legitimately move from a logic of pure equivalence to an instrument to be used in the reform of national regulatory policies. While mutual recognition aimed at simple equivalence will only require national regulators to recognize the rules of other states that achieve the same degree of protection of the goals pursued by their domestic rules, a stricter form of mutual recognition, as usually conceived in the European Union, requires them to take into account new interests beyond those taken into account to determine the goals pursued by the original national policy. In the European Union, that is justified by the political dimension of its economic integration, which can be said to require national political processes to expand, in certain instances, their democratic constituencies to include the interests of nationals of other member states.

Mutual recognition has, therefore, at least two types of functions beyond that linked to the process of regulatory competition. On the one hand, it is a translator of different national regulatory languages: it helps member states to realize that, in some instances, different rules do not mean, in fact, different policy objectives and that they actually share the same regulatory goal (though the regulatory words may vary, their purpose is the same). In these cases, mutual recognition also impacts on the power of a state but mostly at a domestic level. It shifts the balance of power within the state political process. On the other hand, there are instances where mutual recognition goes further: when it requires member states to change their regulatory ideals in order to attend also to the broader goals of economic integration required by a non-fragmented market. In these instances, member states are forced to incorporate in their regulatory analysis the costs arising from their regulations to the interests of nationals of other member states.

Thus, it is important to highlight that mutual recognition cannot be simply presented as not interfering with national sovereignty and policy autonomy. The right question is instead, what kind of transfers of power does mutual recognition entail and when are they justified?

MUTUAL RECOGNITION AND IDENTITY

Finally, all contributions stress the connection of mutual recognition to questions of identity and mutual trust. Two closely linked issues prevail here: first, the extent to which the viability of mutual recognition does depend on a certain degree of policy and systems identity between the participating states; second, the extent to which, while attempting to promote mutual trust among the participants (Nicolaïdis 2007), mutual recognition also depends on the pre-existence of such mutual trust.

These two issues are, in my view, also linked to different forms of mutual recognition which emerge from the contributions: norms recognition (functional equivalence); policy recognition (mutual recognition of different goals); and systems recognition (mutual enforcement and systems recognition). These require different degrees of mutual trust and pre-existent identity.

Rules disparities which do not reflect different goals are the easier disparities to overcome by mutual recognition as highlighted in Pelkmans' (2007: 702) discussion on the equivalence of national regulatory objectives which is often hidden behind different rules. Often, in these cases, the process of national regulatory reconstruction forced by mutual recognition leads the national regulators to be confronted with identical policies hidden behind different national rules. In this case, systemic trust is promoted by the identification of policy coincidence. It will be in these instances that mutual recognition will be more easily adopted and legitimated. States are not required to change their policy goals. They are only required to recognize different rules that pursue the same goals. The existent policy identity facilitates the mutual recognition of different rules. It will often be in a context of this type that a pure form of mutual recognition will be adopted. Usually, judicial enforcement of the principle of mutual recognition is sufficient in these cases. In requiring proper justification for divergent national rules it allows an easy identification of the policy consensus underlying those different rules.

Mutual recognition immediately becomes more difficult once it is attempted in a context of differentiated goals and limited policy identity. In such a context, different rules do pursue different goals. What happens is that, in some instances, those different goals may be the product of insulated national political processes which do not take into account the broader goals of the integrated polity. Mutual recognition may still be possible and desirable once a broader set of goals is taken into account by national political processes. However, it will usually take the form of managed mutual recognition highlighted by Nicolaïdis and Schmidt (2007). Sometimes also, this form of mutual recognition can be judicially promoted by balancing the application of the principle of mutual recognition with public interest exceptions. This forces states to internalize in their decision-making process a broader set of interests while also authorizing some exceptions to mutual recognition, if states still justify them as necessary and proportional to the pursuit of legitimate goals. At other times, however, judicial enforcement will not be sufficient and it has to be supported and/or preceded by a certain degree of harmonization. The supranational deliberative process which is put in place by the need to harmonize may provide a better forum to agree on new policies. If that is the case, managed mutual recognition is also conducive to policy identity but through deliberation at a different level than the state.

The more difficult context for mutual recognition is that exemplified by Lavenex (2007). It is the case of mutual recognition that requires a broad systems recognition. In the area of justice and security discussed in her contribution, member states have to do more than simply recognize other norms as equivalent to their own. They have to accept and enforce other systems of law. This requires a higher degree of mutual trust than in the area of economic integration. The mutual recognition of judicial decisions is not based simply on the mutual recognition of each applicable norm but on the assumption that the other's judicial and legislative decisions are legitimate in systemic terms. It is the entire system which must be recognized as a system affording all the appropriate protections, notably in the area of fundamental rights. This involves the recognition of rules, goals and the processes and institutions through which they are adopted and implemented in another system. Other forms of mutual recognition also entail some recognition of the other's system, only the latter is, in reality, deduced from the existence of policy coincidence or overcome if goal differentiation takes place in a non-systemic area (a more limited or less sensitive policy). Instead, where that is not the case it is to be expected that national political processes and national courts may show some resistance to the idea of mutual recognition. The problem is that the same variable that pushes for mutual recognition (the difficulty to achieve a political consensus on common rules) also makes it more difficult to enforce it (because of the lack of sufficient mutual trust).

This paradox of mutual recognition can also be presented from a normative standpoint by stating that, while its broader normative foundation may lie in the promotion of the recognition of the other, it is more likely to be workable and legitimate where the pre-existent identity is stronger. The greater the initial degree of policy or systemic divergence, the greater the likelihood that mutual recognition will face resistance and the greater the justification to impose on a state the recognition of the other's policies. The paradox, as was stated, is that it is also where divergence is greater that mutual recognition is more needed as an instrument for economic and political integration. This is the case for pragmatic reasons but also for normative ones. Such divergence creates regulatory and political obstacles to the pursuit of other legitimate goals linked to integration: it is precisely in these instances that the information and transaction costs arising from national treatment will be higher. Furthermore, national treatment will often be used as an instrument of resistance to the idea of inclusiveness inherent in the process of integration.

A variant on this problem is presented by Genschel (2007: 753) who highlights that, in the tax domain, the fact that mutual recognition is not distributionally neutral exacerbates the problem of mutual trust. In reality, mutual recognition is likely, as we have seen, to have distributional consequences in all domains, both between states and within states (between different groups of citizens). Where that is the case, the issue of mutual trust becomes a question of solidarity. This requires us to consider what broader goals need to be provided to support mutual recognition, particularly when it moves beyond functional equivalence. To what extent, when mutual recognition has redistributive consequences, does it need to be grounded in some form of political commitment entailing some degree of solidarity between the participants in this form of governance? If so, how should these redistributive consequences be measured and regulated? These raise deep normative questions on what recognition entails, something that Kalypso Nicolaïdis (2007) addresses.

Finally, because, as was said, harmonization will also be more difficult where the conditions for mutual recognition will be less favourable (transactions and information costs in the supranational political process will be very high by virtue of the high degree of policy and systemic divergence), the favourite solution in the European Union has been a form of managed mutual recognition (Nicolaïdis and Schmidt 2007). Often, however, managed mutual recognition, either through the adoption of minimum standards or by references to general clauses and principles, leads to a broad application of a rule of reason subject to judicial adjudication. Such a form of mutual recognition largely delegates, de facto, the final responsibility on when and how mutual recognition should be applied to the judicial process.

Instances of political delegation in the judicial processes, where there is unresolved political disagreement, are not new. Moreover, they can be an appropriate form of rationalizing political conflicts, by agreeing on principles and on a process to balance between those principles outside the passion of ordinary politics. However, this places a particularly high burden on courts which the political process should support in legitimacy terms. Instead, the risk is that the very contested nature of the politics of these issues may lead the political process to challenge the judicial outcomes. In the end, the European judiciary can be placed in the difficult situation of being forced to arbitrate between quite divergent political views that, while entrusting to the Court that task, at the same time constantly challenge the legitimacy of its outcomes.

In this respect, a system of managed mutual recognition can only be successful, in the long term, if the delegation it entails in the judicial process is fully assumed by the political process and supported by the legitimacy it accords to the judiciary. Mutual recognition will also be more successful where existing alternative institutions are available to co-manage mutual recognition and guarantee that the political process can always regain control over the policy issues that it, frequently and implicitly, delegates to courts. The legitimacy of mutual recognition requires it to operate in a context where other viable choices are available in terms of institutional alternatives or forms of governance. It is only in this context that the preference for the mechanisms of participation and representation that it entails can be properly legitimated. However, it is precisely where that is not the case that mutual recognition tends to be chosen as a kind of fall-back solution to the problems of stalled integration. It is this dilemma that makes mutual recognition so appealing but at the same time so contested.

Biographical note: Miguel Poiares Maduro is Advocate General at the European Court of Justice.

REFERENCES

Genschel, P. (2007) 'Why no mutual recognition of VAT? Regulation, taxation and the integration of the EU's internal market for goods', *Journal of European Public Policy* 14(5): 743–61.

Héritier, A. (2007) 'Mutual recognition: comparing policy areas', *Journal of European Public Policy* 14(5): 800–13.

Lavenex, S. (2007) 'Mutual recognition and the monopoly of force: limits of the single market analogy', *Journal of European Public Policy* 14(5): 762–79.

Nicolaïdis, K. (2007) 'Trusting the Poles? Constructing Europe through mutual recognition', *Journal of European Public Policy* 14(5): 682–98.

Nicolaïdis, K. and Schmidt, S.K. (2007) 'Mutual recognition "on trial": the long road to services liberalization', *Journal of European Public Policy* 14(5): 717–34.

Pelkmans, J. (2007) 'Mutual recognition in goods. On promises and disillusions', *Journal of European Public Policy* 14(5): 699–716.

Reich, N. (1992) 'Competition between legal orders: a new paradigm of EC law?', *Common Market Law Review* 29: 861–96.

Schmidt, S.K. (2007) 'Mutual recognition as a new mode of governance', *Journal of European Public Policy* 14(5): 667–81.

Trachtman, J. (2007) 'Embedding mutual recognition at the WTO', *Journal of European Public Policy* 14(5): 780–99.

Index

For Product Safety Concerns and Information please contact our EU
representative GPSR@taylorandfrancis.com Taylor & Francis Verlag GmbH,
Kaufingerstraße 24, 80331 München, Germany

Batch number: 08158497

Printed by Printforce, the Netherlands